The Macintosh Bible Guide to ClarisWorks 3

The
Macintosh Bible
Guide to
ClarisWorks 3

by

Charles Rubin

PEACHPIT PRESS

THE MACINTOSH BIBLE GUIDE TO CLARISWORKS 3
Charles Rubin

Peachpit Press
2414 Sixth St.
Berkeley, CA 94710
(510) 548-4393
(510) 548-5991 (fax)

Peachpit Press is a division of Addison-Wesley Publishing Company.

Cover design by YO, San Francisco

Cover illustration by John Grimes

Interior design by Olav Martin Kvern

Production by Byron Brown

ISBN 1-56609-180-2

0 9 8 7 6 5 4 3 2 1

Printed and bound in the United States of America.

Printed on recycled paper

Contents

· ·

PART 2   **THE SIX APPLICATIONS**

CHAPTER 4   **The Word Processor**...83

PART 3   **ADVANCED TECHNIQUES**

CHAPTER 11   **Spreadsheet and database functions**........................311

CHAPTER 12   **Using frames** 371

Acknowledgments

. . . .

Many thanks to Ted Nace for giving me the opportunity to write about this delightful program.

For the book's overall design and production quality, I'm grateful to Roslyn Bullas, Cary Norsworthy, Byron Brown, and Ole Kvern. These are the people who really make books.

For the book's success, I thank Keasley Jones, Gregor Clark, Trish Booth, John Grimes, Bernhard Schmidt, and everyone else at Peachpit Press. The Peachpit gang has restored my faith in the idea that it's possible to be pleasant, helpful, efficient, and highly competitive, all at the same time.

Introduction

ClarisWorks is the best-selling integrated
program for the Macintosh, and has been
since it was introduced in 1991. ClarisWorks
has outrun some well-established competition
in the Mac integrated software derby because
it offers the best balance of features,
simplicity, and plain old bang for the buck. ➤➤

- ClarisWorks handles all the major personal computer productivity tasks—word processing, spreadsheeting, charting, database management, graphics, and communications—in one relatively inexpensive program.

- It has lots of common commands among its different tools, so it's much easier to learn than a handful of separate programs.

- It uses far less memory than several separate programs.

- It lets you combine data in ways that are difficult or impossible with stand-alone programs.

ClarisWorks does most of the things you'll want to do with your Mac in the simplest possible way.

Why this book?

If it's all so simple, why do you need this book? There are lots of reasons.

Simplicity

The ClarisWorks 3.0 package comes with a condensed manual, an on-line help system and on-screen introduction, and a collection of Assistants, scripts that automate complex tasks or the creation of documents such as newsletters and databases. You may often find yourself using two or three of these sources to get the answers you want as you work with the program. This book puts the answers in one place, logically organized and clearly explained.

Economy

Software companies inevitably get involved in feature wars that result in new versions of their products becoming ever more powerful and complex, even in a market category like integrated programs, which are supposed to be simple. For Mac owners, version 3.0 of

ClarisWorks has only minor changes compared with version 2.1, mostly the new help features that are covered in Chapter 3. But as with the previous edition of this book, I've tried to explain the most popular features first—the ones you'll use the most—and have put the more advanced and seldom-used information in a separate section where it won't get in your way.

I've also tried to save you time by not belaboring the obvious. Even if you're new to the Macintosh, there are lots of basic concepts that you come to understand fairly quickly, and which therefore don't have to be repeated endlessly. This book isn't bloated with repetitive instructions about closing windows, clicking Cancel buttons, and so on.

If you're totally new to the Macintosh, you should practice the basic exercises in your Mac's manual to learn about windows, dialog boxes, clicking, and selecting before you get into this book. This book assumes that you understand the basics of using the mouse and keyboard.

Objectivity

The ClarisWorks manuals are written at Claris, which naturally feels that this is the greatest product in the universe and that all of its features make perfect sense. In this book we'll look at Claris-Works in a more realistic light, covering its disadvantages as well as its advantages and learning how to make the best of the situation regardless. In most chapters you'll find loads of tips for working smarter as you go along, as well as troubleshooting sections that zero in on common problems and offer quick solutions.

About ClarisWorks 3.0

ClarisWorks versions 2.0 and 2.1 were so far ahead of the other Mac integrated programs that Claris decided to focus on making this new version easier to learn. Perhaps the most important reason for this new version is that the exact same program is now available for both the Mac and Windows environments, so users of different computers in an office can share ClarisWorks files without having to translate them.

Here's what's new in ClarisWorks 3.0 for the Mac.

- ClarisWorks Assistants, a new feature of the help system that guides you through complex tasks. Some Assistants help you create budgets, presentations, address lists, and newsletters. Others help you insert tables into documents, find documents, and perform other chores.

- New preferences options you can choose for the spreadsheet and for the program's behavior in general.

- A separate word count command so you can tally words in a document without having to use the spelling checker, as before.

- New commands for copying summary calculations and for deleting records from the database.

- Some minor changes in how existing features are implemented, such as a button to make stationery documents instead of a menu option, and a few changes in command names.

- 75 clip art images included with the package to help you dress up your documents with graphics, and 7 new fonts for text.

Like version 2.1, ClarisWorks version 3 is native for Power Macintosh computers, so this version runs much more quickly than its competitors. Overall, ClarisWorks 3 performs most key functions from two to ten times more quickly than Microsoft Works version 4, and it remains the only integrated Mac program that will work on a Mac Plus.

How to use this book

This book is divided into three sections. Part 1 covers basic features of the program, Part 2 covers each of the six ClarisWorks applications, and Part 3 covers advanced features. The best approach to this book depends on how much you know already.

If you're new

If you're new to ClarisWorks, it's best to start at the beginning. Start up the program and run the Introduction to ClarisWorks (see *Using the Help system* in Chapter 3), and then browse through the rest of the information in Part 1 of this book. Then, learn more about the applications one at a time. Pick the application you want to know about first, then learn and practice with it before you go on to learning about others. Try creating documents of your own—letters, budgets, database files, or graphics, for example—as you read the chapter about each tool. Think of a real project you want to tackle and then try it as you learn about the application you'll use to do it.

 If you haven't yet installed ClarisWorks, or if you're having trouble getting it to run, see Appendix A.

Allow plenty of uninterrupted time to learn each application. Don't expect to learn ClarisWorks five minutes at a time between meetings or chores. Set aside at least an hour at a time and concentrate on learning the application you've chosen.

On the other hand, don't spend lots of time learning features you don't think you'll use. There's no test at the end of each chapter, and this isn't a contest to see how much you can learn. Once you feel you've learned what you need to know to get your work done, you've done enough.

If you're upgrading from ClarisWorks version 1, 2, or 2.1

If you're upgrading from version 1 of ClarisWorks, skim through each chapter and then turn to the sections that describe features that are new in version 3. Also, watch for the tip and warning icons scattered throughout the book to pick up some quick pointers about making the most of the program. If you're upgrading from version 2 or 2.1, focus on the changes in Chapters 2 and 3.

For future reference

Once you've done the initial learning, you can use this book as a reference.

- Check the table of contents to zoom in on sections covering the different functions of each application.

- Turn to the Troubleshooting section at the end of a chapter to find quick answers to specific problems you may be having.

- Check Appendix B for a list of keyboard commands.

- Consult the index to locate references to individual commands, concepts, and procedures.

Learning a new program is a journey from anticipation and ignorance through bewilderment, challenge, and frustration. The destination is mastery, a feeling of accomplishment, and the ability to solve problems and make your life easier with your new skills. If the going gets heavy at times, remember that there are lots of wonderful things in life that have nothing to do with ClarisWorks, this book, the Macintosh, or computing in general. So try to have fun with it, and when you can't, take a break—it'll all be waiting for you the next time you sit down at your Mac.

P A R T 1

Basics

Introducing ClarisWorks

ClarisWorks combines all the most common computer applications—word processing, spreadsheeting, database management, drawing, painting, and communications—in one integrated program. Having all these applications together makes it easy to work with data in different ways. In this chapter, we'll look at ClarisWorks in overview and see how it makes integrating data so easy. ➵

What's so great about integration?

One of the frustrating things about computers is that they don't work with the different types of data in our world as easily as we do ourselves. With a pencil and paper, you can switch easily from making a drawing to writing a sentence to adding up a couple of numbers. You do all these things on the same piece of paper with the same pencil, and you're hardly aware that you're switching from one type of data to another.

But computers aren't so smart. They enforce rigid data classifications such as text, numbers, and graphics, and they require different kinds of programs for dealing with each data type. Without an integrated program, you have to use a different program each time you want to work with data in a different way, and you can end up spending a lot of time figuring out how to combine numbers with text or graphics by merging documents or cutting and pasting. ClarisWorks helps make computing more natural by offering all the most common methods of data manipulation in one simple program and making it very easy to move from one data type to another.

Here are the major integration features of ClarisWorks and how they work to make your computing life easier.

Six data environments

ClarisWorks combines, or integrates, six of the most popular personal computer applications in one program. Each application has its own document type, or its own data handling environment.

The word processor

In the word processing environment you work with text, so the menus available have lots of features that make it easy to create text documents such as letters and reports. A word processing document looks like this:

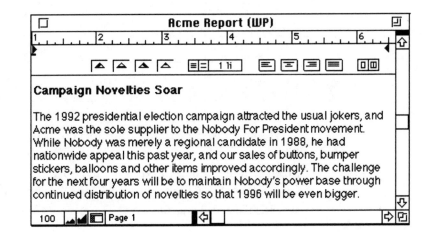

We'll explore the ClarisWorks word processor in Chapter 4.

The spreadsheet

The spreadsheet environment is for calculating numbers and producing charts based on numeric data. A spreadsheet document looks like the figure at the top of the next page:

	1993 Budget (SS)				
B5	×✓	3500			

	A	B	C	D	E
1	Expenses	January	February	March	April
2	Salaries	$10,200	$11,300	$12,400	$12400.00
3	Benefits	$4,500	$4,700	$4,800	4800
4	Materials	$3,000	$4,000	$5,000	5500
5	Rent	$3,500	$3,500	$3,500	3500
6	Advertising	$5,000	$5,400	$4,700	4900
7	Kickbacks	$1,000	$1,000	$1,000	1000
8	Utilities	$225	$230	$215	210
9	Insurance	$200	$200	$200	200
10	Telephone	$550	$575	$540	490
11					
12	Total	$28,175	$30,905	$32,355	33000

The spreadsheet can store numbers or text, and it can also store formulas that automatically produce calculations. Also, you can produce many different types of charts from numbers in a spreadsheet. See Chapters 5 and 6 for more on working with spreadsheets and charts.

The database

The database is for storing and manipulating collections of facts, such as address files, sales order files, and inventories. You can perform calculations on numeric or text data, select and display groups of facts in different ways, and produce printed reports. A database document might look like the figure at the top of the next page:

Employees (DB)

FirstName	George
LastName	Barrios
Street	24 First Ave
City	San Mateo
State	CA
Zip	95505
Phone	916-555-8876
Department	Marketing

Records: 27

Selected: 1

Sorted

See Chapter 7 for more on using the database.

The drawing program

The drawing program lets you create and manipulate objects with drawing tools. Objects you draw are made up of lines, and once you've drawn an object you can select it and resize it. A drawing document looks like this:

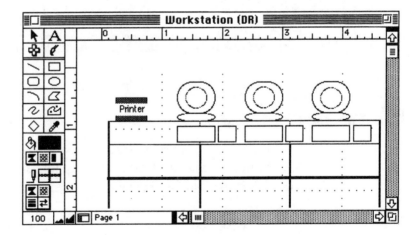

For more on drawing, see Chapter 8.

The painting program

The painting program lets you create graphics with painting tools. Unlike objects in a drawing document, painted graphics aren't made up of lines; they're made up of patterns of dots called *bitmaps*. A painting document looks like this:

See Chapter 9 for more on painting.

The communications program

The communications program allows you to exchange data with other computers via direct cables or telephone lines. A communications document looks like the figure at the top of the next page:

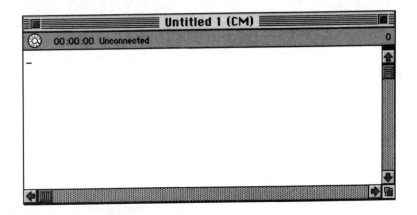

Rather than creating text, numbers, facts, or graphics on the screen with the communications program, you transmit data to other computers or receive it from them. The blank area of the document above is where you see incoming or outgoing text as you receive or transmit it. Chapter 10 explains the communications program in detail.

Graphic objects and frames

Being able to create six different document types is a good start toward integration, but ClarisWorks goes a lot farther. Along with the individual document types just described, you can create *objects* and *frames* inside most document environments. You can draw objects (lines, ovals, rectangles, or polygons) inside any word processor, spreadsheet, or database document at any time. You can also create frames in which you can use word processing, spreadsheet, or painting tools even if you're not in those document types.

Integrated drawing tools

Although there's a separate drawing application in ClarisWorks, you can also draw objects inside a word processing, spreadsheet, or database document at any time. This allows you to combine text, numbers, or data with colorful graphics without having to create separate documents and then manually combine them. Here's an example:

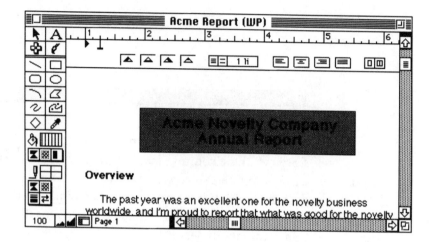

The title in this word processing document has a gray box around it for emphasis. The box is a *graphic object* drawn with the rectangle tool and filled with a gray fill pattern (see *The tool panel* on p. 21 in Chapter 2).

The box is a separate object that can be moved, resized, or otherwise manipulated independently from the text it surrounds. In fact, every object you draw is placed in a separate layer of the document. In the example above, the text has been set to the color black, and the box has been placed in a layer behind the text, so that the black text appears on top of it.

You can put objects like this on top of or underneath the text or numbers in any word processor, spreadsheet, or database document by using the tools in the ClarisWorks tool palette. For more information, see *Managing objects in layers* on p. 248 in Chapter 8.

Frames

Spreadsheet, text, and paint frames give you all of ClarisWorks' spreadsheeting, word processing, and painting power even when you're not working in a spreadsheet, word processor, or paint document. For example, the word processor document below contains a spreadsheet frame with some calculated numbers in it.

```
┌──────────────── Acme Report (WP) ────────────────┐
```

The past year was an excellent one for the novelty business worldwide, and I'm proud to report that what was good for the novelty business was good for Acme Novelty. In this report, you'll find all the usual tedious breakdowns of expenses and income, but here's the bottom line:

	A	Sales	Expenses	Gross Profit
1		Sales	Expenses	Gross Profit
2	1991	$1,024,560	$662,900	$361,660
3	1992	$1,720,411	$1,014,380	$706,031
4				

The frame above was created with the spreadsheet tool in the tool panel (see *The tool panel* on p. 21 in Chapter 2). The spreadsheet frame itself is an object, and it can be selected, moved, or resized like a rectangle you might draw with the drawing tools. However, when you work inside the frame the spreadsheet's menus become available and you can work with numbers just as if you were in a spreadsheet document. For more about using frames, see Chapter 12.

In the example above, the spreadsheet's row and column headings are showing, as are the grid lines that separate the cells, but you can hide all these items so only the data shows. See Chapter 12 for more information.

You can create frames inside word processor, spreadsheet, database, draw, or paint documents, so you can work with data the way you want, wherever you are at the time.

Because you use the word processor, spreadsheet, or painting program's features to work in their respective frames, you should learn about the ClarisWorks word processor, spreadsheet, and painting programs in Chapters 4, 5, 6, and 9 before you begin working with frames.

Common commands and tools

ClarisWorks is fairly easy to learn and use because it has many commands and tools that are the same in each of its applications. As we'll see in Chapters 2 and 3, the commands to print a document, manage document views, or display ClarisWorks's Help system are the same in all document types. And as we'll see in Chapter 2, many of the features of document windows and tools are also the same in every application.

The limits of ClarisWorks integration

ClarisWorks has very good integration among its applications, but the integration isn't totally seamless or universal. The communications application behaves a lot differently from the other applications, and you can't create frames or draw objects in communications documents. There are also some differences in the way frames are handled in paint documents. We'll cover those in Chapter 12.

By now, you should have a good general idea of how Claris-Works integrates data. In Chapter 2, we'll see how to work with documents.

CHAPTER 2

Working with documents

Whenever you work with data in ClarisWorks, you work in a document. Depending on the type of work you want to do, you open or create one of six document types. Although each ClarisWorks application has its own document type, many features are common to all document types. In this chapter, we'll look at the basics of working with documents. ➻

From here on, we'll assume that you've already installed Claris-
Works and that you know how to start the program. If you need
help with these procedures, see Appendix A.

Making new documents

To work with any ClarisWorks application, you can:

- Create a document with that application's type;

- Open a document that you created before; or

- Make a frame for the application you want to use inside the
document you currently have open.

In this section, we'll cover the procedures for making new
documents. For information on opening existing documents,
see p. 24. To learn about using Assistants to help you create new
documents, see Chapter 3. Frames are covered in Chapter 12.

The Welcome dialog box

When you first open the ClarisWorks program, it displays a
Welcome dialog box like the one at the top of the next page:

This screen assumes you're new to ClarisWorks, so it offers you the option to run an onscreen introduction to the program by double-clicking the top icon or (since this icon is already selected) by simply pressing ⌈Return⌉. To make a new document or open an existing one instead, you double-click one of the other two buttons below.

Once you've become familiar with the program, you can opt to have ClarisWorks move straight to the New Document dialog box when it starts up by clicking in the box at the bottom to place an X in it.

The New Document dialog box

If you double-click the second button in the Welcome dialog box (or choose the *New...* command from the File menu at any time), you see the New Document dialog box, which looks like the one at the top of the next page:

```
┌──────────────────────────────────────────────────────┐
│  New Document                                          │
│  ────────────────────────────────────────────────     │
│                                                        │
│   ┌───┐   Start with a        ┌──────────────────┐▲    │
│   │   │   Blank Document       │A Word Processing │     │
│   └───┘                        │🖎 Drawing        │     │
│                                │🖌 Painting       │     │
│                                │▦ Spreadsheet     │     │
│   ┌───┐   Start with           │▤ Database        │     │
│   │▤ │   an Assistant          │📞 Communications │     │
│   └───┘   or Stationery        └──────────────────┘▼    │
│                                                        │
│   Create a new word processing document.               │
│                                                        │
│                              ┌────────┐ ┌────────┐    │
│                              │ Cancel │ │   OK   │    │
│                              └────────┘ └────────┘    │
└──────────────────────────────────────────────────────┘
```

The list of options at the right depends on which of the two buttons at the left is selected. In the example above, the Start with a Blank Document button is selected, so the list shows the six different types of documents you can create with ClarisWorks. To make a new document, you point to the document type you want in the list and then double-click on it, and the new document will open on your screen.

If you select the Start with an Assistant or Stationery button at the left, the list will show the names of ClarisWorks Assistants and stationery documents you can use to help you create new documents, or stationery files that are already set up for different types of projects. For more information on stationery, see p. 30. For more on Assistants, see Chapter 3.

You can have as many documents open at a time as your Mac's memory will allow—usually a dozen or more—and you can easily switch from working with one document to another (see *Changing the active document* on p. 35).

The document window

Each application's document window has some unique features, but all ClarisWorks document windows have many features in common, as you can see in the word processing window below:

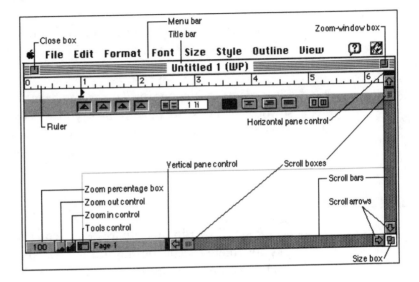

The menu bar

At the top of every ClarisWorks screen you'll find a menu bar. The menu names change depending on which document type you're using and what you're doing in that document. Sometimes menu names are dimmed, meaning the commands on that menu aren't available at the moment, and sometimes individual command names are dimmed on a particular menu because those commands aren't currently available.

The title bar

Below the menu bar is the document window itself. Each document window has a title bar. New documents have the generic name *Untitled <Number>*, where the number indicates the order in which new documents have been opened during the current session. There's also an abbreviation that indicates the document type.

You can move a document around the screen by dragging its title bar. To close a document, either click the close box or choose the *Close* command from the File menu. The zoom-window box at the right end of the title bar changes the window size from the maximum size it can be on your screen to a smaller size, if you've set a smaller size using the size box at the lower left corner of the window.

> **Tip**
>
> Most menu commands in ClarisWorks have ⌘-key alternates so you can choose them with the keyboard. If you're doing a lot of typing, it's faster to use the keyboard to choose commands. See the keyboard guide in Appendix B for a list of all the keyboard alternates.

The rulers

Beneath the title bar in this window is the ruler. Every Claris-Works document except communications documents has a ruler. (In fact, drawing and painting documents have both vertical and horizontal rulers.) Rulers aren't always displayed automatically when you first open a document. You can display or hide a document's rulers at any time by choosing *Show Rulers* or *Hide Rulers* from the View menu.

You can also change the way the ruler appears in a document. Choose *Rulers...* from the Format menu and then make the changes you want in the dialog box that appears. You can change the ruler's unit of measurement (inches, millimeters, centimeters, picas, or points), the number of divisions (tick marks) it has, or whether the ruler is for text (one ruler at the top of the document) or graphics (rulers at the top and the left side of the document).

The scroll bars

At the bottom and the right side of the document are the typical scroll bars, scroll boxes, and scroll arrows you'll find in most

Macintosh document windows, as well as the usual size box at the lower right corner. The scroll bars let you navigate through a document that's more than one screen long or wide, and the size box lets you resize the document window. (If you don't know how to use these controls, consult your *Macintosh User's Guide*.)

The pane controls

The horizontal and vertical pane controls allow you to divide the window into separate panes. It helps to split a window when you want to view two different parts of a large document at the same time.

When you drag one of these controls into the middle of the document window, ClarisWorks adds an extra set of scroll bars for the new pane you've created, like this:

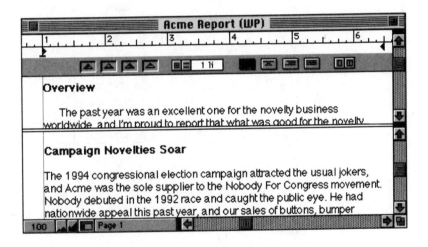

You can then scroll each pane independently. To work with data in a particular pane, just click inside that pane to move the cursor there.

To remove a pane divider, drag the divider itself or the pane control to the top, bottom, left, or right edge of the window.

The zoom controls

Each new ClarisWorks document window starts out at actual size, so the zoom percentage box shows 100 percent. Click the zoom in and zoom out controls to magnify or reduce the size of everything inside the window. When you click repeatedly, you zoom in or out further each time.

Magnifying a window helps when you're working on a detailed graphic and need to make fine adjustments. Reducing a window makes it possible to see all of a large layout—even a multipage layout—on your screen at once.

You can also zoom a window to a specific size by clicking on the zoom percentage box itself. You'll see a pop-up menu like this:

```
   25%
   33%
   50%
   67%
   75%
 • 100%
   200%
   400%
   Other...
```

You can choose a percentage from this menu to change the window's zoom percentage. If you don't see one you like, choose the *Other...* command to display a dialog box like the following one:

```
  View scale        100

       Cancel       OK
```

Here, you can type in a custom percentage value and then click OK to set it.

Zooming windows only changes the size of data on your screen. To change the size of a document as it prints, change the value in the Reduce or Enlarge box in the printer's Page Setup dialog box. (Not all printers have this capability.)

The tool panel

In every ClarisWorks application except communications, you use the tool panel to create spreadsheet or text frames or graphic objects. The tool panel looks like this:

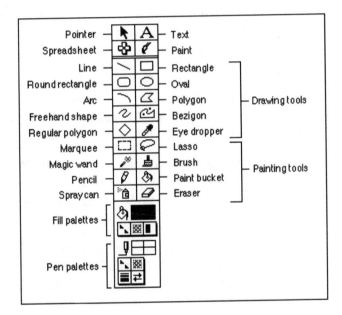

To use any tool, click on it to select it, then click or drag in the document. (See Chapters 8 and 9 for more on drawing and painting.)

Each tool is automatically deselected after you use it once. To lock a tool so you can use it over and over without selecting it each time, double-click on it.

If the tool panel isn't showing, click the tools control or choose *Show Tools* from the View menu. To hide the tool panel, click the tools control or choose *Hide Tools* from the View menu.

The tools

Most of the tools in the panel are for drawing or painting, so we'll cover them in detail in Chapters 8 and 9, but here's a brief overview, starting from the top of the panel.

The *pointer* is the tool you use to select objects or frames you've created with the other tools. This tool is usually selected as the default.

The *text* tool lets you add text to documents. When you select this tool and click or drag in the document, you create a text frame and the word processor's menus become active.

The *spreadsheet* tool lets you create spreadsheet frames. When you select this tool and draw a rectangle in the document, a spreadsheet appears inside the rectangle and the spreadsheet's menus become active.

The *paint* tool lets you create paint frames. When you select this tool and draw a rectangle in the document, you create a paint frame and the paint program's menus appear at the top of the screen.

The *drawing* tools let you draw objects if you're working in a word processor, spreadsheet, database, or drawing document. These tools are available in all except communications documents, but when you're working in a painting document or a paint frame, the drawing tools create painted shapes (bitmaps) rather than draw objects. For more on these tools, see Chapter 8.

The *painting* tools only appear in the tool panel when you're in a paint document or you're working inside a paint frame. For more on these tools, see Chapter 9.

The *fill* tool's three palettes let you add colors or patterns to the objects you draw or paint. The rectangle next to the paint bucket icon shows the current fill color or pattern. See Chapter 8 for more information.

The *pen* tool's four palettes let you select the color, pattern, thickness, and style of lines you draw (including the lines that make up the borders of shapes). The rectangle next to the pen icon shows the current line color, pattern, and thickness. See Chapter 8 for more details.

Floating palettes

Each of the seven fill and pen palettes pops up when you click it. Once you've displayed a palette, however, you can display it in a window by itself by dragging it out into the document. Just drag to the right until the palette outline appears in the document and then release the mouse button. The palette appears as a window by itself, like this:

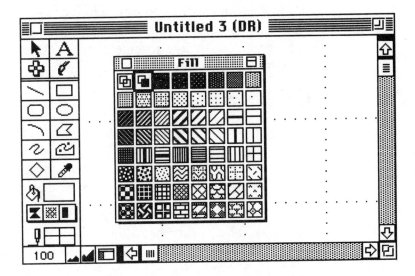

Just as with any window, you can drag a floating palette window by its title bar to move it, and you can close it by clicking the close box at the left side of the title bar. However, floating palette windows also have a *gravity zoom box* at the right side of the title bar. When you click this box, the palette shrinks so you can see only its title bar, like this:

Gravity zooming also moves the window to the upper right corner of your screen. Naturally, clicking the gravity zoom box again opens the palette and returns it to its original position on the screen.

Opening, closing, and saving documents

You can always display the New Document dialog box by double-clicking its icon on the Welcome screen or you can have it appear each time you start the program (see p. 16), but if you want to create, open, close, or save documents at any other time, you use commands on the File menu.

Making more new documents

To make a new document once you're working in ClarisWorks:

1. Choose the *New...* command from the File menu. Claris-Works displays the New Document dialog box.

2. Select the button for the type of document you want to create (blank or stationery), and then double-click on the specific document type or name in the list at the right. ClarisWorks displays a new, blank document of that type on the screen.

Opening documents

To open a document that was previously saved on your disk:

1. Choose the *Open...* command from the File menu. You see a dialog box like this:

```
┌─────────────────────────────────────────────────────────┐
│                                                           │
│    ┌──────────────────────────────┐                       │
│    │ 🗁 ClarisWorks 3.0 Folder ▼ │                       │
│    ┌────────────────────────────┬─┐   ⊂⊃ Macintosh HD    │
│    │ 🗀 Clip Art              │⇧│                         │
│    │ 🗋 Read Me               │ │   ┌──────────────┐      │
│    │                          │ │   │    Eject .    │     │
│    │                          │ │   └──────────────┘      │
│    │                          │ │   ┌──────────────┐      │
│    │                          │ │   │   Desktop    │      │
│    │                          │ │   └──────────────┘      │
│    │                          │ │                         │
│    │                          │ │   ┌──────────────┐      │
│    │                          │ │   │    Open      │      │
│    │                          │⇩│   └──────────────┘      │
│    └────────────────────────────┴─┘   ┌──────────────┐    │
│                                         │   Cancel     │   │
│                                         └──────────────┘   │
│    **Document Type**          **File Type**               │
│    ┌────────────┐             ┌──────────────────┐        │
│    │ All Types ▼│             │ All Available  ▼ │        │
│    └────────────┘             └──────────────────┘        │
│                                                           │
└─────────────────────────────────────────────────────────┘
```

This type of dialog box is often called a *directory dialog box,* because it shows all the files and folders inside the current folder (or directory) of your disk, and it allows you to select a file or switch to a different disk or folder. The current folder's name is shown on the pop-up menu above the file list, and the current disk's name is shown above the Eject button.

This dialog box usually shows all the ClarisWorks files in the current location. If you want to open a file that wasn't created in ClarisWorks, see *Importing documents,* next.

2. If the document you want to open isn't on the list, choose a different folder or a different disk.

3. When you find the name of the document you want, double-click on it and the document opens.

If the list of files is quite long and you want to restrict the number of items on it, choose a specific ClarisWorks document type from the Document Type menu. The list will then show only documents of that type.

If you don't have ClarisWorks running, you can start the program and open a ClarisWorks document at the same time by double-clicking that document's icon on the desktop.

Importing documents

To import a document that was created with another program, you use the same procedure as you do to open a file. First choose the ClarisWorks document type from the Document Type menu, then choose the document's file type from the File Type menu.

ClarisWorks comes with a selection of translator files that allow you to import files from most popular programs. The selection of file types you see on the File Type menu depends on which translators you have installed.

Inserting a document into the active document

Along with opening a document by itself, you can also insert a document into another document you already have open. For example, if you're working on a report document in the word processor and you have part of the report stored as a separate document, you might want to insert it into the active document. Here's the procedure:

1. Open the document into which you want to insert the new document, if it isn't already open.

2. Move the insertion point to the location in the document where you want the inserted document to appear.

3. Choose *Insert...* from the File menu. You'll see a directory dialog box.

4. Locate the document you want to insert and then double-click on its name. ClarisWorks inserts the document.

Closing documents

To close a document, either choose *Close* from the File menu or
click the document window's close box. If you've made changes to
the document since you opened it, ClarisWorks gives you the
option of saving them, like this:

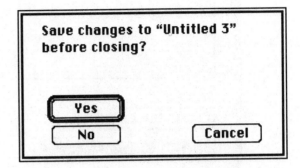

Press the Return key or click the Yes button to save the changes.
If the document is a new one, you see a directory dialog box in
which you can name the new document and choose a disk
location for it. If the document is an existing one, it will be saved
with the same name at the same location.

Saving documents

To save a document, choose *Save* from the File menu. If the
document is a new one, you'll see a directory dialog box in which
you can name the new document and choose a disk location for it,
like the one at the top of the next page:

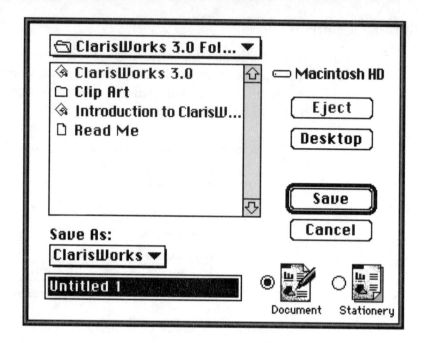

If the document is an existing one, it will be saved with the same name at the same location.

If you're working with a document that was previously saved and you want to save it with a different name, in a different format, or to a different location, choose *Save As...* from the File menu. You see a directory dialog box like the one above so you can choose a different location, type a different name, or select a different format for the file.

> *Tip*
>
> To use a ClarisWorks document with another program, choose *Save As...* and then use the Save As pop-up menu in the dialog box to select a format that can be used by the other program. If the other program's native format isn't listed on the menu, choose a standard format it can import, such as RTF or text. For example, to save data from a spreadsheet or database file so it can be used in another spreadsheet or database program, you would probably choose the Text format from the Save As pop-up menu to save the file in text format. Text format can be read by most programs on every computer, from a desktop system to a mainframe.

Saving summary information

The new *Document Summary* command on ClarisWorks 3.0's File menu lets you save information about a document without including it in the document itself. To do this, open the document you want to make notes about and then choose *Document Summary* from the File menu. You'll see the Document Summary dialog box, like this:

```
┌─────────────────────────────────────────────────────┐
│  Document Summary                                     │
│                                                       │
│        Title: [                                    ]  │
│                                                       │
│       Author: [ Charlie Rubin                      ]  │
│                                                       │
│      Version: [                                    ]  │
│                                                       │
│     Keywords: [                                    ]  │
│                                                       │
│     Category: [                                    ]  │
│                                                       │
│  Description: [                                    ]  │
│               [                                    ]  │
│               [                                    ]  │
│                                                       │
│                        ( Cancel )  (( OK ))           │
└─────────────────────────────────────────────────────┘
```

The Author space is automatically filled in with the name under which your copy of ClarisWorks is registered. Every box here has a title, but you can put whatever information you want in each box. For example, you might record the number of hours you've spent working on a document (if you're being paid by the hour to work on it), or the number of words in the document, or some notes about what information the document contains. Document summary information is stored with the document when you save it, and it can always be displayed with the *Document Summary* command.

Reverting to the last saved version of a document

Sometimes you'll open an existing document, make some changes, and then decide you don't like those changes. If you've only made one small change, you can edit the document to remove that change or choose *Undo* from the Edit menu to cancel a change you've just made (see *Undoing changes* on p. 59 in Chapter 3). However, if you've made several significant changes to a document and you want to toss them all out, choose *Revert* from the File menu.

When you choose the *Revert* command, ClarisWorks presents a dialog box asking if you want to revert to the last saved version of the document. Click the Yes button or press the (Return) key. Claris-Works closes the current document without saving the changes you've made and then automatically opens the last saved version of the same document.

Using stationery

Stationery documents open as Untitled documents, but they contain some custom text, data, or format settings that you want each new document to have. For example, if you store your return address and telephone number at the top of a word processor document, you could save the document as stationery and then open a new, Untitled page with your return address already on it each time.

Opening stationery

ClarisWorks comes with several pre-defined stationery documents for different purposes. To use a stationery document, display the New Document dialog box and click the Start with an Assistant or Stationery button. You'll see a list of Assistants in the list at the right, like the one at the top of the next page:

New Document

Start with a
Blank Document

Start with
an Assistant
or Stationery

Category: General ▼

- ⌨ Name & Address List
- 🖥 Calendar
- 🖥 Envelope
- 🖥 Home Finance
- 🖥 Newsletter
- 🖥 Create One Month Calendar
- 🖥 Presentation

This Assistant will help you create a name and address database.

Cancel   OK

Assistants are different from stationery because each one helps you through the creation of a document by asking you questions. You can tell the documents displayed above are Assistants because they have a unique icon next to them. (See Chapter 3 for more on Assistants.)

To open a stationery document, choose a different category from the pop-up menu above the list of documents. The list will change to show the names of stationery documents. Here's the list when you choose the None category:

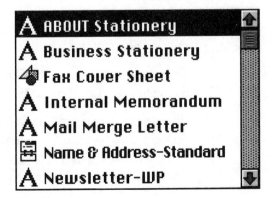

To open a particular stationery document, just double-click on its name. It opens as an Untitled document.

Stationery documents appear in this list only if they're stored inside the *ClarisWorks Stationery* folder, which is located inside the *Claris* folder inside your Mac's System Folder. However, you may end up saving stationery documents to other folders on your disk. You can always tell a stationery document from a normal document in the list in a directory dialog box because it has a stationery pad icon next to it, rather than a standard document icon, like this:

```
┌─────────────────────────────────────┬───┐
│ ▢ Acme Report                       │ ⇧ │
│ ▣ Letterhead                        ├───┤
│                                     │   │
└─────────────────────────────────────┴───┘
```

In this example, the *Letterhead* document is a stationery document.

Making stationery

You can create stationery documents with any of ClarisWorks' applications, and if you save them inside the ClarisWorks Stationery folder inside the Claris folder in your System Folder, they'll appear on the list you see when you choose the Stationery option in the New Document dialog box, as explained above. To make a new stationery document:

1. Open a new document and enter the data or make the formatting adjustments you want to save in the stationery.

2. Choose *Save As...* from the File menu to display the Save As dialog box, as shown on p. 28.

3. Click the Stationery button in the lower right corner of the dialog box to save the document as stationery. As you do, you'll see that ClarisWorks automatically selects the *Claris-Works Stationery* folder inside your System Folder as the

document's destination, so your new stationery will be added to the Stationery list.

4. Type a name for the stationery document.

5. Click the Save button or press [Return]. The document is saved as stationery, and it remains Untitled on your screen. (To change the document's name on the screen, save it as a normal ClarisWorks file.)

Making a stationery folder

You can save stationery documents anywhere you like on your disk, but their names won't appear on the Stationery list in the New Document dialog box unless they're saved inside the *Claris-Works Stationery* folder. In a normal ClarisWorks installation, this folder is created automatically because ClarisWorks comes with about two dozen stationery documents already set up for you. However, if you didn't install the *ClarisWorks Stationery* folder when you installed ClarisWorks (maybe you wanted to save some disk space), you'll have to create one in order to have stationery listed in the New Document dialog box.

To make a stationery folder, use the Finder to display the Claris folder inside your System Folder, open the Claris folder, and choose the *New Folder* command from the File menu. A new Untitled folder will appear, and you can then change its name to *ClarisWorks Stationery*. With the folder there, you can then save stationery documents to it so their names will automatically appear on the Stationery list.

Changing stationery documents

At some point you may want to change the stationery document itself. For example, if you move you'll want to change the address and telephone number on your letterhead stationery document. To change a stationery document:

1. Open the stationery document. It opens as an Untitled document.

2. Make the changes you want.

3. Choose the *Save As...* command from the File menu and save the document as a stationery document with the same name as the original stationery document. You'll be asked if you want to replace the existing document. Click the Yes button or press Return to replace the older document with the new, changed one.

Managing document views

You can have more than one document open in ClarisWorks at a time, and you can also change the view of any document by showing or hiding the tool panel or ruler, or by opening multiple views of the same document. The Views menu contains the commands for managing document views.

About document views

When you create or open a document, it appears in its own window on the screen, and the document's name appears at the bottom of the View menu. If you have more than one document open, the windows are stacked on top of each other, and the one that's on top of the stack is the *active document*, where your keyboard and mouse actions will take effect.

As you open successive documents, ClarisWorks overlaps their windows on the screen so you can see a portion of each window, like this:

Because of window overlapping, windows get progressively smaller as you open several of them. Click the zoom-window button to expand a window to its maximum size on the screen.

Changing the active document

There are two ways to bring a different document to the top of the stack and make it the active document:

- Click in an area of the document you want to activate, if part of it is sticking out from underneath any documents on top of it; or

- Choose the document's name from the bottom of the View menu.

Using the Page View

The Page View shows your document as it will print on paper, including the margins and edges of each page. The Page View is automatically turned on in word processor documents so you can easily see where one page ends and the next one begins. In other document types, Page View is normally turned off. To turn on Page View, just choose *Page View* from the View menu.

You can't turn Page View on in the database's Layout mode or in communications documents, and you can't turn Page View off in word processor documents (although you can hide the page margins—see Chapter 4).

Using multiple document views

Along with opening several documents at a time, you can also open more than one view (or window) for any document. To open a new document view, make that document the active one and then choose the *New View* command from the View menu. The second view opens on top of the first view, like the one at the top of the next page:

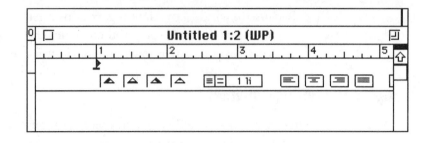

When you open multiple views of a document, the document name changes so you can tell which view is which. You can have as many views open as your Mac's memory will permit. Each view of a document is totally independent in terms of how the window is displayed and which view options are set, but any changes to the data or objects inside the document are reflected in all the views.

To close a document view, just click the close box or choose the *Close* command from the File menu, just as you would to close any document window.

Why multiple document views?

• Display different pages of a document in separate, full-sized windows.

• Display a document's Page View in one window and its normal view in another window.

• Zoom in for close work in one view and display a second view at actual size so you can see how changes will really look.

• Show a database document's Layout mode in one view and its Browse mode in another, so you can see how changes in Layout will look in Browse.

Arranging windows on the screen

With multiple documents and document views available, you could easily have a dozen or so different windows to manage on your screen. You can always activate any window (bringing it to the top of a stack of windows) by clicking in it (if you can see part of it to click in) or by choosing its name from the View menu; but the View menu also contains two commands that automatically arrange windows on the screen.

The *Tile Windows* command resizes all the windows you have open and arranges them in rectangular tiles, like the following:

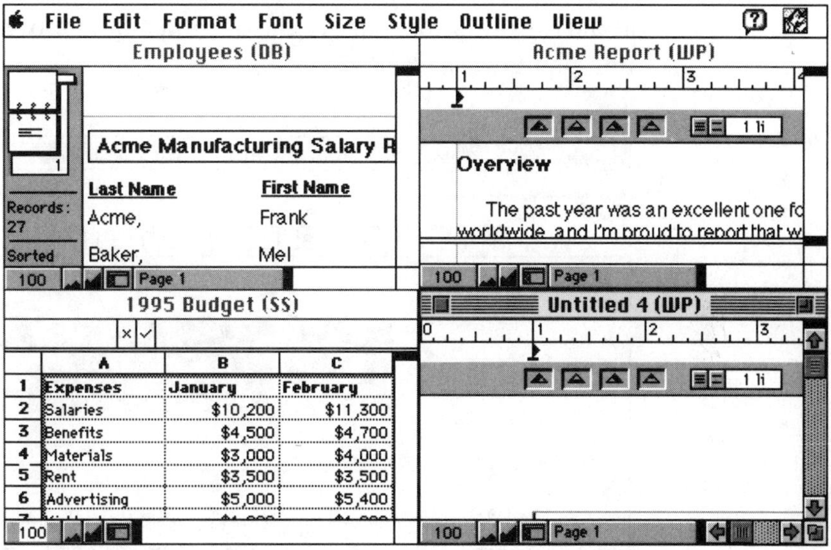

The size of each window's tile depends on how many windows you have open—with a dozen windows open, the tiles are much smaller than the ones shown above.

The *Stack Windows* command returns your group of document windows to a stack (one on top of the other), just as they were when you originally opened them.

Using headers and footers

Any ClarisWorks document (except communications documents) can have page headers and footers, which are special areas at the top and bottom of every page that display the document title, author's name, print date, and/or page number. The basic procedure for inserting page headers and footers is the same in each document type, although there are some issues specific to each document type that we'll discuss in later chapters.

To add a header or footer, choose *Insert Header* or *Insert Footer* from the Format menu. ClarisWorks inserts the header or footer at the top or bottom edge of the document and moves the insertion point there, like this:

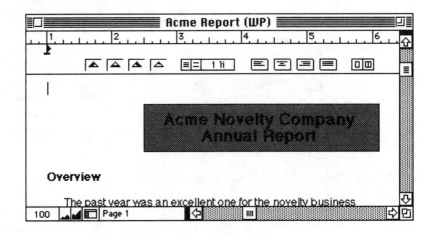

The example above is a word processing document, but if you're working in a spreadsheet, database, draw, or paint document when you insert a header or footer, ClarisWorks switches to the text tool and puts the word processor's menus in the menu bar so you can enter or format text in the header or footer. When the insertion point is in a header or footer area, you can use all the same editing and formatting tools you use in the word processor.

Once you insert a header or footer, the command on the Format menu changes to *Remove Header* or *Remove Footer*, and you choose that command to delete a header or footer.

To return to the document's normal spreadsheet, database, drawing, or painting environment, just click in the document outside of the header or footer area.

Adding document page numbers or dates

To add automatic page numbers or a date in a header or footer, choose *Insert Date* or *Insert Page #* from the Edit menu. Once you've included automatic page numbers in a document, you can determine the starting page number by choosing the *Document...* command from the Format menu. Normally, page numbers in a document start at 1, but the *Document...* command's dialog box has an option in which you can enter a different starting number. For example, if your document is the second chapter (and the 25th page) in a book, you could set its starting page number as 25. See *Setting a starting page number* on p. 41.

Setting margins and display options

Along with changing a starting page number, the *Document...* command on the Format menu lets you set the margins and other display options for each document page. The *Document...* command's dialog box looks like the one at the top of the next page:

```
┌─────────────────────────────────────────────────────┐
│  Document                                             │
│ ┌─Margins────────────┐ ┌─Display──────────────────┐  │
│ │ Top      [1 in    ] │ │  ◉▤   ○▤▤   ○[3]        │  │
│ │ Bottom   [1 in    ] │ │  ☒ Show margins          │  │
│ │ Left     [1 in    ] │ │  ☒ Show page guides      │  │
│ │ Right    [1 in    ] │ │  ☐ Title page            │  │
│ └─────────────────────┘ └──────────────────────────┘  │
│                                                        │
│   Starting page #  [1  ]      ( Cancel )   ( OK )     │
└─────────────────────────────────────────────────────┘
```

The options for setting and displaying margins and for setting a starting page number are common to all ClarisWorks documents, so we'll look at these here. However, each application has other document formatting options as well. See Chapters 4 through 10 for more on these options.

Setting margins

To set a document's margins, select the *Top, Bottom, Left,* or *Right* box and type a value. (You can also press the ⌗Tab⌗ key to skip from one box to the next.) The default margin values you'll see depend on which type of document you're working with.

The margin measurements are shown in inches, picas, points, centimeters, or millimeters, depending on which unit of measurement you've set with the *Rulers...* command on the Format menu (see p. 18).

Displaying margins

The *Show Margins* and *Show Page Guides* checkboxes let you show or hide page margins and page guides. These options are only active when the document is set to page view, and they may or may not be checked, depending on which document type you're working with.

In a word processing document, for example, Show Margins and Show Page Guides are normally checked, so your document shows the page margins and page guides, like this:

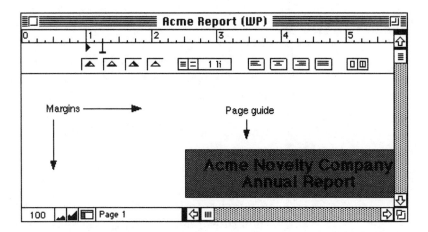

When you uncheck the Show Margins box, the page margins aren't shown, so there's more room in a window to display the text itself.

Setting a starting page number

The *Starting Page #* box lets you set the starting page number when you include automatic page numbers in a document. To set a different starting page number, just click in the box and type a different number.

Printing

The File menu's *Page Setup...* and *Print...* commands allow you to choose printing options for all ClarisWorks documents. The options available with these commands are standard across most Macintosh applications, so if you're already familiar with printing from a Mac, you can skim through this section. If you're new to the Mac, we'll cover the basics here, but you should also check your *Macintosh User's Guide* for more information.

Choosing a printer

When you first install ClarisWorks, the program doesn't automatically know which printer you want to use, so you need to select one with the Chooser.

1. Choose *Chooser* from the menu. The Chooser dialog box appears.

2. Click the icon for the printer you want to use.

3. If you chose a LaserWriter, you see the printer's name at the right side of the Chooser dialog box. (If you're on a network, there may be more than one printer connected, and you see more than one name.) Click on the name of the printer you want to use.

   If you chose a StyleWriter or ImageWriter, click the button at the right to identify the port to which the printer is connected.

4. If you chose a LaserWriter, click the Active button to turn on AppleTalk if this button isn't already selected.

5. If you chose a LaserWriter or StyleWriter, a Background Printing option appears at the right. Click the On button to turn on background printing (which tells the Mac to send print jobs to the printer by itself while you get on with other work).

6. Click the close box to put the Chooser away. Your printer is now selected.

Page setup options

Before you print a document, you can choose the type of paper you're printing on and other options with the *Page Setup...* command. The specific dialog box you see when you choose *Page Setup...* from the File menu depends on which printer and system software version you're using. The LaserWriter Page Setup dialog box for a Mac using System 7 software looks like the one below. We'll cover the options in this box that are the same or similar in other printers' Page Setup dialog boxes.

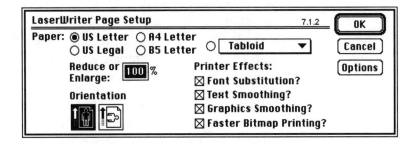

In the *Paper* section, the buttons let you select a predefined paper size. The four letter and legal sizes are standard U.S. and European paper sizes, and the *Tabloid* option is a pop-up menu that lets you select other sizes, including envelopes. The default setting is US Letter, which is 8½" by 11".

The *Reduce or Enlarge* box lets you shrink or expand the size the document's text, graphics, or other data will have when it prints. The default setting is 100% (actual size).

The *Orientation* icons in the Page Setup dialog box let you choose which direction your layout will print on the page. Clicking the horizontal icon causes your data to print across the paper's length, rather than across its width, giving you more horizontal room on a page for spreadsheet data, columnar reports, and other wide documents.

The *Printer Effects* options and the additional choices you see when you click the Options button are specific to LaserWriter printers. See your *Macintosh User's Guide* or your LaserWriter manual for more on these options.

Page Setup options can affect the arrangement of a document's contents on the page. Check the format of your document in Page View after changing Page Setup options, but before printing, to make sure the document still looks the way you want it to.

Printing options

After you've chosen the document setup options you want with the *Page Setup…* command, you're ready to print. To do this, you choose the *Print…* command, which produces a dialog box with more options of its own. Fortunately, you'll use the default settings in this dialog box most of the time.

The Print dialog box has different options, depending on which printer you've selected with the Chooser. The LaserWriter dialog box looks like the following one. Again, we'll go over the printing options that are the same or similar in all print dialog boxes. For information on options not covered here, consult your printer's manual.

```
┌────────────────────────────────────────────────────────────┐
│ LaserWriter  "CJS "shared" LaserWriter IINT"    7.1.2   ┌─────────┐ │
│                                                         │  Print  │ │
│ Copies:[1]           Pages: ◉ All ○ From:[   ] To:[   ] └─────────┘ │
│                                                         ┌─────────┐ │
│ Cover Page:   ◉ No ○ First Page ○ Last Page            │ Cancel  │ │
│                                                         └─────────┘ │
│ Paper Source: ◉ Paper Cassette  ○ Manual Feed          │
│ Print:        ◉ Black & White   ○ Color/Grayscale      │
│ Destination:  ◉ Printer         ○ PostScript® File     │
└────────────────────────────────────────────────────────────┘
```

The *Copies* box shows the number of copies you want printed. Type a different number than 1 here if you want multiple copies.

The *Pages* option is normally set to All, so every page in the document is printed. To print specific pages, type the page numbers you want printed in the From and To boxes.

The *Paper Source* options let you choose between a printer's built-in paper cassette (or sheet feeder) and its manual (or single-sheet) feeder.

Printing mail merge documents

Mail merge documents contain data from a ClarisWorks database file that is automatically merged with the other contents of the document when it's printed. For example, you might type a form letter and merge names and addresses from a database address file into it to produce personalized letters for several people in a mailing list.

To print a mail merge document, you must use the *Mail Merge...* command on the File menu. If you print a mail merge document with the *Print...* command, ClarisWorks will print the document, but it won't merge the database data into it. For more on mail merge, see Chapter 14.

Troubleshooting

You click the *Show me an onscreen tour of ClarisWorks* button on the Welcome screen and you see the message, "Not enough memory to run MacroMind Player." Choose Control Panels from the menu, open the Monitors control panel, and make sure the option is set to display 256 colors, not Thousands or Millions. If it's already set for 256 colors, close the Memory control panel, quit the program, and increase the program's memory size as explained on p. 457 in Appendix A.

You can't find a document's name in the Open dialog box. Make sure you're looking inside the right folder or on the right disk. If you are, choose the specific document type and file type from the pop-up menus. See p. 25.

You *still* can't find a document's name in the Open dialog box. The file may not be in a format that can be opened by ClarisWorks. If you have the program that created the file, try using it to save the file in a format Claris-Works can open. Check the File Type pop-up menu in the Open dialog box for a list of formats ClarisWorks supports.

You can't find a stationery document in the New Document dialog box. Be sure you have the Start with an Assistant or Stationery button selected, and check the Category pop-up menu above the list of documents to make sure it's set to None. If you still can't find the document, make sure the stationery document is saved as stationery, and that it's stored inside the ClarisWorks Stationery folder inside the Claris folder in your System Folder. See p. 33.

New paint documents are too small. Paint documents are sized to fit the available memory. Try closing other ClarisWorks documents or resetting ClarisWorks' memory size. See Appendix A.

You can't find a document on the screen. It's probably covered up by another one. Choose its name from the bottom of the View menu. If the name isn't there, the document isn't open.

A document won't print. Make sure you have a printer selected with the Chooser (p. 42) and that the printer is plugged into your Mac and is turned on. If you've chosen the Manual Feed option in the Print dialog box, the printer may be waiting for you to insert a sheet of paper.

3

Other shared features

Along with the basics of document handling, ClarisWorks has several other features that work the same way in most or all of its applications. ➤➤

- The Help system;

- Selecting data and using the Clipboard;

- The *Undo* command;

- Finding and replacing data;

- The writing tools; and

- Setting preferences.

We'll look at these features in this chapter. Mail merge, publish and subscribe, macros, and mailing documents are also common to all ClarisWorks documents, but these are more advanced features, so we'll cover them in Part 3.

Using the Help system

ClarisWorks comes with one of the most comprehensive Help systems available for a Macintosh program. This system is always available, and includes the Introduction to ClarisWorks, a Help file organized by topics, Balloon Help, and ClarisWorks Assistants.

There are two ways to access the ClarisWorks Help system:

- Choose *Help* from the menu to display a submenu of options; or

- Choose one of the Help options from the menu (if you're using System 7 or later).

The menu looks like the one at the top of the next page:

```
┌─────────────────────────────────────┐
│  About Balloon Help...               │
├─────────────────────────────────────┤
│  Show Balloons                       │
├─────────────────────────────────────┤
│  ClarisWorks Help Contents           │
│  Search for Help On...               │
│  Topics A-Z                          │
│  How to Use Help                     │
├─────────────────────────────────────┤
│  Introduction to ClarisWorks         │
├─────────────────────────────────────┤
│  ClarisWorks Assistants...           │
└─────────────────────────────────────┘
```

Using Balloon Help

When you choose *Show Balloons*, the Mac displays little pop-up balloons that explain different items on your screen. In Claris-Works, these balloons explain different controls you'll find inside a document window, such as the tab, alignment, and line spacing controls in a word processing document. Try Balloon Help for yourself to see how it works. When you get sick of balloons popping up all over the place as you move the mouse (and you will, believe me), just choose *Hide Balloons* from the ⟨?⟩ menu.

About the ClarisWorks Introduction

For a quick, self-guided tour of ClarisWorks right on your computer, you can use the Introduction to ClarisWorks. You can start the intro by choosing its command from the or ⟨?⟩ menu, or you can double-click the option to run the introduction on the ClarisWorks Welcome screen.

About the Help window

The ClarisWorks Help window is the gateway to the rest of the help functions you see on the and ⟨?⟩ menus. You can view the contents of the help file by topics, by subject categories, and by searching for a particular keyword. The ClarisWorks Help window is also where you get information about how to use the help system. The window looks like this:

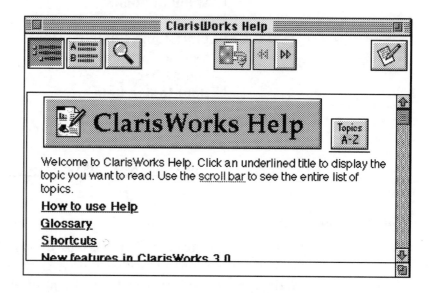

In addition to choosing one of the Help system options from a menu, you can jump directly to the Help window by pressing ⌘ ⟨?⟩; or by pressing the Help key on the Mac extended keyboard, if you're using one.

This window displays a list of topics in general categories such as drawing, painting, spreadsheet, and database. To see a list of topics under one of these general categories, just click on its name. You'll then see a list of more specific topics. You can then click on a topic to display text about it. To learn more about using Help, for example, click the How to use Help topic at the top of the contents list to display a list of Help topics, then click on the particular topic you want to read about.

The other buttons at the top of the Help Contents window correspond to other commands on the ⌘ or ⟨?⟩ menu. Here's what they do:

The Contents button takes you to the Help Contents screen if it's not displayed already. Clicking this button is the same as choosing *ClarisWorks Help Contents* from the or ? menu.

The Keywords button displays an alphabetical list of specific features in ClarisWorks and matches them to a topic name so you can locate the help text that covers it, like this:

ClarisWorks Help
Keywords   **Help Topics**

Keywords

&(ampersand)
*(multiplication sign)
+(plus sign)
-(minus/negative sign)
/(division sign)
12-hour clock format
24-hour clock format
3-dimensional charts
<(less than)
<=(less than or equal to)
<>(not equal to)
=(equal sign)
>(greater than)
>=(greater than or equal to)
ABS (Absolute Value) function
absolute references
ACOS (Arc Cosine) function

Help Topics

Numeric operators

Scroll the list at the left to find the feature you want to learn about and then select its name. The topic name that covers that feature will appear in the list at the right. You can then double-click on the topic name to display its text.

The Search button lets you locate information by searching for keywords you type in. When you click this button, you see a search dialog box like this:

ClarisWorks Help

Search for | |

Search in ☐ Topic titles

☒ Help text   **Start Search**

Topics

You can click the checkboxes to search for information among the topic titles in the Help file, or among the actual help text. When you type in matching text and click the Start Search button, ClarisWorks displays a list of topics that match the text you typed. You can then click on one of the displayed topics to view it. Clicking this button is the same as choosing *Search for Help On...* from the or ⁇ menu.

The Previous Topic button displays the last topic you viewed. So, if you were looking at a topic and then you went back to the main contents screen or the list of alphabetical topics, you could jump back to the topic you last viewed by clicking here.

The Forward and Backward buttons display the next topic in a category.

The Topics A-Z button displays a list of topics in alphabetical order, like this:

```
┌─────────────────── ClarisWorks Help ───────────────────┐
│                                                         │
│  ┌────┐ ┌────┐ ┌──┐        ┌──┐ ┌──┐ ┌──┐      ┌──┐   │
│  │    │ │    │ │🔍│        │  │ │◄◄│ │▷▷│      │📝│   │
│  └────┘ └────┘ └──┘        └──┘ └──┘ └──┘      └──┘   │
│                                                         │
│ ┌─────────────────────────────────────────────────┬─┐ │
│ │ Click a letter to see an alphabetical list of Help topics. Then click an │▲│ │
│ │ underlined title for more information.            │ │ │
│ │ A B C D E F G H I J K L M N O P Q R S T U V W X Y Z │ │ │
│ │                                                   │ │ │
│ │ About borders                                     │ │ │
│ │ About cell references                             │ │ │
│ │ About charts                                      │ │ │
│ │ About communications                              │ │ │
│ │ About communications documents                    │ │ │
│ │ About databases                                   │ │ │
│ │ About drawing                                     │ │ │
│ │ About formulas                                    │ │ │
│ │ About frames                                      │ │ │
│ │ About functions                                   │▼│ │
│ │ About layout parts                                │ │ │
│ │ About letters                                     │▣│ │
│ └───────────────────────────────────────────────────┴─┘ │
└─────────────────────────────────────────────────────────┘
```

You can click an alphabet letter to show the topic list for that letter, and then click on any topic heading for help with that topic. Clicking this button is the same as choosing the *Topics A-Z* command from the or ⟨?⟩ menu.

The Notes button displays a dialog box where you can type your own notes about a particular topic, like this:

Notes for: Contents

Cancel

OK

You get a different, blank notes box for each topic you display, so there's plenty of room to make notes for yourself. The notes are automatically stored with the topic you made them about, so you can always display them again by clicking the Notes button.

Explore the help system for yourself. You'll quickly see how useful it is.

You can print out any screen from the Help window by simply displaying it and choosing the *Print...* command from the File menu.

Using ClarisWorks Assistants

Assistants are pre-recorded scripts that automatically perform a complex chore in ClarisWorks. ClarisWorks has two kinds of Assistants. The ones you choose from the New Document dialog box guide you through the creation of whole documents, such as newsletters, address files, and so on. The ones you choose from the or menus help you perform specific tasks inside a document you already have open.

For help in making a new document, click the Start With an Assistant or Stationery button in the New Document dialog box. You'll see a list of Assistants in the list at the right (see p. 62 for an example of this screen). Once you double-click on an Assistant name, you'll see a dialog box that explains what the Assistant does, like this:

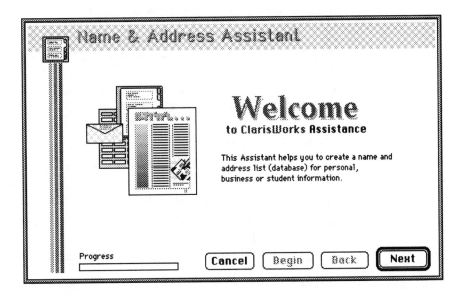

You click the Next button to continue creating the document. The Assistant will display one screen after another, giving you choices about how the document should look. Once you've made all the choices, the Assistant creates a new Untitled document and opens it on your screen. The whole process is self-explanatory. Try an Assistant yourself to see how it works.

When you choose the *ClarisWorks Assistants...* command from the or menu, you see a dialog box like this:

```
╔══════════════════════════════════════════════════╗
║ ░░░░░░░░░░░░░░ Select Assistant ░░░░░░░░░░░░░░     ║
║ ┌──────────────────────────────────────────────┐  ║
║ │  Category: |General ▼|                        │  ║
║ │  ┌──────────────────────────────────────┬──┐ │  ║
║ │  │ Address Envelope                     │▲ │ │  ║
║ │  │ Find ClarisWorks Documents           │  │ │  ║
║ │  │ Insert Footnote                      │  │ │  ║
║ │  │ Insert Footnote                      │  │ │  ║
║ │  │ Make Table                           │  │ │  ║
║ │  │ Make Table                           │▼ │ │  ║
║ │  └──────────────────────────────────────┴──┘ │  ║
║ │  To use this assistant, select the text for the addressee │  ║
║ │  first.                                       │  ║
║ │                                               │  ║
║ │           ( Cancel )      ╔══════════╗        │  ║
║ │                           ║    OK    ║        │  ║
║ │                           ╚══════════╝        │  ║
║ └──────────────────────────────────────────────┘  ║
╚══════════════════════════════════════════════════╝
```

The list shows Assistants for different operations. This list appears when you're in a word processing document–you'll see a different list when you're in other documents. To get help with one of the operations listed, you just double-click on its name and follow the instructions on the screen. (The double entries for Insert Footnote and Make Table are a bug–choosing either one of them performs the same operation.)

The Category pop-up menu above the list doesn't change. Eventually, Claris hopes to add more Assistants and group them into categories you'll be able to choose from this menu.

Try these Assistants for yourself and see what they can do.

. . . .

Selecting, cutting, copying, and pasting data

You select, cut, copy, and paste data in ClarisWorks the same way you do in every Mac program. If you're familiar with these operations from using other programs, enough said. If not, here are some basic points to keep in mind as you use ClarisWorks.

Select it first

Before you can work on anything on the Mac, whether it's a disk, folder, window, icon, number, string of text, or graphic object, you have to select it. You can tell when something is selected because it turns dark.

There are several ways to select things on the Mac, depending on what you're selecting.

- Point and click to select an icon, filename, or button.

- Click, hold down the mouse button, and drag a selection rectangle around a group of objects, or drag across text, database records in Browse mode, or spreadsheet cells.

- (Shift)-click on additional items to add them to a selection. If you already have one item selected, (Shift)-clicking adds the next item you click on to the group of selected items. If you're selecting text, you can select one character at the beginning of a paragraph (or document, for that matter), scroll to the end of the paragraph or document, and then (Shift)-click to select all the text between your first and last click points.

Copying versus cutting

Once you've selected text, numbers, data, or graphic objects, you can copy or cut them. Copying leaves the selection where it is; cutting removes the selection.

To copy a selection, press ⌘C or choose *Copy* from the Edit menu. ClarisWorks makes a copy of the selection and stores it in a portion of the Mac's memory called the Clipboard; you can then paste the selection in another location. (See *Pasting data*, next.)

To cut something, press ⌘X or choose *Cut* from the Edit menu. ClarisWorks cuts, or removes, the selection from its place in the document and places it on the Clipboard. You can then paste the selection into another location.

If you haven't selected anything in a document, both the *Copy* and *Cut* commands are dimmed on the Edit menu, because there's nothing selected for ClarisWorks to copy or cut.

The Clipboard retains whatever data you copy or cut until you copy or cut something else. To see the Clipboard's contents at any time, choose *Show Clipboard* from the Edit menu. The Clipboard window opens at the bottom of your screen.

Pasting data

Once you've copied something to the Clipboard, you can paste it to a different location. Just move the insertion point to the place where you want to paste the data and then press ⌘V or choose *Paste* from the Edit menu. (If you haven't copied or cut anything to the Clipboard since you started ClarisWorks, the *Paste* command is dimmed because the Clipboard is empty.)

Because you can have many different document windows open at a time, you can easily move data from one document to another by cutting and pasting. Just select the data in one document and copy or cut it, then activate a different document window, move the insertion point to the place where you want it, and paste the data there.

And, because the Clipboard retains whatever you cut or copy to it until you cut or copy something else, you can put a copy of the same data in several different places by pasting over and over. For example, you might want to paste the same city name into the City field of several database records. You can do that by copying the name once, then pasting it in the City field of each record where you want the same data to appear.

 ClarisWorks pastes data into documents with different results, depending on the type of document you're pasting into. Also, there are additional commands on the Edit menu for pasting in special types of information, depending on which document type you're working with. For more information on these differences, see Chapters 4 through 10.

 If you keep changing data in one document and having to recopy and paste it into another document, try using publish and subscribe instead to create an automatic data link. See Chapter 15.

Undoing changes

Everybody makes mistakes, but the *Undo* command on the Edit menu can save you. ClarisWorks keeps track of the very last keyboard or mouse move you made. To cancel this last action, choose *Undo* or press ⌘Z.

 If you forget to use *Undo* and decide you want to go back to the last saved version of your document (which is like undoing everything you've done since you last saved it), choose *Revert...* from the File menu.

Finding and replacing data

Once you've got a lot of text or data in a document, you may want to quickly locate specific words or number, or automatically change a particular word or number to something else. The

Find/Change submenu off the Edit menu is the key to these operations. When you point to *Find/Change* and hold down the mouse
button, you see a submenu like this:

```
┌──────────────────────┐ ┌────────────────────────────┐
│ Find/Change      ▶ │ │ Find/Change...      ⌘F │
└──────────────────────┘ │ Find Again          ⌘E │
                         │ Find Selection   ⇧⌘E │
                         └────────────────────────────┘
```

You can find or replace text anywhere in a word processor,
spreadsheet, database, or draw document. This includes data in
database fields, text in text frames or on database layouts, or numbers in spreadsheet cells. When you choose the *Find/Change...*
command from the submenu, ClarisWorks displays the
Find/Change window, like this:

```
┌─────────────────────────────────────────────────────┐
│ ▣▢▬▬▬▬▬▬▬▬▬▬▬▬ Find/Change ▬▬▬▬▬▬▬▬▬▬▬▬▬ │
│  Find                         Change                  │
│ ┌────────────────────────┐  ┌──────────────────────┐ │
│ │                        │  │                      │ │
│ └────────────────────────┘  └──────────────────────┘ │
│ ☐ Whole word   ☐ Case sensitive                      │
│ ┌────────────┐ ┌──────────┐ ┌─────────────┐ ┌───────────┐ │
│ │ Change All │ │  Change  │ │ Change, find│ │ Find Next │ │
│ └────────────┘ └──────────┘ └─────────────┘ └───────────┘ │
└─────────────────────────────────────────────────────┘
```

To find text, a number, a date, or a time, type it in the *Find* box
and click the *Find Next* button or press Return. ClarisWorks
searches the document. When there's a match to the Find box's
data, ClarisWorks selects it in the document, and the Find/Change
window remains open on the screen. (Since it's a window, you can
drag it around the screen to reveal selected data underneath it.) If
there's no match to the Find data, you see a message saying so.

When it gets to the end of a document, ClarisWorks automatically resumes its search from the beginning of the document
again, and it will cycle through the document endlessly as long
as you keep clicking the Find Next button. It pays to watch the
document so you don't waste time locating the same strings
over and over.

If you want ClarisWorks to be more particular when searching for data, click the *Whole Word* box (so it matches whole words only) or the *Case Sensitive* box (so it matches the case of the text in the Find box).

Replacing data

To replace data in the Find box with other data, type replacement data in the *Change* box. Once you've entered replacement data, click a button to find or replace information.

- Clicking the *Find Next* button finds and selects the first occurrence of Find data.

- Clicking the *Change* button replaces a selected occurrence of Find data with the Change data.

- Clicking the *Change, Find* button replaces a selected occurrence of Find data with the Change data, and then automatically finds the next occurrence of Find data.

- Clicking the *Change All* button replaces all occurrences of the Find data with the Change data.

When you're finished finding or replacing data, click the Find/Change window's close box to put it away.

The data you type in the Find box remains there even after you put the Find/Change window away. To search again for the same thing, choose the *Find Again* command from the Find/Change submenu. ClarisWorks automatically searches for the same criterion without displaying the Find/Change window.

If you'd rather not type in a Find string, select the data you want to search for and then choose *Find Selection* from the Find/Change submenu. ClarisWorks searches for your selection without displaying the Find/Change window.

Finding invisible characters

ClarisWorks word processor documents have invisible characters such as spaces, tabs, and returns that separate one paragraph from another. Sometimes it's useful to find and replace these invisible characters.

For example, suppose a document that you received with the communications program has a tab at the beginning of each paragraph, and you don't want one. By searching for a single tab character and replacing each one with nothing, you can have ClarisWorks automatically eliminate all the tabs in the document.

Invisible Characters

This table shows the invisible characters in ClarisWorks, which keys you press to search for them, and what you see in the Find box when you press those keys:

Invisible character	Keys you press	What you see
Return	⌃ ⌘ Return	\p
Tab	⌃ ⌘ Tab	\t
Space	Spacebar	nothing
Nonbreaking space	Option Spacebar	nothing
Column break	⌃ ⌘ Enter	\c
Time	\h	\h
Date	\d	\d
Backslash (\)	\\	\\

To display invisible space, return, and tab characters in your document, choose the *Preferences…* command from the Edit menu and click the *Show Invisibles* box in the text preferences.

What Find finds

The Find function in ClarisWorks always finds *exactly* what you type in the Find box. If you're searching for *$1534* and you type

1534, for example, ClarisWorks won't find what you're looking for because you didn't include the dollar sign.

Also, be careful when searching for times and dates that you've inserted with the Edit menu's *Insert Time* and *Insert Date* commands (see *Inserting dates, times, and page numbers,* on p. 87 in Chapter 4). The times and dates displayed when you choose these commands are markers, not text, so ClarisWorks won't be able to find them even if you type exactly the same times or dates in the Find box. To find times and dates that have been inserted with time or date markers, search for these markers' invisible characters.

Finally, unless you limit the search with the Whole Word or Case Sensitive checkbox, ClarisWorks will find any occurrence of a Find string you type, whether it's part of a word or not, and no matter how it's capitalized. Use the checkboxes in the Find/Change window to locate the data you want more quickly.

Using the writing tools

ClarisWorks has a selection of tools you can use to work with text anywhere except in communications documents. There's a spelling checker, a thesaurus, and automatic hyphenation and word count features. You'll probably use these features most in word processing documents, but it's nice to know you can also use them in spreadsheets, database documents, drawing documents, or text frames anywhere. All these features are available on the *Writing Tools* submenu on the Edit menu.

You can use the spelling checker, thesaurus, word count, or hyphenation on text inside a text frame in a paint document, but only when you first create the frame. Once you've created the text and clicked away from the frame, the text becomes a bitmapped image and ClarisWorks no longer recognizes it. See *Special situations* on p. 375 in Chapter 12.

About the spelling checker

The spelling checker verifies the spelling of text in a document by comparing the words in it with the words in its built-in dictionaries. ClarisWorks uses both a *Main Dictionary* and a *User Dictionary*. The Main Dictionary contains over a hundred thousand words. The Main Dictionary can't be changed, but you can add words to or delete them from the User Dictionary.

When it finds a word in your document that isn't in the Main Dictionary, ClarisWorks gives you three choices. You can correct the word by typing or selecting a new version of it; add the word to the User Dictionary so ClarisWorks won't question it again; or skip over the word (if the spelling is correct but you don't want to add it to the User Dictionary).

Although it only uses one main and one user dictionary at a time, you can install different main and user dictionaries. Claris offers main dictionaries in several languages, and you can substitute any of them for ClarisWorks' standard Main Dictionary. You can also develop several different user dictionaries and have ClarisWorks use different ones at different times. For example, you might have a dictionary filled with technical terms for when you're working on a report, and another filled with the names of friends for when you're checking the spelling of letters.

Finally, ClarisWorks works with user dictionaries from other Claris products, such as MacWrite II, MacDraw Pro, and File-Maker Pro. If you've developed a user dictionary with another Claris product, you can install it as the one ClarisWorks uses. (See *Managing dictionaries* on p. 70.)

What the spelling checker checks

The spelling checker checks the data in documents or selections in different ways, depending on which type of document you're working with. No matter what, though, you activate the spelling checker by selecting a document or text inside a document, holding down the *Writing Tools* command on the Edit menu, and then choosing *Check Document Spelling...* or *Check Selection Spelling...* from the Writing Tools submenu.

In word processor, spreadsheet, and draw documents, the *Check Document Spelling...* command checks the spelling of all the text in the document, including all the text in spreadsheet charts, text frames, and spreadsheet frames.

In the database, *Check Document Spelling...* checks the spelling of data inside database fields when you're in Browse mode, and it checks the names of database fields or other layout text when you're in Layout mode.

To check only some of the text in a document, select only that text and then choose the *Check Selection Spelling...* command.

Using the spelling checker isn't a substitute for proofreading your document. Even if a word is spelled correctly, it may not be used correctly in your document. Be sure to proofread important documents before considering them finished.

Checking spelling

To check the spelling of a selection or a document, select the document window or the text inside it that you want to check, and then choose either *Check Document Spelling...* or *Check Selection Spelling...* from the Writing Tools submenu. ClarisWorks begins checking the document's spelling and soon displays the Spelling window, like this:

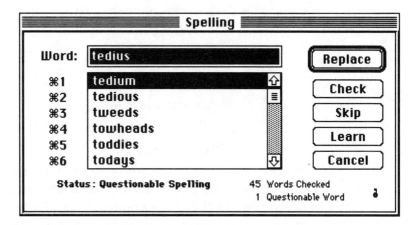

You can drag this window around the screen to reveal text it may be covering up.

In the example above, the word "tedius" has been found questionable, as shown by the message in the Status area at the bottom of the window. The window offers several options for dealing with questionable words.

The *Word* box shows the questionable word. If you want to correct its spelling, you can type your correction into this box, or select one of the alternates listed below it. To select an alternate from the list:

- Double-click on the alternate;

- Select the alternate and click the *Replace* button or press Return; or

- Press the ⌘-number combination next to the alternate.

The replacement word is then put in the document where the original was, and the text around it is automatically reformatted to accommodate the new word.

If you type a replacement in the Word box and aren't sure it's correct, click the *Check* button to verify its spelling. The *Status* area tells you if the spelling is correct; or you see a list of alternate words if the spelling isn't correct.

To have ClarisWorks ignore the questionable word, click the *Skip* button or press ⌘S.

To add the questionable word to your user dictionary, click the *Learn* button or press ⌘L.

The *Cancel* button ends the spelling check, puts the Spelling window away, and returns you to the document.

After you choose an option for each word, you see the next questionable word as ClarisWorks moves through the text in the document. When all questionable words have been found, the Replace button at the upper right of the Spelling window says Done, and you can click it to put the window away.

You can use the spelling checker to look up any word, even if you're not checking a document. Just choose *Check Document Spelling...* from the Writing Tools submenu, type the word you want to look up in the Word menu, and click the Check button.

Along with the status of the current word, the Status area at the bottom of the window shows how many words have been checked so far and how many have been found questionable. If you want to see the questionable word in context with the words that surround it, click the flag icon in the lower right corner of the window. The window lengthens and you see the word in context.

Using the thesaurus

With the thesaurus, you can select a word and find synonyms for it. To use the thesaurus:

1. Select the word in your document for which you want to find synonyms.

2. Choose the *Thesaurus...* command from the Writing Tools submenu. The Thesaurus window appears, like this:

```
═══════════════ Word Finder® Thesaurus ═══════════════
 joke:
  noun    banter, chatter;                                          ⬆
   ∞      antic, escapade, adventure, caper, lark, mischief, prank, trick;  ▤
   ∞      humor, jest, banter, comedy, crack, funniness, gag, quip,
          small talk, wisecrack, wit, witticism;
   ∞      satire, caricature, buffoonery, burlesque, comedy, farce, humor,
          imitation, lampoon, mockery, parody, spoof, takeoff, travesty.    ⬇

 Find: [ joke            ]  ( Lookup ) ( Last Word ) ( Cancel ) ( Replace )
```

As with the Spelling window, you can drag the Thesaurus window around your screen to reveal different parts of the document underneath it.

At the top of the window you see a list of words that are synonymous with the word selected in your document. These are divided into usage categories, such as nouns, verbs, and so on.

The word you selected in your document is also entered automatically in the *Find* box. If you want to find a synonym for a different word, type it here and click the *Lookup* button.

When you see a word you like, double-click it or select the word and click the *Replace* button. The word replaces the one you selected in your document and the Thesaurus window disappears.

The *Last Word* button tells ClarisWorks to list the last ten words for which you looked up synonyms, and lists them in the upper part of the window. To see the synonyms for one of these words again, select the word and click the Lookup button.

Click the *Cancel* button to put the window away without making any changes.

Hyphenating text automatically

ClarisWorks' automatic hyphenation feature helps clean up your documents by hyphenating long words at the ends of lines. Rather than wrapping a long word like "parliamentarianism" down to the next line and leaving a big gap at the end of the previous line, ClarisWorks hyphenates the word to better fill the available space.

To turn on automatic hyphenation, choose *Auto-Hyphenate* from the Writing Tools submenu. A check mark appears next to the command name, and ClarisWorks then hyphenates text as you enter it. If there is already text in a document when you turn the feature on, that text will also be hyphenated. If you edit your document so the position of an automatically hyphenated word changes, ClarisWorks removes hyphens or moves them as necessary.

With the automatic hyphenation feature on, ClarisWorks hyphenates any word that is six or more letters long, but only if there will be at least two letters before the hyphen and three letters after it. ClarisWorks decides how to hyphenate words by using a built-in hyphenation dictionary that is installed automatically when you install ClarisWorks. If you don't like the way Claris-Works breaks up a word, or if you'd like it to hyphenate additional words, you can edit the dictionary. (See *Editing the user and hyphenation dictionaries* on page 72.)

To turn off the hyphenation feature, choose *Auto Hyphenate* again to remove the check mark next to its name on the Writing Tools submenu.

Hyphenating text manually

Along with automatic hyphenation, you can hyphenate words manually in two ways:

- Press - (-) to insert a regular hyphen; or

- Press ⌘- to insert a discretionary hyphen.

A regular hyphen appears no matter where the word is located, while a discretionary hyphen only appears when the word is broken at that point. If subsequent editing moves a word with a discretionary hyphen so that it ends up all on one line, the discretionary hyphen disappears.

Using automatic hyphenation does not remove any regular or discretionary hyphens you've added to a document.

Counting words

The new *Word Count...* command in ClarisWorks 3.0 gives you statistics about the number of characters, lines, words, paragraphs, and pages in a document. To use the command, just display the document for which you want statistics and choose *Word Count...* from the Writing Tools submenu. You'll see a dialog box like the one at the top of the next page:

```
┌─────────────────────────────────┐
│  Word Count                     │
│  ──────────────────────────     │
│  Characters: 7247               │
│      Words: 886                 │
│      Lines: 262                 │
│  Paragraphs: 228                │
│      Pages: 7                   │
│                    ┌────────┐   │
│                    │   OK   │   │
│                    └────────┘   │
└─────────────────────────────────┘
```

The *Word Count…* command always counts all the text in a document with one exception. If you place the insertion point inside a text frame in a spreadsheet, database, or drawing document, it will count only the words inside that text frame.

Managing dictionaries

When you run a spelling check or use the thesaurus or automatic hyphenation, ClarisWorks uses a main dictionary and a user dictionary for spelling, a thesaurus dictionary, and a hyphenation dictionary. If you have more than one of either type of dictionary, you can choose which one ClarisWorks uses in a particular check. ClarisWorks will use whatever dictionaries you've installed until you remove them or install different ones.

To install a dictionary:

1. Choose *Select Dictionaries…* from the Writing Tools submenu. ClarisWorks displays a directory dialog box like the one at the top of the next page:

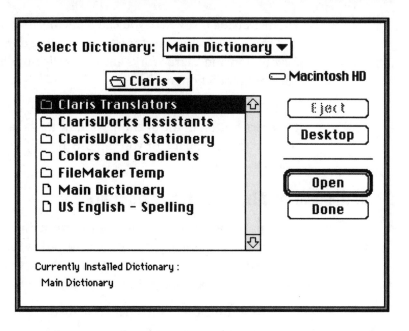

2. Choose the dictionary type you want to install from the Select Dictionary pop-up menu. The status area at the bottom of the dialog box shows the name of the dictionary of this type that's currently installed.

3. Navigate to the location of the dictionary file you want to install, then select the dictionary name. The *Open* button at the right changes to *Select*.

4. Click the *Select* button. ClarisWorks installs the dictionary and puts the dialog box away.

Installing a dictionary automatically removes any dictionary of the same type that's in use. If you have a user dictionary installed and you want to remove it without installing another one, choose *User Dictionary* from the pop-up menu, select the dictionary name, and then click the *None* button that appears at the right.

Creating a new user dictionary

You can also create new user dictionaries by clicking the *New...* button in the Select Dictionaries dialog box. ClarisWorks displays another dialog box where you can name the new dictionary file and choose a location to store it. Once you've done so, click the *Save* button and ClarisWorks automatically installs it as the current user dictionary.

To add words to a new user dictionary, you can either click the *Learn* button in the Spelling window to add a questionable word to the dictionary, or you can use the editing features described next.

Editing the user and hyphenation dictionaries

You can add words to or remove them from the current user or hyphenation dictionary at any time. To add or remove individual words when you're not doing a spelling check, the simplest method is to type the words. Here's the procedure:

1. Select the user or hyphenation dictionary you want to edit, using the *Select Dictionaries...* command, then click the *Edit* button that appears at the right. ClarisWorks displays a dialog box like this:

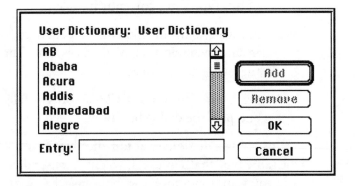

To add a word, type the new word in the *Entry* box and click the *Add* button or press Return. To remove a word, select it in the list of words and click the *Remove* button. To edit a word (or to change the hyphenation of a word in the hyphenation dictionary), you must remove the existing version and then add the new one.

Setting document preferences

Preferences are basic options you can choose for different types of operations in ClarisWorks. You can set preferences any time by choosing *Preferences...* from the bottom of the Edit menu. You'll see a dialog box like this:

There are either six or seven icons in the scrolling list at the left, depending on whether or not you have PowerTalk mail features installed on your Mac. These icons, when selected, display different options for setting general, text, graphics, spreadsheet, palette, communications, and—if you have PowerTalk installed—mail preferences.

To set a preferences option:

1. Click an icon to display the preferences options you want.

2. Click the specific option or options at the right.

3. Click the OK button or press (Return).

The preferences options you first see when you begin using ClarisWorks for the first time are the *default options*–they're set for all new documents. When you change any of the preferences, you change them only for the document you have open at the time. To reset an option so it affects all new documents, choose the new options you want, click the *Make Default* button, and then click OK.

Here's a quick rundown of the preferences options.

General preferences

General preferences control how ClarisWorks deals with documents and displays fonts in its Font menu.

Show Fonts in Font Menu displays each of your installed fonts in its actual typeface in the Font menu, so you can see how each font looks.

Old Version Alert tells ClarisWorks 3.0 to alert you with a message whenever you open a document created with an older version of the program.

Locked File Warning tells ClarisWorks 3.0 to alert you with a message whenever you open a document that is locked and can't be changed. (If a document is locked, you can unlock it by selecting its icon in the Finder, choosing *Get Info* from the File menu, and clicking the Locked checkbox.)

Paint Reduction Warning tells ClarisWorks 3.0 to alert you whenever you open a paint document that can't be made full size because there isn't enough memory available.

[v3.0] Suffix adds this suffix to the name of any document created with an older version of ClarisWorks when you open it with version 3.0. You can then save the converted document without replacing the old one, because the two documents have different names.

Create Custom Icon saves every paint document with an icon that's a miniature representation of the document's contents.

When you view the document in Icon or Small Icon view in the Finder, you see the document itself in miniature.

Create Preview saves every paint document so that a miniature preview version of it appears in the Open dialog box when you select its name. (This feature only works if you're using System 7.5 or later.)

The *On Startup, Show* buttons let you determine which dialog box, if any, appears on the screen when ClarisWorks starts up. As you can see, you can choose the Welcome, New Document, or Open Document dialog boxes, or have nothing except the Claris-Works menus at the top of the screen.

```
Preferences

  ┌─────────────────────────────────────────────────┐
  │  ▲    General                                     │
  │ [General icon]  ☒ Show Fonts in Font Menu         │
  │ [General]       ☒ Old Version Alert               │
  │                 ☒ Locked File Warning             │
  │  ┌───┐          ☒ Paint Reduction Warning         │
  │  │ A │          ☒ [v3.0] Suffix                   │
  │  └───┘                                            │
  │  Text           Saved Documents      On startup, show │
  │                 ☐ Create Custom Icon  ◉ Welcome   │
  │ [Graphics icon] ☒ Create Preview      ○ New Document │
  │                                       ○ Open Document │
  │  Graphics ▼                           ○ Nothing   │
  └─────────────────────────────────────────────────┘

       ( Make Default )   ( Cancel )   ( OK )
```

Text preferences

Text preferences affect text in word processing and database documents, as well as in text frames anywhere.

```
┌─────────────────────────────────────────────────┐
│  Preferences                                      │
│  ┌──────────────────────────────────────────────┐│
│  │ ▲  ┌ Text ─────────────────────────────────┐ ││
│  │ ▓  │                                        │ ││
│  │ ▓  │ General  ☐ Smart Quotes ( ' ' ," " )   │ ││
│  │General│       ☐ Show Invisibles             │ ││
│  │    │          ☐ Fractional Character Widths │ ││
│  │ ┌─┐│          ☒ Auto Number Footnotes       │ ││
│  │ │A││        Starting Footnote # ▐1      ▌   │ ││
│  │ └─┘│                                        │ ││
│  │Text│ Date     ○ 7/26/92                     │ ││
│  │    │ Format   ○ Jul 26, 1992                │ ││
│  │    │          ○ July 26, 1992               │ ││
│  │    │          ● Sun, Jul 26, 1992           │ ││
│  │Graphics│      ○ Sunday, July 26, 1992       │ ││
│  │ ▼  └────────────────────────────────────────┘ ││
│  └──────────────────────────────────────────────┘│
│         (Make Default)  (Cancel)  ( OK )          │
└─────────────────────────────────────────────────┘
```

Smart Quotes replaces the regular straight quote and apostrophe marks with curly ones as shown.

Show Invisibles displays Space, Tab, and Return markers in word processing documents.

Fractional Character Widths adjusts the spacing between characters more precisely for a more professional look.

Auto Number Footnotes works in word processing documents. Footnotes are numbered consecutively when this option is checked; you set the starting number by typing it in the box below.

The *Date Format* buttons let you choose the format that dates will have when you use the *Insert Date* command on the Edit menu in word processing documents or text frames.

For more about these options, see Chapter 4.

Graphics preferences

Graphics preferences control the way graphic objects are selected, drawn, and manipulated.

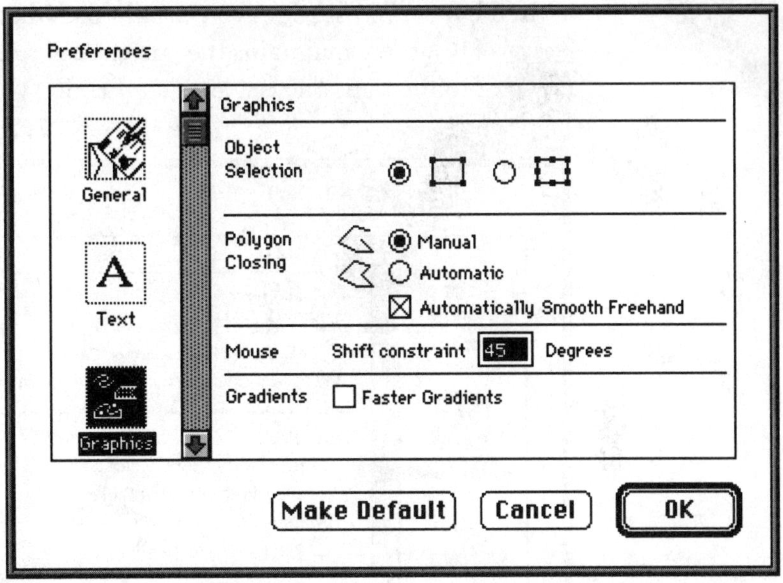

Preferences

Graphics

Object Selection ◉ ▭ ○ ▥

Polygon Closing ◉ Manual ○ Automatic ☒ Automatically Smooth Freehand

Mouse   Shift constraint [45] Degrees

Gradients   ☐ Faster Gradients

General   A   Text   Graphics

(Make Default)   (Cancel)   (OK)

Object Selection sets the number of handles that appear when an object is selected.

Polygon Closing lets you draw polygons more easily by closing them automatically.

Mouse changes the way object movements are constrained when you hold down the s key.

Gradients helps the gradient palettes appear more quickly.

For more information about these options, see Chapters 8 and 9.

Spreadsheet preferences

Spreadsheet preferences give you some options about how the arrow keys and the (Return) and (Enter) keys behave.

In the *Arrow Keys* section, you can choose whether pressing an arrow key selects the next cell in that direction or moves the insertion point in the spreadsheet's entry bar.

In the *Enter Key* section, you can choose whether pressing the
Return or Enter key maintains the current cell selection or moves it
down or to the right one cell after confirming your data entry.

```
┌─────────────────────────────────────────────────────────┐
│  Preferences                                              │
│  ┌──────────┬──────────────────────────────────────────┐ │
│  │          │ Spreadsheet                              │ │
│  │   ╔══╗  ▲│ ──────────────────────────────────────── │ │
│  │   Graphics│ Arrow Keys                               │ │
│  │          │   Pressing arrow keys                    │ │
│  │          │   ○ Always Selects Another Cell          │ │
│  │          │   ◉ Moves the Insertion Point in the     │ │
│  │  ▦▦▦     │         Entry Bar                        │ │
│  │ Spreadsheet│ ──────────────────────────────────────── │ │
│  │          │ Enter Key                                │ │
│  │          │   Press Enter to confirm entry and       │ │
│  │   🎨     │   ○ Stay in the Current Cell             │ │
│  │  Palettes▼│   ◉ Move Down One Cell                   │ │
│  │          │   ○ Move Right One Cell                  │ │
│  └──────────┴──────────────────────────────────────────┘ │
│                                                           │
│        ( Make Default )  ( Cancel )  (( OK ))             │
└─────────────────────────────────────────────────────────┘
```

For more on spreadsheet navigation, see Chapter 5.

Palettes preferences

```
Preferences

  Graphics

  Spreadsheet        ≡       Spreadsheet

  Palettes

                              Arrow Keys
                                Pressing arrow keys
                                ○ Always Selects Another Cell
                                ● Moves the Insertion Point in the Entry Bar

                              Enter Key
                                Press Enter to confirm entry and
                                ○ Stay in the Current Cell
                                ● Move Down One Cell
                                ○ Move Right One Cell

                     ( Make Default )   ( Cancel )    ( OK )
```

Palettes preferences control display options for the fill and pen color palettes and for the Shortcuts palette.

```
Preferences

  Spreadsheet                 Palettes

  Palettes                    Color    ○ Drawing and Text Colors
                                       ● Editable 256 Color Palette

  Communication                        ( Load Palette... )   ( Save Palette... )

                              Shortcuts ● Grow Vertically      Grow    10
                                        ○ Grow Horizontally    Limit:

                                       ☐ Shortcuts Palette Visible on Startup
                                       ☒ Separate Document Shortcuts
                                       ☐ Show Names

                     ( Make Default )   ( Cancel )    ( OK )
```

The *Color* options let you select different numbers of colors on the color palettes for the fill and pen tools. You can also create or edit palettes to add or change the colors on them. See Chapters 8 and 9 for more information.

The *Shortcuts* options control how shortcuts are displayed and used in documents. See Chapter 13 for more information.

Communications and Mail preferences

The Communications and Mail preferences are the two most complex groups of options, and you need to understand the communications program and ClarisWorks' mail features before these make any sense. See Chapter 10 for more about communications and Chapter 17 for more about mail.

PART

2

The six applications

4

The word processor

With the ClarisWorks word processor, you can prepare any sort of written document, from a one-page letter to a book-length manuscript. You type text in a word processing document much as you do on a typewriter, except it's a lot quieter, it's easier to correct mistakes or change text formats, and you can make sure your document is perfect before you commit it to paper. ➤➤

The word processor window

When you open a word processing document, the window looks like this:

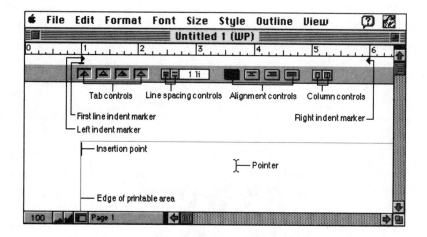

The *insertion point* is blinking at the beginning of the first line of the document. The area in which you can type (the *printable area*) is bounded by the dotted line, and the white space outside the line represents the top, bottom, left, and right page margins. When the pointer is inside the document window, it changes from an arrow to the I-beam you see above.

All the controls below the ruler let you adjust the formatting of the document, setting left and right indents, inserting or adjusting tab stops, setting line spacing or text alignment, or specifying the number of columns in which you want text arranged. See *Formatting paragraphs* on p. 93 for more information.

Entering and changing text

As you type, characters appear in the printable area. When your text reaches the right edge of the document it automatically wraps around to the next line. Try typing a few lines to see for yourself.

ClarisWorks wraps lines at spaces between words. If you don't want two words to be broken up between two lines (proper names, for example), type a nonbreaking space between them by pressing (Option)(Spacebar).

The only time you need to press the (Return) key is when you want to end a paragraph. Pressing the (Return) key moves the insertion point from the current line down to the next one and inserts an invisible *return* (or new paragraph) marker at the end of the line you were on. To insert extra blank lines in a document, press the (Return) key for each blank line you want to add.

To display the invisible return, space, and tab characters, choose *Preferences...* from the Edit menu and click the Show Invisibles checkbox.

Adding text

If you want to add text in the midst of other text in a document, just click to move the insertion point to the place where you want the new text to start and then begin typing. The characters you type are inserted at the insertion point's position, and any text after that automatically moves over or down to accommodate it.

Selecting and editing text

Before you can make any changes to text in a document, you must select it or at least move the insertion point to the place where you want to make the change. To move the insertion point:

- Point to the place where you want the insertion point to appear and click the mouse button.

- Press one of the arrow keys on your keyboard;

- Press the `Tab` key to move to the next tab stop (see *Setting tab stops* on p. 96); or

- Press the `Delete` key (to back up and erase the character to the left).

Moving the insertion point or using the `Delete` key is the best strategy when you want to correct a small error. But if you want to replace several words, it's easier to select the text. Once you've selected text, you don't need to delete it before typing new text—the new text automatically replaces what you've selected. To select text, just drag the pointer over the characters you want to select.

If you want to select several paragraphs, just drag up or down on the screen—the document scrolls automatically. As an alternative, you can `Shift`-click: click at the beginning of the text you want to select, scroll the document if necessary, and then `Shift`-click at the end of the text you want to select. All the text between the first click and the `Shift`-click is selected.

To select an entire document, choose *Select All* from the Edit menu. This is handy when you want to make a character or paragraph formatting change to the whole document, such as changing the font or style of the text.

The word processor also has three mouse-click shortcuts for selecting specific groups of text:

- Double-click on any character in a word to select the whole word;

- Triple-click on any character to select the current line;

- Quadruple-click on any character to select the current paragraph.

Deleting, moving, and copying text

To delete text, just select it and press the [Delete] key.

To remove text from one place and put it somewhere else, select it, choose *Cut* from the Edit menu, click where you want the text inserted, and then choose *Paste* from the Edit menu.

To copy text, select the text, choose *Copy* from the Edit menu, click where you want the copy inserted, and choose *Paste*.

When you paste text into a document, any text after the insertion point moves over and is reformatted automatically.

Inserting dates, times, and page numbers

Along with text, you can also place other types of data in word processing documents. The *Insert Date*, *Insert Time*, and *Insert Page #* commands on the Edit menu place these types of information in your document. When you use one of these commands, ClarisWorks places an invisible character in your document that tells it to read the current date, time, or document page number and display it in the document, like this:

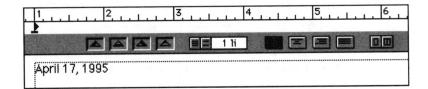

April 17, 1995

Because the information is produced by a single invisible character, however, you can't delete individual characters of the date, time, or page number you see.

To change the format of dates that are inserted with the *Insert Date* command, choose the *Preferences...* command and click the checkbox for the date format you prefer.

Also, because using these commands inserts invisible characters that tell ClarisWorks to read the current date, time or page number, this information changes under different circumstances:

- If you add pages to your document, the page number information automatically changes to reflect the addition.

- If you open the document on a different date or at a different time from when you originally inserted the date or time character, the information is updated to show the current date or time.

Tip   To place a date or time in a document that won't change when the document is opened later, type the date or time with the keyboard.

Pasting graphics and charts

Along with dates, times, and page numbers, you can insert other types of information into a document without typing.

Using the Clipboard, you can paste in pictures or charts that you've copied from another document. Just move the insertion point to where you want the picture or chart to appear, then choose the *Paste* command.

When you paste in a graphic or chart, it becomes part of the paragraph into which you paste it, like the one at the top of the next page:

Public Relations Notes

After months of research, we've determined that Acme needs a new image. As part of that effort, we've come up with this logo:

We really feel the flying horse adds just the right combination of class and whimsy to really define Acme Novelty.

In the above example, the logo is treated as a text character at the beginning of the paragraph's third line. Because the logo is so large, the third line is much taller than the other lines in the paragraph. Unlike a frame or an object you create with the drawing tools, graphics you paste in from the Clipboard are part of the text layer in the document, and they move around the document if you insert or delete text in front of them.

For more formatting flexibility, draw an object or create a frame in your word processing document. If you already have a graphic you want to use, you can paste it into a paint frame. Frames and objects are independent of text, so they don't affect the spacing of text lines.

When the picture or chart is selected, a dotted line appears around it and you can drag the handle in its lower left corner to resize it. You can also cut, copy or paste the graphic just as you would text.

Inserting documents

With the *Insert...* command on the File menu, you can select another document or picture file on a disk and insert it into a word processing document (see *Opening, closing, and saving documents* on p. 24 in Chapter 2). Inserted documents also become part of the text layer of a word processing document, even if the document you insert is a graphic.

Adding footnotes

If your document is a report or research paper, you may want to add footnotes to it. The ClarisWorks word processor has a footnote capability that automatically adds footnotes in the correct place at the bottom of each page where they occur, and also keeps track of footnote numbers for you.

To add a footnote:

1. Move the insertion point to the place where you want the footnote number to appear in your text.

2. Choose *Insert Footnote* from the Format menu. ClarisWorks adds a footnote number at the insertion point in the document, like this:

> the usual jokers[1] , and Acme was

At the same time, ClarisWorks opens a footnote area at the bottom of the page, enters the same footnote number there, and moves the insertion point there so you can type the footnote text, like this:

3. Type the text of the footnote.

4. Scroll back up in your document and click to move the insertion point out of the footnote area and back in to the text.

ClarisWorks automatically makes space for as many footnotes as you need on a page, and it keeps track of the current footnote number so the proper number is inserted at any time, no matter which page of the document you're on.

To remove a footnote, delete the footnote number from the text of the document (not from the footnote area).

You can change the starting footnote number with the *Preferences...* command. See p. 76 in Chapter 3.

Formatting characters

Any character you type in a word processing document can have its own font, size, style, and color. You can set these attributes individually by choosing commands from menus, or you can set them all at once in one dialog box. Also, you can create custom character styles and store them so you can reuse them easily.

Changing fonts, sizes, styles, and colors

To change the font, size, style, or color of text:

1. Select the text you want to change.

2. Choose the font or size from the Font or Size menu, choose the style from the Style menu, or choose the text color from the Text Color submenu off the Style menu.

The fonts, font sizes, and colors available to you depend on which fonts or font sizes are installed in your Mac's System Folder, whether or not you're using a color Mac, and how many colors your Mac is set to display.

If you want to specify a font size that isn't showing on your Font menu, choose *Other...* command from the bottom of the Font menu and then type in the size you want.

Your Mac's ability to display smooth versions of odd-size fonts depends on whether you're using scalable TrueType or Post-Script fonts. If you're not using scalable fonts, odd-size fonts won't look very good. Ask your Apple dealer for information about upgrading to scalable fonts.

Saving custom character styles

If you regularly use a custom character format like Palatino 18 Bold, you can store that format and add it to the bottom of the Style menu. Here's the procedure:

1. Choose the *Define Styles...* command from the bottom of the Style menu. The Define Custom Styles dialog box appears, like this:

```
┌─────────────────────────────────────────────────────┐
│  Define Custom Styles                                 │
│  ───────────────────────────────────────────────     │
│  ┌──────────────────────────────────┐ ⬆   ☒ Plain Text │
│  │                                  │     ☐ Bold        │
│  │                                  │     ☐ Italic      │
│  │                                  │     ☐ Underline   │
│  │                                  │ ⬇   ☐ Strikethru  │
│  └──────────────────────────────────┘     ☐ Outline    │
│                                            ☐ Shadow     │
│  Name │Helvetica 12              │         ☐ Condense   │
│                                            ☐ Extend     │
│  Font │Helvetica ▼│                        ☐ Superscript│
│  Size │12 Point ▼│   Color ■               ☐ Subscript  │
│                                                         │
│  ( Add )  ( Modify ) ( Remove )   ( Cancel )  ( Done )  │
└─────────────────────────────────────────────────────┘
```

2. Choose the font, size, and color you want from the pop-up menus at the left, and choose the styles you want by clicking the checkboxes at the right.

3. Type a name for the style in the Name [...] always suggests the font name and size [...] custom style, but it's more useful to na[...] function in the document, such as "sect[...] "header," and so on.)

4. Click the Add button. The style name appears in the list above the Name box, and is automatically added to the bottom of your Style menu.

 You can also define a custom style by example. Just set the styles you want for a selection of text, leave the text selected, and then choose the *Define Styles...* command. The styles you've set for the currently selected text will be showing in the dialog box.

Applying custom character styles

To apply a custom character style to your document, just select the text and then choose the style's name from the bottom of the Style menu.

Formatting paragraphs

ClarisWorks defines a paragraph as all the text between one Return character and the next. Each paragraph can have its own format settings.

Left and *Right Indents* indent every line in the paragraph from the left or right margin.

First line indents indent only the first line of a paragraph from the left margin.

Line spacing determines the spacing between lines, and also before and after the paragraph itself.

Alignment controls whether the text is aligned on the left or right margin, centered between the two margins, or justified so it's aligned on both margins at once.

Tabs are settings that determine where the insertion point stops each time you press the [Tab] key. You can set left-aligned, right-aligned, centered, or decimal tabs (aligned on a decimal place in numbers), and tabs can have *fill* characters that occupy any blank space between one tab and the next.

These settings apply to an entire paragraph—you can't apply them to just one line of text within a paragraph. ClarisWorks assumes that you want to continue the current paragraph's format settings into any following paragraphs, so if you set a paragraph for double-spacing and then press [Return] and type a new paragraph, the new paragraph will also be double-spaced unless you change its settings.

The default paragraph formats for word processing documents are single spacing, no indents, left alignment, and tab stops every half inch. In this section we'll see how to change them.

Setting indents and line spacing

The most precise way to specify paragraph indents and line spacing is with the Paragraph formats window.

1. Choose the *Paragraph...* command from the Format menu. You'll see the Paragraph window, like this:

Paragraph			
▶ **Left indent**	0 in	**Line spacing**	1 · li ▼
⊥ **First line**	0 in	**Space before**	0 · li ▼
◀ **Right indent**	6.5 in	**Space after**	0 · li ▼

[Apply] [Cancel] [OK]

2. Click in the indent or line spacing box whose setting you want to change, or press the ⟮Tab⟯ key until the box you want is selected.

3. Type the measurement you want (you don't have to type "in" or "cm" after the number you type—ClarisWorks automatically uses the current unit of measurement set for the document's ruler).

4. Click Apply to apply the change and keep the Paragraph window open, or click OK or press ⟮Return⟯ to apply the change and close the window. (You can drag the Paragraph window around to see the effects of different settings on the text underneath it.)

The pop-up menus to the right of the Line Spacing, Space Before, and Space After boxes let you specify spacing measurements in lines, points, inches, millimeters, centimeters, or picas. A "line" is a vertical area the height of the other lines in the paragraph, while the other measurement units let you specify spacing much more precisely.

Clicking and dragging for indents and spacing

You can also set a paragraph's indents and spacing by dragging the indent controls or clicking the spacing controls below the ruler in the document window. The current line spacing is shown to the right of the line spacing controls, and you can click the controls themselves to expand or shrink the line spacing in fixed increments. Try it and see.

To create a hanging indent (where the first line is indented less than the rest of the paragraph), type a negative value in the First Line indent box, or drag the first line indent marker to the left of the left indent marker.

Setting text alignment

To change the horizontal alignment of text in a paragraph, just click one of the alignment controls below the ruler. The darkened icon indicates which alignment setting is currently in effect.

Setting tab stops

Tab stops are another paragraph format you can set either with a dialog box or by dragging icons below the ruler. ClarisWorks automatically sets tab stops every half inch, but you can override these by setting stops of your own. To set a tab stop with the ruler icons, just drag the tab control for the appropriate type of tab stop to the tick mark on the ruler where you want it to be. Once you release the mouse button, the tab marker remains there, like this:

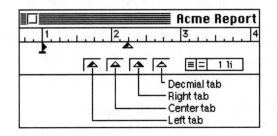

Tab stops you set override any standard ones that would normally occur to the left of the new stop's position on the ruler. In the example above, the first tab stop in this paragraph will now be at 2¼ inches—the standard tab stops at 1, 1½, and 2 inches have been automatically removed, but the standard tabs at 2½ inches, 3 inches, and so on are still in effect.

To move a tab stop, just drag it to a different place on the ruler. To delete a tab stop, drag it back down into the icon area below the ruler.

Formatting tab stops

The tabs you set by dragging the tab controls are "plain," which means that any empty space between them is blank. However, you can have ClarisWorks fill this blank space with dots, dashes or underline characters. This is handy when you've set tabs to create two widely separated columns, such as chapter titles and page numbers in a table of contents.

To format a tab stop you've already set, double-click on the tab marker in the ruler. The Tab window appears, like this:

```
╔══════════════════ Tab ══════════════════╗
║  ┌Alignment────────┐  ┌Fill─────────┐    ║
║   ◉ ▲ Left            ◉ None  ○ ........  ║
║   ○ ▲ Center          ○ ----   ○ _____   ║
║   ○ ▲ Right                              ║
║   ○ ▲ Align On │ . │  Position │2.25 in│  ║
║                                          ║
║        ( Apply )  ( Cancel )  ( OK )     ║
╚══════════════════════════════════════════╝
```

Here you can click a button to select a different type of tab or a tab fill character. The Position box shows the current location of the tab marker you double-clicked on, and you can change the tab's position by typing in a different number here. After you've chosen the options and position for a tab in this box:

• Click the Apply button to set the tab with these options;

• Click the Cancel button to remove the tab at the position shown; or

• Click the OK button or press the (Return) key to set the tab at the current position and put the Tab window away.

Instead of dragging tab markers to the ruler, you can also set tabs by using the Tab window itself. Just choose *Tab...* from the Format menu, type in the position of the tab you want and choose options for it, and then click the Apply or OK button. By clicking the Apply button, you leave the Tab window open and you can set several tabs at different positions, one after the other.

Making tables

You can create a table using tab stops, but since spreadsheets are automatically arranged in rows and columns you can use a spreadsheet frame to format a table more easily. One way is to create a spreadsheet frame using the spreadsheet tool and then add the numbers or text you want in each cell. Using frame options, you can hide the spreadsheet's normal row and column headings and its cell grid. See Chapter 12 for more information.

Another option is the table tool in the Shortcuts palette. If the palette isn't showing, choose *Show Shortcuts* from the Shortcuts submenu off the File menu. (See Chapter 13 for more information.) The table tool looks like this: ▦ . When you click it, ClarisWorks adds a grid of cells to your word processing document, like this:

Double-click inside the grid to activate the spreadsheet's menus, and then add text or numbers to each cell as you would in a spreadsheet (see Chapter 5). Unlike adding a regular spreadsheet frame, though, the grid you add with the table tool is part of the document's text layer—you can't move the table independently of the text as you can a spreadsheet frame. To make the table bigger or smaller, click on it once and drag the selection handle in its lower right corner. (See *Inserting or pasting graphics* on p. 105 for more about the text layer.)

Copying paragraph formats

ClarisWorks automatically applies the format of the existing paragraph to the next paragraph you create. However, if you enter several paragraphs and then later set custom tabs, indents or line spacing in one paragraph, those changes won't be applied automatically to any other paragraph.

To apply format changes in one paragraph to other paragraphs, you can copy the format settings from one paragraph and apply them to another with two simple commands.

1. Move the insertion point to the paragraph whose settings you want to copy.

2. Choose *Copy Ruler* from the Format menu.

3. Move the insertion point to the paragraph (or select the group of paragraphs) to which you want to apply the same settings.

4. Choose *Apply Ruler* from the Format menu.

Formatting documents

Document formatting options apply to your entire word processing document. These include page margins, headers and footers, and columns. The general procedures for setting margin sizes, display options, and starting page numbers were covered beginning on p. 39 in Chapter 2. In this section, we'll look at word processor-specific options for document formatting.

Changing the document display

To change a document's page margins or other general display options, choose *Document...* from the Format menu. The Document dialog box appears, like the one at the top of the next page:

Document

Margins
Top	`1 in`
Bottom	`1 in`
Left	`1 in`
Right	`1 in`

Display

⦿ 📄   ○ 📑   ○ `3`

☒ **Show margins**
☒ **Show page guides**

☐ **Title page**

Starting page # `1`   (Cancel)   (**OK**)

In a word processing document, the Display area of this dialog box has buttons at the top that let you decide how document pages appear on the screen in relationship to each other.

The default setting is one across (you scroll down to view the second page of a document), but you can view documents two or more pages across by clicking the other two buttons. If you click the third button, you can enter a number to view the document three or more pages across. You then scroll to the right to see following pages of the document.

Don't confuse displaying pages side by side with formatting text in multiple columns on a page. For more on formatting text in columns, see *Creating multicolumn documents* on the next page.

Also, the Title Page option in this dialog box determines whether or not ClarisWorks prints page headers or footers on the first page of the document when you include automatic page numbers in a document. See *Setting header and footer options* below for more on this option.

Setting and removing page breaks

As you enter text that fills more than the current page, Claris-Works automatically breaks the page and flows the text onto a new page. Sometimes, however, you'll want to insert manual page breaks to divide text differently. To set a manual page break:

1. Move the insertion point to the line below which you want the page break to occur.

2. Choose *Insert Break* from the Format menu. A new page break appears.

To delete a page break, move the insertion point to the upper left corner of the page below the break and press the Delete key. You can't delete page breaks that ClarisWorks inserts automatically, however.

Setting header and footer options

The basic procedure for adding a header or footer to a document is covered on p. 38 in Chapter 2. When you add a header or footer to a word processing document, however, the *Document ...* command's dialog box has a Title Page checkbox that lets you prevent the header or footer from printing on the document's first page.

Creating multicolumn documents

Word processing documents start out with one column, but you can easily format your text into two or more columns. Like other document formatting options, however, you set the number of columns for a whole document, not for individual pages.

You can add or remove columns from your document in two ways:

- Click the column controls (to the right of the alignment controls) below the document's ruler, or

- Choose the *Columns...* command from the Format menu.

The right-hand column control adds columns, and the left-hand control removes them. For example, if you open a new document and click the right-hand column control once, ClarisWorks adds another column to the document, like this:

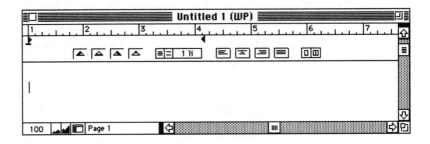

 You can add or remove columns at any time, whether or not your document contains text.

The columns you create with the column control are always of equal widths. Because the insertion point is in the left-most column, the ruler shows left and right indent markers for that column—you can drag these to set indents within this column. The indent markers always appear above the column you're working in.

As you enter text, it flows automatically from the first column to the second, and so on. If you change column widths, ClarisWorks reformats your text automatically to fill up the space in the columns.

Creating variable-width columns

To create columns of unequal width, use the *Columns...* command on the Format menu.

1. Choose the *Columns...* command. You see a dialog box like the one at the top of the next page:

```
┌──────────────────────────────────────────┐
│  Columns                                   │
│                                            │
│  ● Equal width                             │
│  ○ Variable width                          │
│                                            │
│  Number of              [   1        ]     │
│  Column width    [ | ▼ ]    6.5 in         │
│  Space between              0 in           │
│                                            │
│              ( Cancel )  [    OK    ]      │
└──────────────────────────────────────────┘
```

2. Type the number of columns you want in the Number Of box.

3. Click the Variable Width button at the top. The Column Width pop-up menu becomes active.

4. Select the column number whose width you want to set from the Column Width pop-up menu (columns are numbered from left to right across the document).

5. Type the column width measurement in the box next to the pop-up menu. The Space Between measurement automatically adjusts, depending on the width you specify for this and other columns.

6. Select other column numbers from the pop-up menu, enter width measurements for them, and click the OK button when you're done.

Adjusting column widths

Once you've set up columns, you can change their widths or the space between them by using the Columns dialog box as explained in the previous section. But you can also click and drag the column dividing lines:

1. Point to the space between the column whose width you want to change and the one next to it and hold down the [Option] key. The I-beam pointer changes to a double arrow.

2. Hold down the mouse button and drag to the left or right to make the column wider or narrower. The widths of other columns adjust to make room for the changes you make in this column.

You can also adjust the amount of space between columns by pointing to a column dividing line (instead of the space between columns), holding down the [Option] key, and dragging.

 Column borders don't show when you have the Show Page Guides box unchecked in the *Document...* command's dialog box. See *Setting margins and display options* on p. 39 in Chapter 2.

Setting column breaks

Although text flows from one column to the next and automatically adjusts itself to the column widths you set, there are times when you want text to break between columns. For example, if a section in your document ends just two lines before the bottom of a column, ClarisWorks begins the next section in the remaining space in that column, but it would probably look better if you began the new section at the top of the next column.

To control where text breaks to a new column, you can insert a column break:

1. Move the insertion point to the line of text you want to begin at the top of the next column.

2. Choose *Insert Break* from the Format menu. The text on the current line and all text below it moves to the top of the next column.

 If the insertion point is in the right-most column on a page, the *Insert Break* command moves text to the top of the left-most column on the following page.

Working with graphics

There are three ways to add graphics to a word processing document:

- Insert a document containing a graphic.

- Paste in a graphic from the Clipboard.

- Create a graphic with the ClarisWorks drawing tools, or create a paint frame inside the document and then make something inside that.

Inserting or pasting graphics

Inserting or pasting graphics from the Clipboard are the least effective ways to add graphics to a word processing document, because you have less control over the position of the graphic after you paste or insert it, and because the graphic affects the formatting of text around it.

When you paste or insert a graphic, it's placed in the text layer of the document, like this:

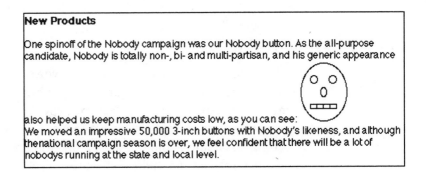

This graphic was pasted from the Clipboard when the insertion point was after the colon in the third line. Because it was pasted, it's treated like one big text character: the line's spacing has been adjusted to accommodate the height of the graphic, and you can't use graphics tools to modify or relocate the graphic.

To delete a graphic you've pasted or inserted, just select it and press the (Delete) key. You can resize a graphic like this by selecting it and either dragging the selection handle that appears at the graphic's lower right corner, or by choosing the *Scale Selection...* command from the Format menu.

When you select an object and choose the *Scale Selection...* command, you see this dialog box:

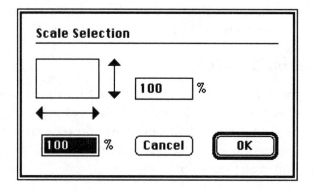

Enter a different horizontal or vertical percentage value to make the graphic taller or wider (*100%* means actual size) and then press (Return).

Creating graphics or frames

When you create graphics or frames in a word processing document, they're placed in the document's graphics layer and are completely independent of the text you type. If you add, delete, or reformat text, for example, your text moves around the screen accordingly. Graphics and frames, on the other hand, remain in the same position even as the text moves.

To move a frame or graphic object, click on the object you want to move. ClarisWorks switches to the draw environment (the I-beam pointer changes to an arrow and the draw menus appear in the menu bar), and you can then resize the object by dragging one of its selection handles, or drag it to a new location. In fact, you can then use any of the draw tools to change the object's fill pattern, line pattern, and other characteristics.

Wrapping text around graphics or frames

The other key advantage to drawing an object or creating a frame in a word processing document is that you can use the draw environment's *Text Wrap...* command to wrap text around the object.

1. Select the graphic object around which you want to wrap text. ClarisWorks switches to the draw environment.

2. Choose *Text Wrap...* from the Options menu. You see a dialog box like this:

```
Text Wrap

  [None]   [Regular]   [Irregular]

     (Cancel)   [ OK ]
```

3. Click the option for the type of text wrap you want, then click the OK button. The text in your document wraps around the graphic object, like this:

New Products

One spinoff of the Nobody campaign was our Nobody button. As the all-purpose candidate, Nobody is totally non-, bi- and multi-partisan, and his generic appearance also helped us keep manufacturing costs low, as you can see:

We moved an impressive 50,000 3-inch buttons with Nobody's likeness, and although the national campaign season is over, we feel confident that there will be a lot of nobodys running at the state and local level.

The Regular text wrap option wraps text around the object's rectangular selection border, while the Irregular option wraps text around the edges of the object itself.

Text wrap is an attribute of the object you select, not of the text around it. In effect, you're setting the object to "repel" text in a certain way. As a result, text will always wrap itself around an object you've set for wrapping, even if you move the object to a different place.

To turn off text wrapping, select the object, choose *Text Wrap…*, click the None option, then click the OK button.

Working with outlines

The word processor has a built-in outlining function that lets you work with text in an outline view, with topics and subtopics. An outline view document looks like this:

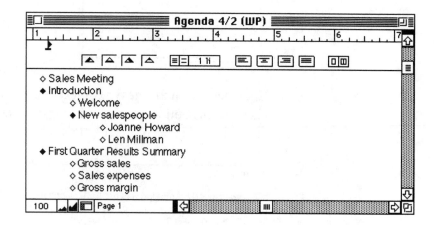

In this example, each topic is indicated with a *topic label* (a diamond in this case), and the outline has two levels of subtopics. When topics have subtopics under them, the topic label darkens to indicate that this is the case.

ClarisWorks offers lots of flexibility in creating and modifying outlines and outline formats. All the outlining commands are located on the Outline menu.

Creating topics and subtopics

To turn on the outliner, choose *Outline View* from the Outline menu. Everything you type will be part of the first topic in the outline until you press Return.

To create a new topic, press Return or choose *New Topic* from the Outline menu. ClarisWorks creates a new topic at the same outline level.

To create a subtopic (which is a topic one level to the right of the current level), choose the *New Topic Right* command or press ⌘R.

To move from a subtopic back up a level and create a topic there (such as moving from *Gross Margin* to *First Quarter Results Summary* in the example above), choose the *New Topic Left* command or press ⌘L.

Selecting and moving topics

The beauty of working with an outliner is that you can easily rearrange the outline, moving topics up or down levels or rearranging their order. You select a topic label by clicking on it, and you can move a topic up or down by selecting it and dragging it. When a topic has subtopics beneath it, selecting the topic also selects the subtopics beneath it.

Instead of dragging topics, you can also use movement commands on the Outline menu.

To move a topic left or right, select it and choose *Move Left* or *Move Right*.

To move a topic up one level in the outline, select it and choose *Raise Topic*.

To change a topic's vertical position in the outline, select it and choose *Move Above* or *Move Below*.

Expanding and collapsing topics

If your outline is long, you may want to condense it by hiding the subtopics under the main topics. To collapse a topic:

- Double-click on the topic label; or

- Choose *Collapse* from the Outline menu.

When a topic is collapsed, its label is dimmed. To expand a topic again, double-click on its label or choose *Expand* from the Outline menu.

Formatting outlines

The diamond labels are the standard topic labels used when you switch to outline view, but you can change topic labels or the whole style of the outline, if you like.

To change the format of one topic label, select the topic and choose a different format from the Topic Label submenu off the Outline menu. Try the different label formats to see how they look.

To change the overall format of an outline, choose a format style from the Outline Format submenu off the Outline menu. Try some different styles to see for yourself.

If you don't like any of the predefined outline formats on the Outline Format submenu, you can create a custom format of your own. Choose *Edit Custom...* from the Outline Format submenu. You see the Level Format dialog box, like the one at the top of the next page:

```
┌─────────────────────────────────────────────────────────┐
│ Level Format                                              │
│ ─────────────────────────────────────────────────────    │
│ ┌──────────────────────────┐  ┌─Text──────────────────┐  │
│ │ Level 1:Helvetica 12    ⬆ │  │ Font  [Helvetica ▼]   │  │
│ │ Level 2:Helvetica 12     │  │ Size  [12 Point ▼]    │  │
│ │ Level 3:Helvetica 12     │  │ Style [Plain Text ▼]  │  │
│ │ Level 4:Helvetica 12    ⬇ │  │ Align [Left ▼]        │  │
│ └──────────────────────────┘  │ Label [Diamond ▼]     │  │
│ ┌─Indent─────────────────┐    │ Color ■               │  │
│ │ ▶ Left indent  [0 in ]  │    └───────────────────────┘  │
│ │ ⊥ First line   [0 in ]  │                               │
│ │ ◀ Right indent [6.5 in] │                               │
│ └────────────────────────┘                               │
│                                                           │
│ ☐ Replace existing styles   (Modify) (Cancel)  (Done)    │
└─────────────────────────────────────────────────────────┘
```

The list in the upper left corner shows different outline levels and the current font and size selected for each. To change a particular level:

1. Select the level (or Shift-click to select several levels).

2. Choose the Text options you want for that level from the pop-up menus at the right.

3. Enter values in the Indent area to specify left, right, and first line indents for the selected level or levels.

4. Click the Modify button to change the outline format.

Once you create a custom outline format, you can select it for other outline levels by selecting the levels you want to change and choosing the *Custom Format* command from the Outline Format submenu. You can only store one custom format at a time; each time you change the custom format it replaces any previous custom format.

Switching out of Outline View

To view your outline as a normal text document, choose the Outline View command from the Outline menu. All topics and subtopics are aligned at the document's left margin, and each topic is a separate paragraph.

About text preferences

We covered the basics of setting document preferences on p. 73 in Chapter 3; now let's look at the text preferences more closely. To display the text preferences option on your screen, choose *Preferences...* from the Edit menu and click the Text icon at the left.

Smart Quotes are curly quotation marks and apostrophes, as shown in parentheses after this option. These look better than straight quotes ('","'). However, smart quotes are created with a different text character than straight quotes. If you save your document in text format and transmit it with the communications program, the smart quotes will be converted to *u*, *m*, or other characters that are part of the standard text character set, making your document harder to read on the computer that receives it. If you know you'll be saving a document in text format, it's best to turn off the Smart Quotes option.

Show Invisibles tells ClarisWorks to display invisible characters such as returns, spaces, and tabs. When this option is checked, these characters show in your document on the screen, but they don't show when you print the document on paper.

Fractional Character Widths tells ClarisWorks to adjust the spacing used for individual characters more precisely, giving your document a more professional, typeset look.

Auto Number Footnotes tells ClarisWorks to automatically number footnotes you insert in a document. When this option is checked (which is the default), you can type a starting footnote number in the box below.

Finally, the *Date Format* options determine how ClarisWorks displays dates that are automatically created with the *Insert Date* command.

When you change the Smart Quotes and Date Format preferences, your changes are not retroactive; any quotation marks, apostrophes, or inserted dates you've already placed in the document will still have the format they had before you changed the preference option.

Troubleshooting

You want to display text all the way to the left edge of the document window. Choose *Document...* from the Format menu and uncheck the Show Margins box.

You want to eliminate the page edges you see between document pages. You can't do this. These appear in Page View, and you can't turn Page View off in the word processor.

You can't select specific characters or put the insertion point between them. This happens with narrow characters (*i, l,* etc.) in certain fonts or when characters are in the Italic style. Click the zoom in control to magnify the document.

You can't click below the last paragraph in a document. The end of the last paragraph is the end of the document. To add text below it, press [Return] to move the insertion point down.

You can't find the tab, spacing, alignment, or indent controls. Choose *Show Rulers* from the View menu.

You can't get indented lines to line up. Don't use the spacebar to offset text from the left margin. This isn't a typewriter. Use tabs.

Tabs or indents change from one paragraph to the next. You have different format options set for the two paragraphs. To make them the same, click in the paragraph whose format you want, choose *Copy Ruler* from the Format menu, click in the other paragraph, and choose *Apply Ruler*.

Line endings or page breaks change when you change fonts. Different fonts have different widths and heights. You may have to reset paragraph indents or page breaks after changing fonts.

Inserting or pasting a graphic screws up a document's line spacing. Select the graphic and remove it with the *Cut* command, then add a paint frame to the document and paste the graphic into the new frame. You can put a frame wherever you want without affecting the spacing of your text.

5

The spreadsheet

The ClarisWorks spreadsheet is the tool you use to arrange and calculate numbers and to produce charts based on those numbers. You can use the spreadsheet to prepare expense budgets or income forecasts, analyze investments, calculate loan payments, and perform many other types of number-crunching tasks.

In this chapter, we'll look at the spreadsheet's calculating features. We'll cover charting separately in Chapter 6. ➠

The spreadsheet window

When you open a new spreadsheet document, it looks like this:

```
┌── Cell address    Cancel button
│   Selected cell  ╱ Accept button      ╭─ Text box    Column heading
```

| Cell address | Cancel button | Accept button | Text box | Column heading |

File Edit Format Calculate Options View (?)

Untitled 1 (SS)

A1 ✗ ✓

	A	B	C	D	E
1					
2					
3					
4					
5		Row heading			
6					
7					
8					
9					
10					

100

A spreadsheet is a matrix of intersecting rows and columns. *Columns* are identified with letters, and *rows* are identified with numbers. Each intersection is called a *cell*, and each cell is identified by a *cell address*. For example, the first cell in the upper-left corner of a spreadsheet has the address A1, because it's at the intersection of column A and row 1.

Tip

A new spreadsheet is 40 columns wide and 500 rows high, but you can change the overall size by inserting or deleting rows or columns (see p. 138), or by using the *Document...* command on the Format menu (see p. 151).

The selected cell or cells in a spreadsheet are indicated by a dotted border (as shown around cell A1 above). The cell's address is shown below the window's title bar.

Also shown below the window's title bar is the *text box*, which displays text or numbers you type in a cell as you type them. Click the *Accept button* to the left of the text box to enter what you've typed in the text box. Clicking the *Cancel button* undoes any changes you've made in the text box.

Selecting cells

You must select a cell before you can enter anything into it. There are several ways to do this.

- Click on the cell.

- Press Tab to move the selection one cell to the right.

- Press Shift Tab to move the selection one cell to the left.

- Press Return to move the selection down one cell.

- Press Shift Return to move the selection up one cell.

- Press one of the arrow keys on your keyboard to move the cell selection in the direction you choose.

- Use the *Go To Cell...* command on the Options menu to move the selection to a specific cell address. (Choose the command, type the cell address in the dialog box that appears, then press the Return key or click OK. The spreadsheet automatically scrolls to and selects that cell.)

 You can also use commands on the Find/Change submenu off the Edit menu to locate a cell by searching for its contents. See p. 59 in Chapter 3.

Sometimes you'll want to select a group of cells. A group of adjacent cells is called a *range*, and is indicated by the first and last cell addresses in the range with two periods between them. For example, the range of cells A1, A2, A3, and A4 has the address *A1..A4.*

A range can include more than one row or column. When it does, the range is defined by its upper-left and lower-right cell addresses. For example, the group of cells from cell A1 to cell D6 would be the range *A1..D6.*

There are several ways to select a range.

- Select an entire column by clicking on the column heading.

- Select an entire row by clicking on the row heading.

- Select a block of cells by dragging the pointer across it.

Entering and changing text and values

Once you've selected a cell, you can enter numbers or text into it by typing. As you type, the data appears in the text box at the top of the spreadsheet window, like this:

□		Untitled 1 (SS)		
A1	×✓ 123			
	A	**B**	**C**	**D**
1				
2				
3				

Notice that the insertion point is blinking in the text box. It appears there as soon as you begin typing. If you make a mistake while you're typing, you can correct it in three different ways:

- Press the Delete key to back up over the mistake and type the correction;

- Drag the pointer across the characters you want to change to select them and then type new ones; or

- Click the Cancel button to the left of the text box or press the (Esc) key to clear the box and then type something else.

Although the characters you type appear in the text box, they don't show up in the cell itself until you confirm or accept the entry. To accept a cell entry:

- Press the (Enter) key or click the Accept button to accept the entry and leave the same cell selected; or

- Press (Return), (Tab), (Shift)(Return), or (Shift)(Tab) to accept the entry and move the cell selection.

You can also accept an entry and leave the same cell selected by pressing a keyboard command to format the cell. For example, press (⌘)(B) to make an entry boldface and accept it at the same time. See Appendix B for a list of all spreadsheet keyboard commands.

Once a cell contains an entry, you change the cell's contents by selecting it and editing the contents of the text box. To change several identical entries in different cells at the same time, use the *Find/Change...* command on the Find/Change submenu off the Edit menu. See p. 60 in Chapter 3.

Entering dates and times

ClarisWorks automatically recognizes dates and times as such when you enter them in the proper format.

Dates can be abbreviated (MM/DD/YY) or spelled out (May 1, 1993). Dates are right-aligned in cells. Although the spreadsheet cell displays the date as you enter it, the date is stored internally as a serial number that equals the number of days since January 1, 1904. For example, if you type *May 1, 1993*, it's stored as 32628. (Dates before 1904 are stored as negative numbers.) Storing dates as serial numbers allows the spreadsheet to make date calculations (see p. 305 in Chapter 11).

Times can be expressed in either 12-hour (8:00 PM) or 24-hour (20:00) format, with or without seconds. Times are also right-aligned in a cell. Although ClarisWorks displays the time as you enter it, it stores a time as a decimal fraction of 1, where 12:00 AM equals zero and 12:00 PM is .5. For example, if you enter *8:00 PM*, it's stored as .833333.

To display the serial date or time value (instead of the formatted date or time) in a cell, change the cell's format to General using the *Number...* command on the Format menu. See p. 143.

Mixing text and numbers in a cell

ClarisWorks knows the difference between text and numbers when you enter them. Numbers, dates and times are right-aligned in cells, and text is left-aligned. You can't perform numeric calculations on text, and you can't perform text calculations on numbers (see *Making calculations*). If you mix text and numbers in a cell (*XD123* or *44 Ave. K*, for example), ClarisWorks treats the entry as text.

While this distinction between text and numbers is the way you'd want it to be in a spreadsheet, there are times when you may want to enter numbers and have the spreadsheet treat them as text. To enter a number as text, type a single quote mark (') as the first character in the entry. ClarisWorks recognizes the quote mark as the signal to treat whatever follows it as text.

What happens to long entries?

In a spreadsheet using the default font, font size, and column width, each cell has room for about 11 numbers or about 17 text characters. However, you can widen columns or decrease the font size to create more room inside a cell.

No matter how wide you make a cell, though, you can't enter more than 255 characters in it. Entries wider than the current

cell's width are treated differently, depending on whether y
entered a number or text.

If you enter more text than will fit inside a cell and the cell to
the right is empty, the text simply overlaps into the next cell,
like this:

□				Untitled 1 (SS)		
B1		×	✓	Worthington Plumbing		
	A		**B**	**C**	**D**	
1			Worthington Plumbing			
2						
3						

If the cell to the right of your entry already contains a number
or text, the long entry is still stored, but the cell only shows as
much as its width permits. In either case, however, the entire entry
always appears in the text box when you select a cell.

Tip You can format cells so that text wraps inside their borders by
choosing the *Wrap* command from the Alignment submenu off
the Format menu. See *Wrapping text within a cell* on p. 142.

If you enter a number that's longer than a cell can display,
ClarisWorks displays the number in scientific notation, like this:

□			Untitled 1 (SS)		
B1		× ✓	1234567894567		
	A	**B**	**C**	**D**	
1		1.23456e+12			
2					
3					

The *e+* in the number means "raised to the power of 10." In
this case, the *1.23456e+12* means 1.23445 raised to the power of
10^{12}. (Each time you raise a value by a power of ten, it's like moving
the decimal point one place to the right.)

If there's not enough room to display a value even by switching to scientific notation, ClarisWorks displays a row of pound signs (#####) in a cell, although the real value will still be stored.

You can always widen a column to make more room for numbers (see p. 146). If you're displaying the result of a calculation, you can use the INTEGER, ROUND, or TRUNC function to display numbers in shortened formats (see Chapter 11).

Making calculations

Placing text and numbers in neat rows and columns is nice, but the real beauty of spreadsheets is their ability to store calculation formulas and then to recalculate values automatically. Here's an example:

1995 Budget (SS)			
B19 ×✓ =B16+B17			
	A	B	C	D

	A	B	C	D
14				
15	Income			
16	Products	32500	33000	30000
17	Services	7500	7500	7000
18				
19	Total	40000	40500	37000
20				

The totals in row 19 of this spreadsheet are produced with formulas. For example, cell B19 *contains* the formula shown in the text box, but *displays* the formula's result.

Once you've entered a formula, you can change any of the values in the cells referred to in the formula, and the formula automatically recalculates and displays the new result.

About formulas

A formula can contain cell references, constants, operators, and functions. You can combine these elements in different ways, depending on the results you want.

A *cell reference* (such as B16 or B17 in the example above) tells the spreadsheet you want to use the value from a particular cell in the formula.

A *constant* is a number you type into the formula. For example, if you want to multiply the contents of cell B16 by 5, you would enter the formula *=B16*5*.

Operators tell the spreadsheet which type of calculation to make. The mathematical operators +, -, *, and / specify addition, subtraction, multiplication, and division, respectively. (You can also use + and - to indicate positive and negative numbers.)

The spreadsheet also has logical operators to specify relationships:

Logical operator	Relationship
>	Greater than
<	Less than
≥	Greater than or equal to
≤	Less than or equal to
=	Equal to
<>	Not equal to

See p. 337 in Chapter 11 for more about logical operators.

Finally, the spreadsheet has one text operator, &, which concatenates (or joins) two strings of text together. See p. 354 in Chapter 11 for more about text formulas.

Functions are predefined formulas that produce various types of calculations. They work like shorthand, producing a specific result such as summing or averaging all the values in a specified group of cells. By using functions, you save yourself the trouble of specifying the entire formula. For example, it's easier to enter *=SUM(A4..A8)* (which sums the values in the range of cells A4 through A8) than it is to enter *=A4+A5+A6+A7+A8.* The spreadsheet has several dozen functions, each of which is specified by its name.

 You can select function names and insert them automatically in a formula with the *Paste Function...* command. See p. 127.

Most functions have *arguments,* which are the cell addresses or values upon which the function acts. In the formula *=SUM(A4..A8),* for example, the range A4..A8 is the argument. Different functions require different types of arguments, and the values or cell references in those arguments must be entered in a specific format. Chapter 11 lists all the function names and shows the formats of their arguments.

Order of precedence

You can make many different types of calculations in the same formula, but some operations are always carried out before others. As a result, you must be careful when entering a formula, because the order of precedence can produce different results. The following list shows the operators in the order in which they're performed within a formula:

% (division by 100 to produce a percent)

+,- (sign of number)

^ (exponentiation)

*, / (multiplication and division)

+, - (addition and subtraction)

Logical operators

Text operator (&)

If two operators are at the same level of precedence, the calculations occur from left to right. For example, the formula *=3+2-4* equals 1 (because equal-level operations occur from left to right), while the formula =3+2*2 equals 7 (because the multiplication occurs before the addition).

To make sure that some calculations are done before others in a formula, use parentheses to enclose the calculations you want made first. The spreadsheet always calculates inside parentheses before it calculates outside them. So, for example, =3+2*2 equals 7, while =(3+2)*2 equals 10.

Entering formulas

To enter a formula, type an equal sign (=) first and then just type the values, constants, operators, or function names that make up the formula. The equal sign tells the spreadsheet you're beginning a formula, but after that it's just like entering a value or text.

If you've entered the formula correctly, it will calculate immediately and you'll see the result displayed in the cell. If you've made an error in the formula, you'll see an error message and you'll have to figure out your mistake. See *Troubleshooting* at the end of this chapter for some common formula problems and solutions.

Setting manual calculation

The spreadsheet is set to automatically recalculate any formula whenever any of the cells referenced in the formula is changed. But if your spreadsheet contains dozens of formulas or calculates large numbers of cells, you may have to wait a few seconds each time the spreadsheet recalculates before you can perform another operation.

If you don't want to be constantly interrupted by automatic recalculations, you can turn this feature off. Just choose *Auto Calc* from the Calculate menu. The check mark next to the command name disappears, and calculations are no longer made automatically.

When Auto Calc is off, you can manually recalculate the spreadsheet any time by choosing *Calculate Now* from the Calculate menu, or by pressing ⌘Shift=.

Clicking to enter cell references

When you type cell references in a formula, there's always the possibility that you'll hit the wrong key and thus enter the wrong cell reference. To eliminate this problem, you can click on or drag across cells to enter their addresses in a formula. Here's an example:

	1995 Budget (SS)		
C19 ×✓			
	A	**B**	**C**	**D**

	A	B	C	D
14				
15	Income			
16	Products	32500	33000	30000
17	Services	7500	7500	7000
18				
19	Total	40000		
20				

To enter a formula in cell C19 that produces a total like the one in cell B19:

1. Select cell C19.

2. Type = to begin the formula.

3. Click on cell C16. ClarisWorks enters the cell address in the text box.

4. Click on cell C17. ClarisWorks inserts an addition operator and adds the second cell address in the text box, like the one at the top of the next page:

1995 Budget (SS)			
C19 ×✓ =C16+C17			
	A	**B**	**C**	**D**

	A	B	C	D
14				
15	**Income**			
16	Products	32500	33000	30000
17	Services	7500	7500	7000
18				
19	**Total**	40000		
20				

Whenever you click on more than one cell address in a formula, the spreadsheet automatically inserts the addition operator between the addresses. If this isn't what you want, you'll have to delete the operators by hand.

5. Click the Accept button or press [Return] to complete the formula. The calculated result appears in cell C19.

Using the *Paste Function...* command

You can also cut down on formula entry errors by pasting function names rather than typing them. Here's another example.

1995 Budget (SS)			
C12 ×✓			

	A	B	C	D
1	**Expenses**	**January**	**February**	**March**
2	Salaries	$10,200	$11,300	$12,400
3	Benefits	$4,500	$4,700	$4,800
4	Materials	$3,000	$4,000	$5,000
5	Rent	$3,500	$3,500	$3,500
6	Advertising	$5,000	$5,400	$4,700
7	Kickbacks	$1,000	$1,000	$1,000
8	Utilities	$225	$230	$215
9	Insurance	$200	$200	$200
10	Telephone	$550	$575	$540
11				
12	**Total**	$28,175		
13				

The formula in cell B12 is *=SUM(B3..B11)*. To enter a similar formula in cell C12:

1. Type = to begin the formula.

2. Choose *Paste Function...* from the Edit menu. The Paste Function dialog box appears, like this:

```
┌─────────────────────────────────────────────┐
│                                               │
│  Paste Function                               │
│  ──────────────────────────────────────────  │
│  ┌─────────────────────────────────────┐ ⬆  │
│  │ ABS(number)                          │ ≡  │
│  │ ACOS(number)                         │    │
│  │ ALERT(value)                         │    │
│  │ AND(logical1,logical2,...)           │    │
│  │ ASIN(number)                         │    │
│  │ ATAN(number)                         │    │
│  │ ATAN2(x-number,y-number)             │ ⬇  │
│  └─────────────────────────────────────┘    │
│                                               │
│           ┌──────────┐  ┌──────────┐         │
│           │  Cancel  │  │    OK    │         │
│           └──────────┘  └──────────┘         │
│                                               │
└─────────────────────────────────────────────┘
```

3. Scroll the list until you see the SUM function, then double-click on it. ClarisWorks enters the function and its arguments in the text box, like the one at the top of the next page:

```
═══════════════ 1995 Budget (SS) ═══════════════
   C12      × ✓  =SUM(number1,number2,...)
```

	A	B	C	D
1	Expenses	January	February	March
2	Salaries	$10,200	$11,300	$12,400
3	Benefits	$4,500	$4,700	$4,800
4	Materials	$3,000	$4,000	$5,000
5	Rent	$3,500	$3,500	$3,500
6	Advertising	$5,000	$5,400	$4,700
7	Kickbacks	$1,000	$1,000	$1,000
8	Utilities	$225	$230	$215
9	Insurance	$200	$200	$200
10	Telephone	$550	$575	$540
11				
12	**Total**	$28,175		
13				

Tip
To scroll quickly in the Paste Function list, type the first letter of the function name. The list scrolls automatically to the first function name that begins with that letter.

When you paste a function, ClarisWorks includes descriptive text in the arguments to help you remember the types of values and the format required. You have to replace this text with cell addresses or constants. In this case, we want to sum the range of cells from C2 to C10.

4. Select all the text between the parentheses and press Delete.

5. Click on cell C2 and drag down to cell C10, then release the mouse button. ClarisWorks enters this range inside the parentheses, like this:

```
═══════════════ 1995 Budget (SS) ═══════════════
   C12      × ✓  =SUM(C2..C10)
```

6. Click the Accept button or press the Return key to enter the formula. The calculated result appears in cell C12.

To enter a SUM formula even more quickly, select a range that includes the cells you want to sum plus one blank cell directly below them, then click the Autosum button $\boxed{\Sigma}$ in the Shortcuts panel. ClarisWorks enters the SUM formula in the blank cell at the bottom of the range and displays the result. See Chapter 13 for more on shortcuts.

As you gain experience with the spreadsheet, you'll discover the most effective way to enter formulas.

Absolute and relative cell references

If you simply type a cell address or select a cell to enter its address in a formula, it's entered as a *relative reference*, which means the address is relative to the position of the formula where you're entering it.

	A	B	C	D
		1995 Budget (SS)		
	B19	× ✓ =B16+B17		
14				
15	Income			
16	Products	32500	33000	30000
17	Services	7500	7500	7000
18				
19	Total	40000		
20				

In the example above, the formula in cell B19 adds the contents of cells B16 and B17. Because B16 and B17 are relative references, however, they will change relative to the formula's position if the formula is copied to another location. If we copy the formula in cell B19 to cell C19, the cell references in the formula will change to C16+C17.

The spreadsheet creates relative cell references by default, because they make it easy to copy a formula. When a spreadsheet has several places that contain essentially the same formula (as in row 19 above), you can simply copy the formula from one cell into others and the references in it will automatically adjust themselves to the positions of the copied formulas.

Sometimes, though, you'll want to use *absolute references* in your formulas, which don't change when a formula is copied. To make a cell reference absolute, type a dollar sign in front of the row and column designations.

The absolute-reference version of the formula in the example above would be =$B$16+$B$17. If you copied this formula from its current location to any other cell, the references would remain $B$16+$B$17.

You can also mix references in a formula, making some cell addresses absolute and others relative, and you can even mix references within one cell address. For example, if you enter the address as $B17, only the column reference is absolute—the row reference is relative and will change according to the position of the formula.

Moving and copying data

As with any ClarisWorks document except communications documents, you can copy, cut, and paste data in a spreadsheet. When you cut the contents of a selected cell or cells, you remove the contents of those cells, but not the cells themselves. To actually remove cells from a spreadsheet, you must delete rows or columns (see p. 138).

Along with the standard cut, copy, and paste functions described in Chapter 3, the spreadsheet offers some special short-cuts and options for pasting data in special ways.

How data is pasted

When you paste more than one cell's worth of data into a spread-sheet, ClarisWorks begins inserting the data at the destination cell you click on (called the *anchor cell*), and then places the rest of it to the right of and below the selected cell. For example, if you copy data from the range of cells A1, A2, B1, and B2 and then click on cell A5 and paste the data, the spreadsheet places the data in cells A5, A6, B5, and B6.

The spreadsheet doesn't move existing data out of the way when it's in the way of data you're pasting in. If there's existing data in the cells where you paste new data, the new data replaces the old data. Choose *Undo* to cancel a paste operation if you mistakenly paste some new data over existing data.

If you cut or copy a formula and then paste it elsewhere, the formula (along with the displayed result) will be copied. To paste only the displayed result of the formula (and not the formula itself), use the *Paste Special...* command described on the next page.

Filling cells

The Edit menu's *Fill Right* and *Fill Down* commands make copying data or formulas easy when you're copying from the current cell into adjacent cells below or to the right.

To copy data into cells to the right:

1. Select the cell whose data you want to copy, then keep the mouse button down and continue selecting the empty destination cells to the right, like this:

≣	1995 Budget (SS)		
B19	×✓ =B16+B17		

	A	**B**	**C**	**D**
15	**Income**			
16	Products	32500	33000	30000
17	Services	7500	7500	7000
18				
19	**Total**	40000		
20				

2. Choose *Fill Right* from the Calculate menu. ClarisWorks fills the destination cells with copies of the original data, like this:

	1995 Budget (SS)		
B19	× ✓	=B16+B17	

	A	**B**	**C**	**D**
15	Income			
16	Products	32500	33000	30000
17	Services	7500	7500	7000
18				
19	Total	40000	40500	37000
20				

(In this case, cell B19 contained a formula with relative references, so the values in cells C19 and D19 are calculated from copies of that formula.)

You can fill cells below the current one the same way. Just select the origin cell and the destination cells in one block, then choose *Fill Down* from the Calculate menu. And you aren't limited to filling just one row or column at a time—you can select several cells in a column or row and then fill a whole group of adjacent cells.

Using special paste options

The *Paste Special…* command on the Edit menu gives you some options about exactly what is pasted from the Clipboard. After you've cut or copied data to the Clipboard, you can paste only the results of formulas or transpose values in rows and columns.

When you choose the *Paste Special…* command, you see a dialog box like the one at the top of the next page:

```
┌─────────────────────────────────┐
│ Paste Special                    │
│ ──────────────────────────────  │
│ ● Formulas and values            │
│ ○ Values only                    │
│ ☐ Transpose                      │
│        ┌──────────┐ ┌──────────┐ │
│        │  Cancel  │ │    OK    │ │
│        └──────────┘ └──────────┘ │
└─────────────────────────────────┘
```

The *Formulas and Values* button is the default, because the spreadsheet normally pastes both formulas and displayed values. At times, though, you'll want to paste a displayed value but not the formula that produced it. In this case, click the *Values Only* button and then click OK.

The *Transpose* checkbox converts data in rows into data in columns, or vice versa.

Moving data

To move data from one cell or cells to another location, you can always cut it from its present location and then paste it into the new location. But the spreadsheet offers a quicker alternative:

1. Select the data you want to move.

2. Choose the *Move...* command from the Calculate menu. You'll see a dialog box like this:

```
┌───────────────────────────────────┐
│                                    │
│   Move to            ┌──────────┐  │
│                      └──────────┘  │
│           ┌──────────┐ ┌────────┐  │
│           │  Cancel  │ │   OK   │  │
│           └──────────┘ └────────┘  │
│                                    │
└───────────────────────────────────┘
```

3. Type the address of the destination cell, then click the OK button. The data is moved to the new location.

Preventing changes in cells

If you've spent a lot of time perfecting the contents of a spreadsheet, you may want to lock some or all of its cells to prevent further changes. To prevent changes in a cell or cells:

1. Select the cell(s) you want to protect.

2. Choose *Protect Cells* from the Options menu. ClarisWorks locks the selected cells so they can't be changed.

You can protect one cell, a group of cells, or all the cells in the spreadsheet this way. Once a cell is protected, ClarisWorks displays a warning message when someone tries to enter data into it.

To unlock a cell, select the cell(s) you want to unlock and choose *Unprotect Cells* from the Options menu.

Sorting data

After you've entered labels or values in a spreadsheet, you may want to rearrange them in numeric or alphabetic order. It's easy to do this with the *Sort...* command. You can sort rows, columns, or even smaller groups of cells within rows or columns.

For example, suppose we have a spreadsheet like the one at the top of the next page:

	A	B	C	D
1		January	February	March
2	**Expenses**			
3	Salaries	10200	11300	11300
4	Health Ins.	2000	2000	2000
5	Disability Ins.	300	300	300
6	Bonuses	0	0	1500
7	Material	5000	5400	4700
8	Rent	3500	3500	3500
9	Utilities	225	230	215
10	Insurance	200	200	200
11	Telephone	550	575	540
12				
13	**Total**	21975	23505	24255

The expense categories aren't in any particular order, and it might be easier to work with them if they were arranged alphabetically. To do this:

1. Select rows 3 through 11 by dragging across these row headings.

2. Choose *Sort...* from the Calculate menu. You'll see the Sort dialog box, like this:

3. Click the OK button or press (Return) to sort the selected rows in alphabetical order.

The Sort dialog box

In the above example we a[...] dialog box, but let's take a [...]

The *Range* box shows the [...] selected. You can type a diff[...]

The *Order Keys* area show[...] (A3) as the 1st sort order key[...] order key, but you can enter t[...] up to three different levels. Th[...] keys tell the spreadsheet to sor[...] .... ascending or descending order.

For example, you might sort some rows based on the contents of cells in three different columns: the first key might be a cell containing a state code, the second key a cell containing a city code, and the third key a cell containing a company name. With these three order keys selected, the rows would be sorted alphabetically by state code, within states by city name, and within cities by company name.

The *Direction* buttons tell the spreadsheet to rearrange your data vertically (down rows) or horizontally (across columns). The default setting is *Vertical,* because you'll typically rearrange rows of data. The *Horizontal* option rearranges the order of columns.

Sorting precautions

Our example showed how easy it is to rearrange entire rows of data, but you can select smaller groups of cells and rearrange them. When you do, however, make sure the results are what you want. In the spreadsheet on p. 118, for example, we could select and sort only cells A3 through A11. If we did that, however, only the labels in column A would be rearranged, while the values in columns B, C, and so on would remain in the same place.

...rting a group of cells screws up your spreadsheet, choose ...ndo Sort from the Edit menu to return the cells to the order they were in before.

Also, be careful when sorting cells that contain formulas, or that are referred to in formulas. Changing cell positions due to sorting changes the cell references in a formula, and may cause the wrong results to appear. For example, if you sort rows 3 through 13 in the spreadsheet on p. 118, the formulas in the Total row (originally row 13) will be moved. Because these formulas contain relative references, the references will change and the Total row will no longer contain complete totals.

The best practice is to do any sorting *before* you enter formulas, and if not, to make sure you check every formula that could be affected after sorting.

Inserting and deleting cells

To insert or delete entire rows or columns of cells, use the *Insert Cells...* and *Delete Cells...* commands on the Calculate menu. Unlike cutting data from selected cells, these commands remove whole rows or columns, along with any data in them. When a row or column is inserted or deleted, rows below (if you're deleting a row) or columns to the right (if you're deleting a column) move and are renumbered to accommodate the change. For example, if you insert a new row above row 2, the old row 2 moves down and becomes row 3.

When you insert or delete rows or columns, any formulas that move as a result are automatically adjusted, even if they contain absolute references.

Inserting rows or columns

To insert a row, select the row below where you want the new row inserted and choose *Insert Cells...* from the Calculate menu. ClarisWorks inserts a new row above the one you selected.

To insert a column, select the column to the right of where you want the new one inserted and choose *Insert Cells....* ClarisWorks inserts a new column to the left of the one you selected.

If you don't have a complete row or column selected when you choose the *Insert Cells...* command, you see a dialog box like this:

Insert Cells

⦿ **Shift cells down**
◯ **Shift cells right**

[Cancel]   [**OK**]

The spreadsheet assumes you want to insert a row, so the *Shift Cells Down* button is automatically selected. To insert a new column, click the *Shift Cells Right* button and then click OK or press (Return).

To insert several rows or columns at once, select as many rows or columns as you want to insert before choosing the *Insert Cells...* command. The spreadsheet then inserts the number of rows or columns that you selected.

Deleting rows or columns

The procedure is similar when you're deleting rows or columns. ClarisWorks deletes rows above the selected row(s) and to the left of the selected column(s). To delete several rows or columns, select as many as you want to delete.

If you select less than a complete row or column to delete, you see a Delete Cells dialog box similar to the Insert Cells dialog box above. *Shift Cells Up* (to delete a row or rows) is the default option. Click the *Shift Cells Left* button to delete a column or columns.

Formatting cells

The spreadsheet's cell formatting options let you control the appearance of data within individual cells. You can set the font, font size, color, style, or alignment of any single cell or group of cells. You can add borders to cells, or change the number, date, or time format for a cell's data. And, if you've set a complex group of formatting options for some cells and want to apply those options to other cells, you can even copy a set of formats from one place to another.

Other formatting options apply to the entire spreadsheet document. We'll explore those under *Formatting documents,* beginning on p. 146.

Setting fonts, sizes, styles and text colors

To change the font, size, style, or text color of a cell, a group of cells, or the entire spreadsheet:

1. Select the cell(s) whose format you want to change.

2. Choose a different font, size, style or text color from the Font, Size, Style, or Text Color submenu off the Format menu.

If you don't like a change once you've made it, just choose *Undo Format* from the Edit menu.

When you make a cell's font larger than 12 point, you'll have to make the entire row taller in order to display the value completely. See *Changing row heights and column widths* on p. 146.

Changing the default font

All new spreadsheets start out with 9-point Geneva as the default font. However, you can change the default to any font or size available on your Mac. To do this:

1. Choose *Default Font...* from the Options menu. You see a dialog box like this:

```
┌──────────────────────────────────────────┐
│  Default Font                              │
│  ─────────────────────────────            │
│                                            │
│  Font                    Size              │
│   ┌───────────────┐┌──┐  ┌─────────────┐  │
│   │ Bookman       ││⇧ │  │ 9           │  │
│   │ Chicago       ││≡ │  └─────────────┘  │
│   │ Cooper Black  ││  │                    │
│   │ Courier       ││  │                    │
│   │ Geneva        ││  │                    │
│   │ Helvetica     ││⇩ │                    │
│   └───────────────┘└──┘                    │
│                      ┌──────────┐┌───────┐ │
│                      │  Cancel  ││  OK   │ │
│                      └──────────┘└───────┘ │
│                                            │
└──────────────────────────────────────────┘
```

2. Choose a different font from the Font list, or type a different font size in the Size box, then press (Return) or click the OK button.

Once you've reset the default font, all new spreadsheet documents will have that font and size.

Changing the alignment of data in cells

Using the Alignment submenu off the Format menu, you can choose whether a cell's contents are left, right, or center aligned. The standard alignment setting for the spreadsheet is General, which aligns text entries at the left edge of a cell and number, date, or time entries at the right edge of a cell. When you enter a formula in a cell, the displayed result is aligned according to the type of data the formula produces. (Some formulas produce text results rather than numbers.)

Right-aligned values and left-aligned text don't always look the way you want, however. When a right-aligned number is in a cell adjacent to a left-aligned text label, the two values tend to run together, like this:

	A	B	C
19	94612	Oakland	
20	94538	Fremont	
21	94109	San Francisco	

To remedy this problem, you can select any cell or group of cells and change the data alignment with the commands on the Alignment submenu. The commands on the menu are General (the default setting), Left, Center, Right, and Wrap. The Wrap option is a special case, so let's take a quick look at that.

Wrapping text within a cell

When text is wider than a cell's width can display, the spreadsheet either flows it into the adjacent cell (if the adjacent cell is empty) or displays only as much as will fit within the cell.

Rather than accepting either of these choices, however, you can wrap the text inside a cell's borders. This option allows text to wrap down to additional lines inside a cell if it's too wide to fit within the cell's border on one line. Here's an example:

E8	× ✓			
	A	**B**	**C**	**D**
1	Consolidated Industries			
2				

The entry in cell A1 (shown in the text box) is too wide to fit within the cell's borders, but it doesn't flow over into cell B1 because the text wrap option is set. To set this option, select the cell and choose *Wrap* from the Alignment submenu.

If you wrap text inside a cell, you won't be able to see the additional lines created by the wrapped text unless you make the row tall enough to display them. See *Changing row heights and column widths* on p. 146.

When you choose the *Wrap* command from the Alignment submenu, the other current alignment option (General, Left, Center, or Right) remains in effect, because wrapping doesn't determine whether data in a cell is left, right, or center aligned.

Setting number, date and time formats

The spreadsheet has several different number, date, and time formats, and you can change them according to the type of data you're working with. If you're working with money figures, for example, it's nice to format the values as dollars and cents.

To change a cell's number format, select the cell (or cells) and choose *Number...* from the Format menu. You see a dialog box like the one at the top of the next page:

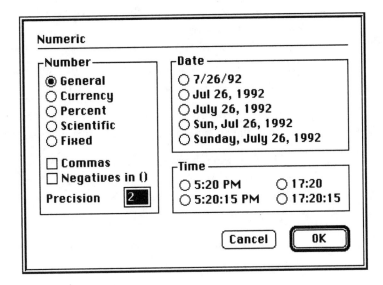

You can also double-click on any cell in order to display this dialog box.

Just click one of the buttons in this dialog box to change a cell's format. If you're setting a number format, you can also enter the number of decimal places you want displayed or check the boxes to display commas or parentheses. Click the OK button when you've set the options you want.

The default number format is *General*, in which the spreadsheet tries to represent numbers you enter as closely as possible to the way you typed them, as long as you're not entering something weird like *$2/4,5.6*, for example.

Currency format adds a dollar sign to any number and automatically sets it to display two decimal places, although you can change this by entering a different value in the *Precision* box.

Percent format multiplies the number by 100 and adds a percent symbol (%) after it. Thus *10* becomes *1000.00%*. (Remember this when you're entering percentage values: to enter a fraction of 1, you must express the value as a decimal fraction. For example, *.65* is formatted as *65.00%*.)

Scientific format is typically used for very large or very small numbers. This is the notation discussed under *What happens to long entries?* on p. 102. Numbers are reduced to the smallest possible value expressed as a power of 10. For example, *1,020,343* is displayed as *1.02e+6*, which means 1.02×10^6.

Finally, *Fixed* format is a number with a specific number of decimal places, which you indicate in the Precision box.

The *Commas* checkbox adds commas to separate thousands in a number, and the *Negatives In ()* checkbox formats negative numbers inside parentheses, rather than with a minus sign in front of them.

The *Date* and *Time* format options in this dialog box are self-evident.

Adding cell borders

Along with the numeric format, font, size, style, alignment, and text color of each cell, you can further enhance a spreadsheet by adding full or partial borders around any cell or group of cells. Borders are especially effective for setting off labels or particularly important values in a spreadsheet, especially when you have the cell grid turned off like this:

	A	B	C	D
1		January	February	March
2	Expenses			
3	Salaries	10200	11300	11300
4	Health Ins.	2000	2000	2000
5	Disability Ins.	300	300	300

(To turn off the cell grid, choose the *Display...* command from the Options menu. See p. 149.)

To set a border:

1. Select the cell or cells you want to have borders on and choose *Borders...* from the Format menu. You see a dialog box like this:

```
┌─────────────────────────────┐
│ Borders                     │
│                             │
│  ☐ Outline                  │
│  ☐ Left      ☐ Right        │
│  ☐ Top       ☐ Bottom       │
│                             │
│     ( Cancel )   ( OK )     │
│                             │
└─────────────────────────────┘
```

2. Click the checkboxes to set the type of border you want, then click the OK button or press the (Return) key.

As you can see, you can put a "border" on only one, two, or three sides of a cell if you like by clicking the right checkboxes. The Outline checkbox puts a border around the whole box.

 When you set an outline border for a group of cells, Claris-Works adds one outline around the entire group, rather than outlining each cell in the group. To outline each cell in a group, click the Left, Right, Top, and Bottom boxes in the Borders dialog box. Also, you can add an outline border to any selected cell or group of cells by clicking the border button [⊞] on the Shortcuts palette. See Chapter 13 for more on shortcuts.

Copying and pasting cell formats

If you've set up a complex format and you want to apply it to a different cell or cells, you don't have to choose those formatting options all over again. Instead, you can copy the format.

1. Select the cell whose format you want to copy and choose *Copy Format* from the Edit menu.

2. Select the cell or cells where you want to apply the format and choose *Paste Format* from the Edit menu.

Formatting documents

In this section, we'll look at formatting options that apply to entire rows, to entire columns, or to the whole spreadsheet document.

Changing row heights and column widths

When you wrap text in a cell or use a particularly large font size, you'll need to make the whole row taller to display all the cell's data. And you can widen columns so the cells in them can display wider data. You can change row heights and column widths either by dragging with the mouse pointer or (if you know exactly how wide or tall you want the column or row to be) by entering a value in a dialog box.

To change a row's height by dragging, just point to the dividing line between the row's number and the row number below it. The pointer changes to a double arrow, like this:

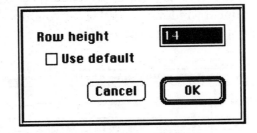

Drag the dividing line up or down to resize the row. If you want to resize several rows at a time, or you'd rather resize one row by entering a value, here's the procedure:

1. Select a cell in the row or rows you want to resize.

2. Choose *Row Height...* from the Format menu. You'll see a dialog box like this:

Row height   ╎14
☐ **Use default**

[Cancel]   [**OK**]

3. The row height value is in points (there are 72 points in an inch). Type a different value and click the OK button.

To reset a row back to the spreadsheet's default height, select it, choose *Row Height...*, click the Use Default checkbox, then click the OK button.

To change a column's width, just drag the dividing line between the column heading and the one to its right. To change the widths of several columns or to reset one column's size precisely, choose *Column Width…* from the Format menu and specify a different value. The default column width value is 72 points, or one inch.

You can hide a row or column completely by setting its width to 0. To reveal the row or column again later, select the rows or columns on either side of the hidden one and set their widths or heights to any positive number.

Keeping row or column titles on the screen

When a spreadsheet is larger than one screen, the column or row titles (which are usually in row 1 or column A) disappear when you scroll down or to the right, and it's easy to lose track of which row or column is which. You can remedy this problem either by using the window's pane controls or by locking the row or column titles on the screen.

The pane controls work best when you want to keep both the column and row titles on the screen, and you want to retain the ability to change the contents of any row or column label. To use the pane controls, drag the horizontal and vertical pane controls in the document window to separate the column and row titles from the rest of the document, like this:

	A	C	D	E	F
	1995 Budget (SS)				
	E20				
1	Expenses	February	March	April	May
2	Salaries	$11,300	$12,400	$12400.00	$12400.00
3	Benefits	$4,700	$4,800	4800	4850
4	Materials	$4,000	$5,000	5500	5750
5	Rent	$3,500	$3,500	3500	0
6	Advertising	$5,400	$4,700	4900	4900
7	Kickbacks	$1,000	$1,000	1000	1000
8	Utilities	$230	$215	210	200
9	Insurance	$200	$200	200	200
10	Telephone	$575	$540	490	510

Now the row and column titles are in separate panes of the document window, and you can scroll the lower right pane to view other numbers without changing the positions of the titles.

If you don't want to separate your document into panes like this, you can lock titles on the screen in another way.

1. Select the cell at the intersection of the column and row you want to lock (you'd select cell A1 in the spreadsheet above to lock both the column and row titles).

2. Choose *Lock Title Position* from the Options menu.

Now the titles in row 1 won't move when you scroll the window down, and the labels in column A won't scroll when you scroll the window to the right. To unlock the titles, choose *Lock Title Position* again.

 Locking titles protects the locked cells so no changes can be made in them.

Setting display options

The *Display...* command on the Options menu lets you set six display options that affect the appearance of your whole document when it's displayed or printed. When you choose this command, the Display dialog box appears, like this:

Display

☒ Cell grid   ☒ Column headings
☐ Solid lines   ☒ Row headings
☐ Formulas   ☒ Mark circular refs

[Cancel]   [OK]

The *Cell Grid* checkbox tells ClarisWorks to display the grid of intersecting lines that separate the spreadsheet's cells. This option is normally checked so the grid lines appear. To view your document without the cell grid, uncheck this box.

The *Solid Lines* checkbox changes the cell grid's dotted lines to solid lines. This box is normally not checked.

The *Formulas* checkbox tells the spreadsheet to display the formulas in cells, rather than the values they produce, as in row 13 below:

	A	B	C	D
2	**Expenses**			
3	Salaries	10200	11300	11300
4	Health Ins.	2000	2000	2000
5	Disability Ins.	300	300	300
6	Bonuses	0	0	1500
7	Material	5000	5400	4700
8	Rent	3500	3500	3500
9	Utilities	225	230	215
10	Insurance	200	200	200
11	Telephone	550	575	540
12				
13	**Total**	=SUM(B3..B11)	=SUM(C3..C11)	=SUM(D3..D11)
14				

This option is handy when you want to view or print a spreadsheet's formulas.

The *Column Headings* and *Row Headings* checkboxes tell the spreadsheet to display its column and row headings. These boxes are normally checked, but you may want to turn the headings off if you're using a spreadsheet frame in a word processing document.

You don't need to turn headings off with the *Display...* command to print a spreadsheet without them—there are checkboxes in the Print dialog box you can click to print without them.

Finally, the *Mark Circular Refs* checkbox tells the spreadsheet to call your attention to any formula containing a circular reference by putting black dots (or bullets) around the cell that contains it. A circular reference in a formula means that the formula refers to itself. For example, if you enter *=A1+A2* in cell A2, you're asking the formula to add its own contents to itself.

Setting document margins, size, and page view options

You can change the amount of data that will print on one page or change the overall size of the spreadsheet document with the *Document...* command on the Format menu. When you choose this command, you see the Document dialog box, like this:

```
┌─────────────────────────────────────────────────────┐
│  Document                                             │
│  ─────────────────────────────────────────────────── │
│  ┌─Margins──────────┐  ┌─Size───────────────────┐    │
│  │                  │  │                         │    │
│  │  Top   [0.5 in]  │  │  Columns across │40│    │    │
│  │                  │  │                         │    │
│  │  Bottom [0.5 in] │  │  Rows down      │500│   │    │
│  │                  │  └─────────────────────────┘    │
│  │  Left   [0.5 in] │  ┌─Display─────────────────┐    │
│  │                  │  │  ⊠ Show margins          │    │
│  │  Right  [0.5 in] │  │  ☐ Show page guides      │    │
│  │                  │  └─────────────────────────┘    │
│  └──────────────────┘                                 │
│  Starting page # [1]                                  │
│                         [ Cancel ]  [   OK   ]        │
└─────────────────────────────────────────────────────┘
```

The *Margins*, *Display,* and *Starting Page #* options here are covered on p. 39 in Chapter 2. (The Display area options are only active when you have Page View turned on—see p. 40 in Chapter 2.)

The *Size* area of this dialog box lets you change the total number of rows and columns in the document. Just click in the *Columns Across* or *Rows Down* box and type a new value, then click the OK button.

Using headers and footers

You add or remove headers and footers in a spreadsheet document just as you do with any other ClarisWorks document. For the basic procedure, see p. 38 in Chapter 2. There are, however, some spreadsheet-specific considerations when you add a header or footer.

When you choose *Insert Header* or *Insert Footer* from the Format menu in the spreadsheet, ClarisWorks automatically switches to the text tool, displays your document in page view (so you can see the page margins, which is where the header and footer are located), and moves the text insertion point into the new header or footer, like this:

| **File** | **Edit** | **Format** | **Font** | **Size** | **Style** | **Outline** | **View** |

1995 Budget (SS)

	A	B	C	D	E
1	Expenses	January	February	March	April
2	Salaries	$10,200	$11,300	$12,400	$12400.00
3	Benefits	$4,500	$4,700	$4,800	4800
4	Materials	$3,000	$4,000	$5,000	5500
5	Rent	$3,500	$3,500	$3,500	3500
6	Advertising	$5,000	$5,400	$4,700	4900
7	Kickbacks	$1,000	$1,000	$1,000	1000

100   Page 1

Here, the insertion point is in the header just above the upper left corner of the spreadsheet's row and column headings. Notice that the word processor's menus are in the menu bar, because the text tool is active. You use the word processor's commands to format the text in the header.

To insert page numbers in the header, choose *Insert Page #* from the Edit menu. To change the starting page number that's inserted when you use this command, choose *Document...* from the Format menu and type a different value in the Starting Page # box.

Once you're through entering and formatting the header, click anywhere inside the spreadsheet's cell area to return to the spreadsheet environment.

Printing

The basic procedure for printing a spreadsheet document is the same as for other ClarisWorks documents, and is covered on pp. 41–45 in Chapter 2. However, let's look at a couple of spreadsheet-specific considerations.

Viewing and setting page breaks

Spreadsheets can be both wider and longer than the paper you're printing on, so a spreadsheet document has both horizontal and vertical page breaks. ClarisWorks sets page breaks automatically according to the size of your document's margins and the size of the paper you're using. (See *Page setup options* in Chapter 2 for more on setting paper sizes and see *Setting document margins, size, and page view options* on p. 151 for more on setting margins.)

The automatic page breaks are normally invisible, but you can show them by choosing *Page View* from the View menu. For example, here's a break between four different pages:

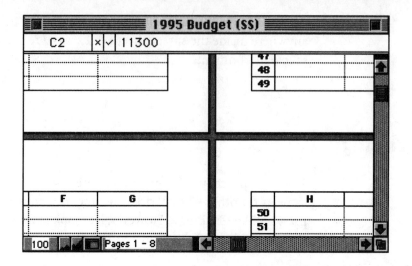

You may want to set your own page breaks to divide data more sensibly between pages. For example, if a yearly budget will print ten months on one page and two months on the next, it might be better to set a page break after the sixth month, so that each page shows half a year's activity.

To set a page break, select the cell in the lower right corner of a page and then choose *Add Page Break* from the Options menu. For example, if you want a new page to begin on row 18 at column O, you'd select cell N17.

Any page breaks you add to a document are indicated with dashed lines, like this:

	M	N	O	P
13	26780	285995		
14				
15				
16	32000			
17	7500			
18				
19				
20				
21				

To remove a manual page break, select the cell just above and to the left of the break (in the example above, that would be cell N17) and choose *Remove Page Break* from the Options menu. To remove all the page breaks you've added to a document (returning it to the default page breaks), choose *Remove All Breaks* from the Options menu.

Setting the print range

ClarisWorks assumes that you want to print all of your spreadsheet document unless you tell it otherwise. But because spreadsheets can be very large and you may want to print only a small group of cells from one page, you can set a print area. To do this:

1. Select the cells you want to print.

2. Choose *Print Range...* from the Options menu. You see a dialog box like the one at the top of the next page:

```
┌─────────────────────────────────────────┐
│  ┌─────────────────────────────────┐     │
│  │                                 │     │
│  │  Print Range                    │     │
│  │  ─────────────                  │     │
│  │  ○ All cells with data          │     │
│  │  ● Cell range   [A1..D12    ]   │     │
│  │                                 │     │
│  │         ( Cancel )  ⟮  OK  ⟯     │     │
│  │                                 │     │
│  └─────────────────────────────────┘     │
└─────────────────────────────────────────┘
```

The range you selected is showing in the *Cell Range* box.

3. Click the OK button. This print area remains selected until you use the *Print Range...* command again.

To go back to printing the whole document, choose *Print Range...*, click the *All Cells With Data* button, and click the OK button.

Spreadsheet options in the Print dialog box

When you choose the *Print…* command from a spreadsheet document, you'll see three additional options at the bottom of the Print dialog box: *Print Column Headings, Print Row Headings,* and *Print Cell Grid.* These are normally checked, so the document's row headings, column headings, and cell grid will be printed. You can uncheck any of these boxes to hide row or column headings or the cell grid when the document is printed.

Troubleshooting

You can't find the selected cell. A cell is selected in a part of the spreadsheet that's not showing on the screen. Check the cell address at the upper left corner of the window to see which cell is selected.

You want to finish a formula but ClarisWorks keeps adding cell references to it instead. You have to click the Accept button or press ⌞Tab⌟ or ⌞Return⌟ to complete a formula. If you click inside any cell before a formula is complete, ClarisWorks adds that cell's address to the formula.

A cell doesn't show all its contents. The cell is too narrow to show everything. You should still be able to see all the cell's contents in the text box at the top of the window. To display everything in the cell, widen the column or select the cell and choose a smaller font size from the Size submenu off the Format menu.

A formula produces the wrong result. Select the cell and check the formula in the text box. Make sure the cell references, constants, and operators are the ones you want. If you've sorted the spreadsheet, inserted or deleted rows or columns, or pasted a formula to a new location, make sure this hasn't screwed up the references in the formula so it calculates the wrong cells. Also, check the order of precedence for operators, and use parentheses to force the order of calculations if necessary (see p. 124).

There's an error message in the cell. Different error messages mean different things. See *Troubleshooting* on p. 404 in Chapter 11.

A cell is outlined with bullets (little black dots). This means the cell's formula contains a circular reference, so the formula calculates itself. Check the cell references in the formula.

A number in a cell turns into a row of pound signs (#####). The cell is too narrow to display the number, so you need to widen the column it's in. This happens a lot when you change the format from General to Currency or Percent, because these formats add extra characters.

You set a number, date, or time format for some cells, and an adjacent cell doesn't have the same format. You have to set data formats individually for each cell. If you want to format a whole column or row the same way, select the column or row by clicking on its heading, then choose the format you want.

The insertion point is blinking in a blank area above or below the cells. You're working in a header or footer. Click inside any cell to return to the spreadsheet.

There's lots of white space around the cells and the edges of the window. Page View is on. Choose *Page View* from the View menu to turn it off.

The wrong rows or columns appear on a printed page. Set a page break to divide up cells between pages differently, or set a print range to print only specific cells.

6

Spreadsheet charting

With the charting features in the ClarisWorks spreadsheet, you can turn numbers into pie, bar, line, and other types of charts. Charts display your data visually so you can easily emphasize differences between one group of numbers and another, or highlight trends that aren't easily noticeable when you look at the numbers themselves. ➥

In this chapter we'll look at ClarisWorks' charting options, including making and revising charts, choosing the appropriate chart type, moving charts to other documents, and printing charts.

Making a chart

To make a spreadsheet chart:

1. Select the group of spreadsheet cells you want to chart. If possible, make your selection so it includes the row and column labels that identify the data. (We'll see why in a minute.) For example, to chart four categories of expense data from three months in a budget spreadsheet, the selection would look like this:

	1995 Budget (SS)				
A1	×✓ Expenses				
	A	**B**	**C**	**D**	
1	**Expenses**	**January**	**February**	**March**	**April**
2	Salaries	$10,200	$11,300	$12,400	$1
3	Benefits	$4,500	$4,700	$4,800	
4	Materials	$3,000	$4,000	$5,000	
5	Rent	$3,500	$3,500	$3,500	
6	Advertising	$5,000	$5,400	$4,700	
7	Kickbacks	$1,000	$1,000	$1,000	

2. Choose *Make Chart...* from the Options menu. You see the Chart Options dialog box, like the one at the top of the next page:

```
┌══════════════════ Chart Options ══════════════════┐
│ ┌─Modify──┐  ┌─Gallery ─────────────────────────┐ │
│ │ ┌─────┐ │  │  ┌──┐   ┌──┐   ┌──┐  ┌──┐  ┌──┐  ┌──┐ │ │
│ │ │     │ │  │  │▐█│   │◢◣│   │◢◤│  │⋰⋱│  │◕ │  │⋮⋮│ │ │
│ │ └─────┘ │  │  └──┘   └──┘   └──┘  └──┘  └──┘  └──┘ │ │
│ │ ┌─────┐ │  │  Bar    Area   Line  Scatter Pie Pictogram │
│ │ │ Axis│ │  │                                   │ │
│ │ └─────┘ │  │  ┌──┐   ┌──┐   ┌──┐  ┌──┐  ┌──┐  ┌──┐ │ │
│ │ ┌─────┐ │  │  │▟▖│   │◢◣│   │╲╱│  │××│  │ʈʈ│  │▟▖│ │ │
│ │ │Series│ │  │  └──┘   └──┘   └──┘  └──┘  └──┘  └──┘ │ │
│ │ └─────┘ │  │  Stacked Stacked X-Y  X-Y  Hi-Low Stacked │
│ │ ┌─────┐ │  │  Bar    Area   Line  Scatter      Pictogram │
│ │ │Labels│ │  │                                   │ │
│ │ └─────┘ │  │  ⊠ Color        □ Shadow          │ │
│ │ ┌─────┐ │  │  □ Horizontal   □ 3-dimensional   │ │
│ │ │General│ │  └───────────────────────────────────┘ │
│ │ └─────┘ │                                          │
│ └─────────┘              ┌──────┐   ┌──────────┐      │
│                          │Cancel│   │    OK    │      │
│                          └──────┘   └──────────┘      │
└────────────────────────────────────────────────────┘
```

3.   Choose the type of chart you want to create by clicking its option in the Gallery area at the right, then click the checkboxes to set options for that chart type (The options change depending on which chart type you choose. See *Changing a chart definition* on p. 164 for more information.)

4.   Click the OK button or press [Return] to draw the chart. The chart appears on the screen on top of the spreadsheet data, like the one at the top of the next page:

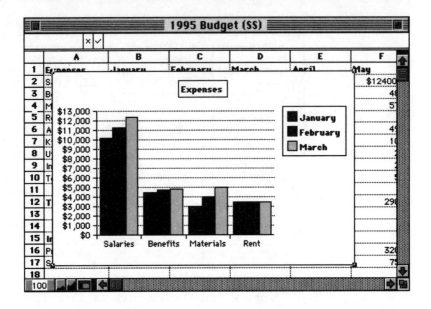

Each expense row we selected in the spreadsheet has become a group of bars, with each column representing one bar. The row labels in column A have become the labels for each group. Also, because the text *Expenses* was in the upper-left cell in the group we selected, it has been used as the chart's title. If column A or row 1 in our selection had been blank, this chart would have no data labels, legend labels, or title.

Notice that the chart is a draw object that has been placed in a separate graphics layer on top of the spreadsheet data. When a chart is selected, you can use draw tools to move or resize it or to modify its appearance. For example, you could draw an arrow pointing to a particular bar. To return to the spreadsheet's environment, click anywhere in the document window outside the chart.

Switching back to the spreadsheet environment doesn't make the chart go away, so if you want to work on cells that are located underneath a chart, drag the chart out of the way first.

The appearance of this chart and others you create with the spreadsheet is initially determined by the contents of the cells you select in the spreadsheet itself. Once the chart is created, however, you can use dozens of options to change how it looks, as we'll see.

You can create as many charts in each spreadsheet document as you like.

Charts are linked to spreadsheet data

Once you create a chart, any changes to the contents of the spreadsheet cells depicted in the chart will be reflected in the chart itself. For example, if we changed a Benefits expense value for January in the spreadsheet on page 160, the January bar in the Benefits category of the chart would grow or shrink accordingly.

When you paste a copied chart into another document, its link to the data in the original spreadsheet is broken, so changes to that spreadsheet's data are no longer reflected in the chart. See *Using draw tools to modify a chart* on p. 182.

Basic charting terms and concepts

Before we get into the details of modifying charts, let's get some basic terms and concepts straight. Let's take another look at the chart we just drew:

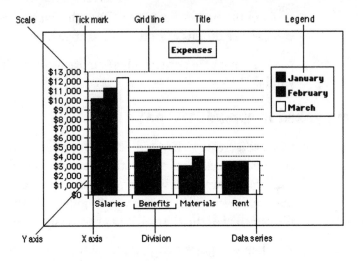

This bar chart displays three months' worth of data from four different expense categories. This type of chart plots the changes in values over time, so it's known as a *time series* chart.

Every time series charts has two axes, a horizontal *x axis* that typically represents categories (or *divisions*) of data, and a vertical *y axis* that typically contains a *scale* of values. The values are separated by *tick marks* on the scale, and in this case *grid lines* extend from the tick marks across the chart so you can more easily tell how much each bar represents.

The chart *title* is shown at the top, and its *legend*, a guide showing which bar pattern represents which data series, is shown at the right.

• •

Changing a chart definition

A chart's definition determines how that chart represents the data you've selected. The bar chart shown above was created with the spreadsheet's default chart definition options, but you have lots of flexibility for representing data in different ways. To change a chart's definition:

1. Select the chart whose definition you want to change.

2. Choose *Modify Chart...* from the Options menu. You see the Chart Options dialog box, as shown on p. 161.

You can also double-click in a blank area of the chart to display the Chart Options dialog box with the Gallery options showing.

There are five groups of options you can view or change in the Chart Options dialog box, depending on which of the buttons at the left you click. When you first choose the *Modify Chart...* command, the Gallery options are the ones you see, so we'll look at those first.

Choosing a chart type

The *Gallery* options in the Chart Options dialog box determine the type of chart used to represent your data. Depending on which chart type you select, the checkbox options below the gallery are different. Here's a rundown on each of the twelve chart types and their options, and how you might use them.

Bar charts are best for comparing changes in values over time. Each row or column of data is shown as a different data series (or type of bar), like this:

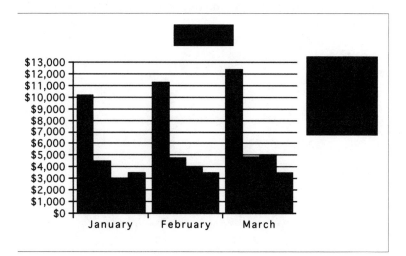

Compare this chart with the one on p. 164. Notice that the bars here represent expense values, and the divisions represent months. ClarisWorks is preset to create data series from columns (which is why the different bars in the chart on p. 164 represent months, rather than expense categories). But most spreadsheets track expenses in rows, so you'll want rows, not columns, to be used for each series. You can use the General options in the Chart Options dialog box to have ClarisWorks make data series from rows. See *Setting general options* on p. 181.

When you choose a bar chart type, the checkbox options below the gallery in the Chart Options dialog box are:

- Color (to display the chart in color);

- Horizontal (to flip the chart's axes, so the bars run horizontally instead of vertically);

- Shadow (which puts shadows behind the bars); and

- Three-dimensional (which adds depth perspective to the bars).

Try these options out for yourself.

Stacked bar charts combine all the data in each division into one bar, like the one at the top of the next page:

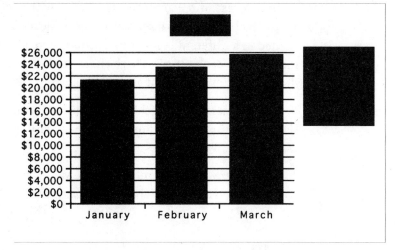

In this case, each stacked bar totals all the expenses for each division, or month, and the segments in each bar show how each expense contributes proportionally to the month's total. The checkbox options for stacked bar charts are the same as they are for bar charts.

Area charts show each data series as a line with the area below the line filled in, like this:

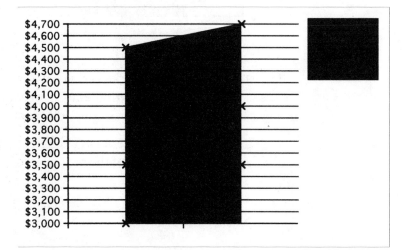

In this case, there are three data series with two values in each series (each value is marked with an x). The area below each line is shaded in a different color, and because there are three data series, they overlap each other. (These charts look better in color, but they're still hard to read if you ask me.)

In area charts, the checkbox options are horizontal, color, and shadow. (A three-dimensional area chart with overlapping series would be too weird.)

Stacked area charts combine all the values from the data series you select and adjust the chart scale accordingly, like this:

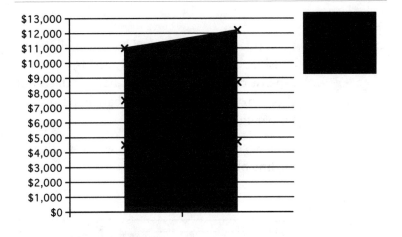

Like stacked bar charts, stacked area charts are best for showing how each of several series contributes to an overall total. Stacked area charts have the same checkbox options as area charts.

Line charts plot each data series as a different pattern or color of line, like the one at the top of the next page:

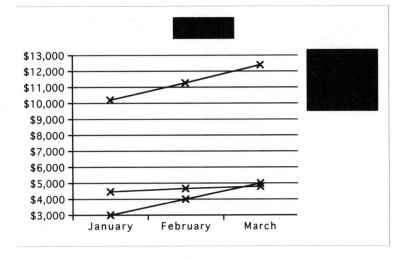

In this case, each series has three values in it, each of which is shown by an x. The lines are much easier to distinguish in color, but you should display the chart in black and white if you plan to print it in black and white, so you'll know how it will look.

ClarisWorks is preset to display each series with an x symbol, but you can use a different symbol for each series by changing the chart's Series options. See *Setting the series pattern or symbol* on p. 177.

Line charts can also be made horizontal, displayed in color, or shadowed, but the shadow option makes it look like you're seeing double.

X-Y line charts are covered on p. 171.

Scatter charts plot values as individual points, but with no lines connecting them or bars beneath them. For example, the line chart above looks like the one at the top of the next page as a scatter chart:

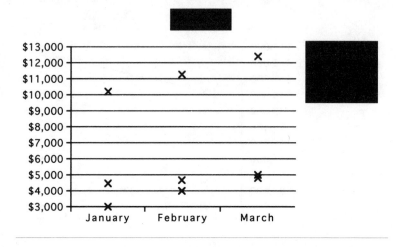

Scatter charts have the same checkbox options as area charts.

Pie charts plot one column or row of data, and represent each value in that column or row as a percentage of the whole pie. For example, five expense figures from one month in a budget spreadsheet might look like this:

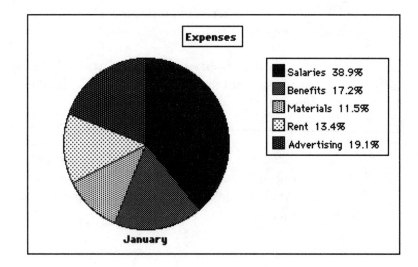

Here the values were in a column labeled *January*. The selected area in the spreadsheet included column A (which contains the expense category labels and the chart title in cell A1), and column B (which contains the values). You can also create multiple pies in the same chart by selecting more than one column. For each column you select, ClarisWorks displays a separate pie.

In addition to the basic horizontal, color, and shadow check-box options, pie charts also have options called Scale Multiple and Tilt.

- *Scale Multiple* only works when you're displaying more than one pie in the same chart. When you check this option, ClarisWorks scales the pies to different sizes, according to the overall total of values in each pie. A pie whose slices total a higher value will be larger than a pie whose slices total a smaller value.

- *Tilt* displays the pie chart with its top tilted away from you. Try this one to see it for yourself.

To explode one or more slices in a pie chart, change the series options. See *Setting pie chart series options* on p. 179.

X-Y line charts and *X-Y scatter* charts plot pairs of values as single points. One column of values is the X axis and the other is the Y axis, and each pair of points is plotted according to its X and Y coordinates. By plotting two values as one point, you can compare one pair of values with another. X-Y line charts connect each pair of values with a line, and X-Y scatter charts just plot the values without the line connecting them. For example, a spreadsheet might track changes in employee productivity like the one at the top of the next page:

	A	B	C
1	Shift Hour	Units/Hour	
2	1	20	
3	2	25	
4	3	26	
5	4	22	
6	5	21	
7	6	20	
8	7	18	
9	8	16	
10			

An X-Y line chart could plot the pairs of values on a line, like this:

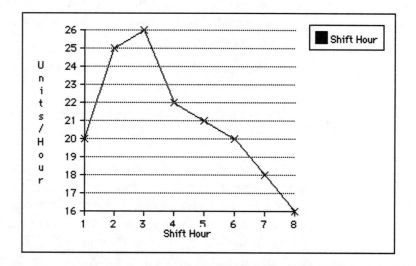

An X-Y scatter chart would plot the pairs of values without the line. When you display X-Y charts, the checkbox options are color display, shadowed display, and a square grid, which makes the tick mark separations on the X axis the same as those on the Y axis. (In the above example, using the square grid option would shrink the X axis, bringing the tick marks closer together to match those on the Y axis.)

Hi-Low charts are another way to plot pairs of values. Instead of arranging them according to coordinates on both the X and Y axes, however, Hi-Low charts plot both values on the Y axis, and each pair of values is a different division on the X axis. For example, a spreadsheet might track listing and sale prices of houses like this:

	A	B	C
1	Property Sales (000)	List Price	Sale Price
2	Madison	240	200
3	Lester	220	180
4	Wilton Ct.	210	170
5	Rodeo	199	190
6			

By selecting cells A1 through C5 and choosing the Hi-Low chart type from the gallery, you could make a chart like this:

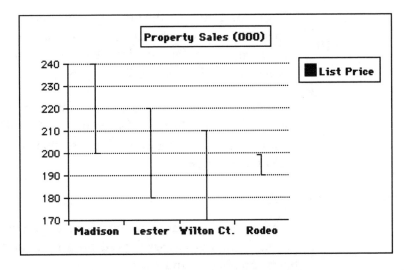

The upper and lower values (from columns B and C) in each row are plotted as the end points of each vertical line. With Hi-Low charts, you have the standard Horizontal, Color, and Shadow checkbox options.

Pictogram charts are bar charts that use graphic symbols to make up the bars instead of just filled rectangles, like this:

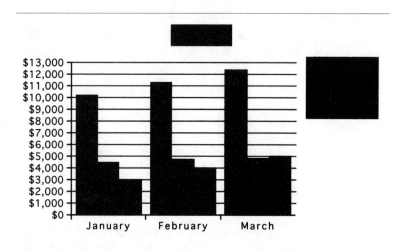

The arrow symbol is the preset graphic option for pictogram charts, but you can change the symbol, and you can have a different symbol for each data series. See *Setting the series pattern or symbol* on p. 177.

Stacked pictogram charts are just like stacked bar charts or stacked area charts. Instead of separate bars for each series, the whole division is one bar divided into segments that represent the value of each series.

Setting axis options

To change the appearance of a chart's scale, you use the axis options. These options aren't available for pie charts, because pie charts don't have X and Y axes.

When you click the *Axis* button in the Chart Options dialog box, you see the axis options, like the ones at the top of the next page:

```
┌─ Axis ──────────────────────────────────┐
│  ○ X axis    ◉ Y axis                    │
│ ─────────────────────────────────────── │
│  Axis label  ┌──────────────────────┐   │
│              └──────────────────────┘   │
│  Tick marks ┌Outside ▼┐   Minor ┌─────┐ │
│             └─────────┘          └─────┘ │
│  ⊠ Grid lines                            │
│  Minimum    Maximum    Step size   □ Log │
│  ┌──────┐  ┌──────┐  ┌──────────┐ ┌────┐ │
│  └──────┘  └──────┘  └──────────┘ └────┘ │
└──────────────────────────────────────────┘
```

You can also double-click on a chart axis to display these options in the Chart Options dialog box.

The buttons at the top let you change either the X or the Y axis for the chart. The *Y axis* is the default option here.

Axis Label is the current label for this axis. Click in the box and edit the label or type a new one.

Tick Marks controls the type of tick marks on the axis. The pop-up menu lets you choose the position of the tick marks: Outside, Inside, or Across the axis line, or None.

The *Minor* box lets you specify the number of minor tick marks you want placed between the major ones that ClarisWorks adds automatically.

The *Grid Lines* checkbox lets you show or hide grid lines that extend across the chart from each tick mark.

The *Minimum, Maximum,* and *Step Size* boxes let you specify minimum, maximum, and step interval values for the axis by entering those values here. ClarisWorks normally sets the scale according to the minimum and maximum values in the range you selected, and chooses a step interval by dividing the total axis range into equal values.

The Log checkbox and text box let you choose a logarithmic scale instead of a numeric one. Once you click the Log checkbox, ClarisWorks automatically suggests a log base of 10 in the text box below. In this case, the scale increases by orders of magnitude, so the tick marks will be 1000, 10,000, 100,000, and so on. You can enter a different log base if you like.

Changing a series display

When you want to change how one or more data series in a chart are displayed, use the series options. Click the Series button in the Chart Options dialog box and you see a set of options like this:

> Double-click on a series indicator in a chart's legend to display the series options in the Chart Options dialog box.

The *Edit Series* pop-up menu lets you select a particular data series to work on. The All option is selected automatically, so any changes you make to the other options below will affect every data series. When you choose a particular data series from this menu, you change only its options. (If you selected row or column labels when you created the chart, those labels are the names of the series. If you didn't, series are labeled *Series 1*, *Series 2*, and so on.)

Once you've chosen a series to work on, the options you see below depend on the type of chart you're working with. The *Display As* pop-up menu lets you display any selected series as a bar, pictogram, line, area, or scatter chart. Since you can modify just one series in a chart, this means you can combine chart types in one chart, plotting one data series as a line and another as a bar, for example.

The *Label Data* checkbox and buttons let you add a label to the series. The label ClarisWorks uses is the highest value in the series. In a bar that goes up to 125 on the Y axis, for example, the label will be *125*. Click the Label Data checkbox and then click a button below to set the label's position relative to the series marker (the bar, line mark, or whatever).

Setting the series pattern or symbol

The *Sample* box shown earlier appears when you're working on a series displayed as a bar or a pictogram. This option shows the current color, pattern, or graphic symbol used for the bar. In a pictogram series, you can change the symbol used by selecting the Sample box and pasting a different symbol from the Clipboard.

Below the Sample box are two checkboxes that control how pictogram symbols appear in a bar. Normally, ClarisWorks stretches or compresses a graphic symbol to fit different bar sizes. The *Repeating* checkbox tells ClarisWorks to repeat a graphic symbol inside the bar instead. The *% Overlap* box tells ClarisWorks to overlap a repeating symbol and lets you specify the percentage of the symbol that is overlapped. For example, if you type *50* in the box, the Sample box shows the symbol repeating and half-over-lapped, like the one at the top of the next page:

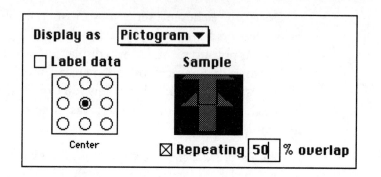

When you're working with a series displayed as a line or area, you can change the symbol used for the series, along with its pattern or color. If you're modifying a line or area series, the options look like this:

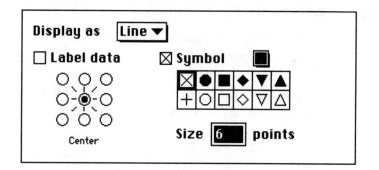

The *Symbol* box is normally checked, and the symbol option is preset to the X, which is outlined above.

- To eliminate symbols (and just display a line or area without them), uncheck the Symbol box.

- To change the symbol used, click on a different one in the palette.

- To change the symbol's color or pattern, click on the pop-up palette to the right of the Symbol checkbox and choose a different one.

- To change the symbol's size, type a different value in the *Size* box at the bottom.

Setting pie chart series options

When you're working with a pie chart, each data series is displayed as a slice of the pie. You can use the series options to modify pie slices and add emphasis to your chart. When a pie chart is selected, the series options look like this:

Display as [Pie ▼]

☒ **Label data**   ☐ **Explode slice**

  ◉ **% in legend**
  ○ **% in slice**
  ○ **% in both**

To modify one pie slice, you must first select the series that slice represents from the Edit Series pop-up menu at the top of the dialog box.

- To hide the pie's data labels, uncheck the *Label Data* checkbox.

- To explode a pie slice, setting it apart from the rest of the pie, click the *Explode Slice* checkbox.

- To display series percentages inside each pie slice, click the *% In Slice* button.

- To display series percentages both in each slice and in the legend, click the *% In Both* button.

Modifying chart titles and legends

To change the text or formatting of a chart's title or legend, use the labels options. (To change axis labels, you use the axis options. See p. 174.) When you click the Labels button in the Chart Options dialog box, the options look like the ones at the top of the next page:

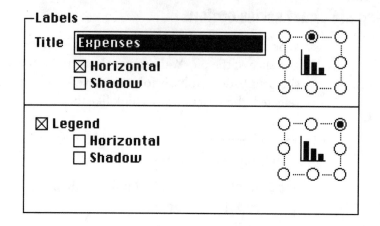

Normally, ClarisWorks uses the text in the upper left cell of the range you selected as the chart title. If the range you selected contained text in the upper left cell, that text is showing in the *Title* box here.

- To add a title or edit the present one, just click in the box and make the changes.

- To eliminate a title, delete the text from the Title box.

- To change the font or size of the title, select the text in the Title box and choose a font, size, or style from the Format menu.

- To display the title vertically, uncheck the *Horizontal* checkbox.

- To place a shadowed box around the title, click the *Shadow* checkbox.

- To change the position of the title, click one of the position buttons at the right.

The legend labels identify each data series in a chart, and they come from the first cell in each series (the top cell in a column or the left-most cell in a row). ClarisWorks normally displays a legend at the upper right corner of the chart.

- To hide the legend, uncheck the *Legend* checkbox.

- To display the legend horizontally, click the Horizontal checkbox.

- To put a shadow behind the legend, click the Shadow checkbox.

- To change the legend's position, click one of the position buttons at the right.

Setting general options

The last group of options in the Chart Options dialog box don't fall into a particular category, so they're called General options. When you click the *General* button in the Chart Options dialog box, you see the General options, like this:

```
┌─General ──────────────────────────────────────┐
│  Chart range  ▐A1..D5▌                          │
│                                                 │
│  Series names              Series in            │
│  ┌──────────────────┐ ⇧    ○ Rows      ▦        │
│  │ January          │      ◉ Columns   ▦        │
│  │ February         │                           │
│  │ March            │      Use numbers          │
│  │                  │ ⇩    as labels in          │
│  └──────────────────┘      ☐ First row          │
│  Each series is a set of data values in a  ☐ First column │
│  row or column. Series names are                │
│  listed in the legend.                          │
└─────────────────────────────────────────────────┘
```

The *Chart Range* box shows the range of cells currently selected for the chart. You can modify the range by typing in new cell addresses at either the beginning or the end of the range shown, or by deleting it and typing in a completely new range. The beginning and ending range addresses must be separated by two periods.

The *Series Names* list shows the names of the series, which are taken from the first cell in each series. If the first cell in each series doesn't contain text, then the series are labeled *Series 1, Series 2,* and so on.

The *Series In* buttons let you decide whether data series are made up from rows or columns. Using columns as series makes more sense when your spreadsheet is arranged so that each column is a month and each row is an expense category.

The *Use Numbers As Labels In* checkboxes tell ClarisWorks to use values (instead of text) as series labels. Normally, ClarisWorks ignores values if they're in the first cells in a series and labels the series *Series 1* and so on. If you check one or both of these boxes, however, ClarisWorks uses numbers in those cells as the labels for series.

Using draw tools to modify a chart

While you have lots of chart formatting options right inside the spreadsheet environment, you have far more options if you use the draw environment. When you're sure the chart plots the values you want and you're ready to make some serious visual modifications to a chart, move it to a draw document.

1. Select the chart in the spreadsheet and choose *Copy* from the Edit menu.

2. Open a new draw document and choose *Paste* from the Edit menu.

Once you paste a chart anywhere, the pasted copy of the chart is no longer linked to the original spreadsheet, so changing values in the original spreadsheet will no longer change the chart.

Ungrouping a chart

When you first paste a chart into a draw document, it's one object with selection handles at its corners, just as it is in the spreadsheet.

To change individual components of the chart, like putting a new pattern into a pie slice or a bar, you must ungroup the object to break it up into smaller component objects. Choose *Ungroup Picture* from the Arrange menu. You'll see selection handles around individual data series, axes, or lines in the legend.

Once a chart is ungrouped, you can select smaller components and ungroup them further to modify individual objects within them. For example, when you first ungroup a chart, the legend is all one object. If you select the legend and choose *Ungroup* from the Arrange menu, each line in the legend becomes one object, like this:

This is fine if you want to change a whole line (the series symbol and the series name), but to change just the name of the series, or the pattern of the symbol, you must select one line and choose *Ungroup* again. Then the series symbol and the text in the name become two different objects, and you can select just one of them and change it.

Remember, once an object is ungrouped, you can move it, resize it, change its font, font size, or style, or change its pattern or color. This has lots of possibilities. You can select one pie slice, change its pattern, and "explode" it farther from the pie than the Chart Options dialog box's normal Explode Slice option. Or you can select one line in a legend and change the font, size, or style of just that one line.

Once you've made the changes you want, you can select the object and those around it and group them again.

If lots of objects are close together when you ungroup them and you have trouble selecting just one to work on, click the zoom-in control in the window's lower left corner to magnify the document.

Printing charts

You can print a chart by simply printing your spreadsheet document, but this isn't the best way to go for lots of reasons.

First of all, you'll probably want to print a chart by itself, but when you print from a spreadsheet document, you'll print the chart along with any spreadsheet data that happens to be on the same document page. If the chart is covering up any numbers, it will cover them up in the printout, too.

It's not always easy to tell which page is which in a spreadsheet document, so even if you move the chart to a blank area of the spreadsheet and set page breaks so the chart is on its own page, it can be hard to tell which page of the document the chart is on so you can print just that one page.

Even if you can print the chart on a page by itself, you'll have to uncheck the options in the Print dialog box to print the row and column headings and cell grid if you don't want them to show up.

Normally you'll want to print a chart either as part of a word processor document or by itself on a page as an illustration for a report or perhaps as an overhead slide. To print a chart for either of these uses, copy it from the spreadsheet document and paste it into the type of document that best suits your purposes.

To include a chart in a word processing document:

1. Select the chart and copy it to the Clipboard.

2. Open the word processing document and display the tool panel.

3. Click on the graphics tool to switch to the draw environment.

4. Paste the chart in the document.

When you paste a chart in the draw environment, it's treated as an object separate from the word processor text, so you can move it independently of the text and even wrap text around it. See Chapter 4 for more on using graphics in word processor documents.

To print a chart on a page by itself, paste the chart into a new draw document and then print that document page. The drawing environment is the best one for printing a chart by itself because you can use the draw tools to modify the chart easily.

Troubleshooting

You can't see all of a chart in the spreadsheet window. Resize the window, if necessary, and then drag the chart to the middle of the window.

Labels or titles aren't included in a chart. The range of cells you select has to include cells with labels at the beginnings of each row or column. If it doesn't, no labels will appear under bars, and the legend will say *Series 1* and so on. If the upper left or left-most cell in the range you select is blank, the chart won't have a title. To add labels to groups of bars, either make a new chart that includes cells with labels, or copy the chart to a draw document, ungroup it, and change the series names with the text tool. To add a chart title, use the Labels option in the Chart Options dialog box.

Month names or other column labels end up in the legend, but you wanted them underneath groups of bars. Select the General options in the Chart Options dialog box and click the Series In Columns button.

The chart scale is too broad. If it's hard to see small changes in bar or line positions because the scale increments are too far apart, change the scale with the Axis options in the Chart Options dialog box, or select a different range of values in which the highest and lowest value are closer together.

You can't find a chart you drew before. It's probably underneath another chart. Drag other charts around the screen to reveal what's underneath them.

There are too many charts on the screen. Select and delete any charts you don't need anymore. If you want to store a lot of charts for later use, move them all to an unused part of the spreadsheet. By resizing each chart so it's only an inch square or so, you can line up a lot of charts in a fairly small area. You can also enter a label in a cell above each chart to identify it. When you need to view a chart again, just resize it. Finally, by entering a label like *Charts* in a cell at the top of the chart storage area, you can quickly move to that area using the *Find/Change* command.

Bars, pie slices, or area segments are in the wrong pattern or color. To change elements like this, copy the chart to a draw document, ungroup it, and then select and change the individual bar or pie slice. However, you can change the symbol on a pictogram chart by selecting the sample in the Series options part of the Chart Options dialog box and pasting in a new one.

7

The database

The ClarisWorks database is the application you use to store collections of facts, such as names and addresses, inventory items, or sales records. Once data is in a database file, you can sort it, select specific facts, or format the data for printing or viewing in many different ways. ➤➤

Basic database concepts

Before we get into the specifics of the ClarisWorks database, it's important to understand some basic concepts about how databases work. Here's a section from an address database file:

FirstName	LastName	Phone
Theo	Clifton	818-555-0987
Fred	Smith	510-555-1234
George	Barrios	916-555-8876

Each database file you create is made up of *records*. A record is one group of facts, such as one address or one invoice. There are three records in the example above.

Each record is divided into *fields,* which are individual categories of information. Before you can store records, you must define the fields into which you'll separate information. Fields can contain text, numbers, dates, or times, or formulas that calculate data from other fields in the file. There are three fields (FirstName, LastName, and Phone) in the example above.

In the ClarisWorks database, the fields you define appear on the screen in *layouts.* Along with fields, layouts can contain text and graphics, and you can create as many different layouts for a file as you like. The arrangement of a layout determines how your data looks on the screen and how it appears when printed on paper.

Different layouts can contain different groups of fields, so you can display your data in different ways. For example, you might have one layout that's a telephone list like the one above, another that looks like a card file and which also contains fields for the person's address, and another that looks like a mailing label.

Using the database's layout tools, you can rearrange fields, resize them, change the font, size, or style of the data in them, add text to identify them (like the boldfaced field names above the records in the example above), or add graphics you create with the ClarisWorks paint or draw tools.

About database modes

The ClarisWorks database has three distinct operating modes, and you use different modes to work with a file in different ways. In fact, the database program's menus change, depending on which mode you're in.

You use *Browse* mode to view records, enter or change records, sort records in different orders, and print records. You can browse records with any layout you've set up for the file.

You use *Find* mode to select groups of records based on specific criteria.

You use *Layout* mode to create or change layouts.

When you create a new database file or open an existing one, ClarisWorks selects Browse mode so you can work with the data in the file. To switch from one mode to another, choose the mode name from the top of the Layout menu.

Although these modes restrict your activities in the database, there are some tasks you can perform at any time, such as opening and closing files, printing files, and defining fields.

Making a new database file

To create a database file, you must make a new file and then define the fields that will contain your data.

1. Choose the *New...* command from the File menu and then double-click on the Database document type in the New Document dialog box. ClarisWorks opens a new database file and, since you must define fields before you can store data, it automatically displays the Define Fields dialog box, like this:

```
┌──────────────────────────────────────────────────────────┐
│ Define Fields                                              │
│  Name                        Type                          │
│  ┌──────────────────────────────────────────────────┐ ⬆  │
│  │                                                    │    │
│  │                                                    │    │
│  │                                                    │    │
│  │                                                    │ ⬇  │
│  └──────────────────────────────────────────────────┘     │
│                                                            │
│  Name │                                            │       │
│  ┌Type──────────────────────────┐   ┌ Create ┐ ┌Options...┐│
│  │ ● Text    ⌘1  ○ Time     ⌘4 │                          │
│  │ ○ Number  ⌘2  ○ Calculation ⌘5│  ┌ Delete ┐ ┌ Modify ┐ │
│  │ ○ Date    ⌘3  ○ Summary  ⌘6 │   ┌────────────────────┐ │
│  └──────────────────────────────┘   │      Done          │ │
│                                      └────────────────────┘ │
└──────────────────────────────────────────────────────────┘
```

2. The cursor is blinking in the Name box. Type a name for the new field.

3. Click a button in the Type area to set the field's data type.

4. Click the Create button at the right or press Return. The field's name and type appear in the field list, like this:

```
┌──────────────────────────────────────────────────────────┐
│ Name                        Type                           │
│ FirstName                   Text                        ⬆  │
│                                                            │
│                                                            │
│                                                            │
│                                                         ⬇  │
└──────────────────────────────────────────────────────────┘
```

5.   Click the Options… button or press the Return key to set any options for the field you've created, if you like. (See *Setting the field type* on p. 196 and Setting entry *options* on p. 197.)

6.   Repeat steps 2 through 5 for the other fields you want to define, then click the Done button when you're finished. ClarisWorks displays the database document window in Browse mode.

Working with data in Browse mode

When you've finished defining fields in a new file, ClarisWorks switches you to the database's Browse mode so you can enter data. Here's the Browse screen in a file that contains three records:

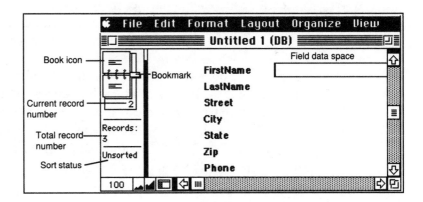

Each field's name is shown in the work area at the right, next to a box that shows the size of the field's data space. The field that's currently selected for data entry is outlined in black.

Viewing records

When you first create a database file, the fields are shown in a *standard layout* like the one above, with the fields stacked on top of each other in the order in which you created them. After you've created other layouts, you can browse records in any of them by choosing the layout name from the bottom of the Layout menu.

Records in a file are displayed in a scrolling list. To move from one record to the next:

- Click or drag in the vertical scroll bar;

- Click the upper or lower pages in the *book icon* at the left to move to the previous or next record;

- Drag the *bookmark* to move proportionally through the file; or

- Choose *Go To Record…* from the Organize menu, enter the number of the record you want to display, and press (Return).

The *current record number* shows which of the file's records you currently have selected.

The database is preset to show records in a continuously scrolling list, so you may see more than one record on the screen at a time. To display records individually, choose *List View* from the Layout menu to remove the check mark from it.

Below the book icon, you can see the total number of records in the file and the file's *sort status*. The records are stored in a file in the order in which you create them; this is the file's *unsorted* status. Files are always unsorted when you open them, and you must use the *Sort Records…* command on the Organize menu to sort records in a different order. See *Sorting records* on p. 209 for more information.

The other window controls in Browse mode (the zoom percentage, zoom in and zoom out, show/hide tools controls, and scroll bars) are the same in every database mode, as discussed in Chapter 2.

Entering and changing data

The simplest way to enter data is to type it: click inside a field's data space to select it and then type the data. To confirm your entry and select the next field at the same time, either click in the next field or press the ⟨Tab⟩ key. You can also move from the current field to the previous field by pressing ⟨Shift⟩⟨Tab⟩.

Another way to enter data is to select a value from a predefined list. If the field was defined with a value list, the list of values will pop up when you select the field. To enter a value from the list, either double-click on the value or select it and press ⟨Return⟩. See *Setting entry options* on p. 197 for more on defining a value list.

A third way to enter data is to paste it from the Clipboard. If you have one value, text string, date, or time on the Clipboard, you can select a field and choose *Paste* from the Edit menu to enter it.

Finally, you can use the *Find/Change* command on the Edit menu to locate a specific piece of data in several records and replace it with something else. See p. 60 in Chapter 3 for more on the *Find/Change* command.

Changing the tab order

When you use the ⟨Tab⟩ key to move the insertion point from one field to the next in Browse mode, ClarisWorks follows the order in which you originally created the fields. Even though you can rearrange the positions of fields in Layout mode, the tab order remains the same.

To change the tab order, choose *Tab Order…* from the Layout menu. You'll see the Tab Order dialog box, like this:

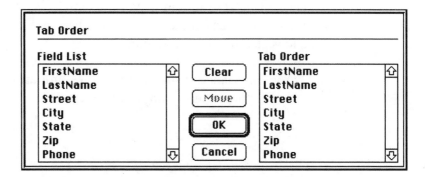

The current tab order is shown in the Tab Order list at the right, and the Field List shows the names of every field in your file, in the order in which they were created.

The simplest way to change the entire tab order is to click the Clear button to clear the Tab Order list and then double-click on the names in the Field List in the new order you want. (You can also click a name and then click the Move button.) As you double-click on each field name, it's added to the Tab Order list.

If you just want to remove one field from the Tab Order list, double-click on its name there, or click it and then click the Move button.

When the Tab Order list is the way you want it, click the OK button to put the dialog box away.

Your file can have several different layouts that show fields in different locations, but changing the tab order changes it for every layout in your file; you can't set a different tab order for each layout.

Adding new records

ClarisWorks automatically creates one new record when you finish defining fields for a new file. To add a new record, choose *New Record* from the Edit menu. You see a new, blank record on the screen and the total record number at the left increases by one.

Each record you add to a file is added to the end of the file and given the next record number. For example, if your file contains three records and you add a record, it becomes record number 4 and is placed after record number 3.

You can change the order in which records are displayed by sorting them. See *Sorting records* on p. 209.

Selecting, copying, pasting, and deleting records

Typically you'll work with one record at a time, entering or changing information in one field. However, if you want to copy the data from several records or delete several records from a file, you must select entire records, rather than one field in one record.

To select a record, click outside of any of its fields. The whole record turns dark to show that it's selected. To select a group of records, either select the first record and then drag the pointer up or down to select the group, or Shift-click after selecting the first record to extend the selection.

To deselect a record, ⌘-click on it, or click inside any of its fields to select that field instead.

Once you've selected a record, you can copy its data by choosing *Copy* from the Edit menu. If you choose the *Paste* command after copying a record, a new record is added to the file and the data on the Clipboard is pasted into it. Of course, you can also paste the data into other ClarisWorks documents.

To delete a record or records from a file, select the record(s) and choose *Cut* from the Edit menu (to remove the record and place its data on the Clipboard), or choose the *Delete Record* or *Clear* command from the Edit menu (to delete the data permanently).

 If you cut or clear a record by mistake, choose the *Undo Cut* or *Undo Clear* command at the top of the Edit menu to put it back.

Duplicating records

Sometimes you have a lot of information in one record that's the same in a new record you want to create. For example, you may have two address records for different people at the same company at the same address. To save yourself some typing, you can duplicate the record and then change the name information only. Just display the record on the screen (or select the record or a field in it if you're viewing records in a list) and choose *Duplicate Record* from the Edit menu.

More about defining fields

At the beginning of this chapter we covered the basics of creating a database file and defining fields. Now let's look more closely at the options you have when defining fields.

Naming fields

Field names can be up to 63 characters long, and can contain spaces, commas, or other punctuation characters.

Setting the field type

Fields can be set to text, number, date, time, calculation, or summary types. A field's type determines what kind of data you can enter and what you can do with that data.

Text fields are for storing letters or numbers that you don't do math with, like zip codes. A text field can contain about 500 characters, depending on the font, size, and style of text in it. Text fields can be as wide or tall as your overall layout's size permits. (See *Changing field and text formats* on p. 220.)

Number fields can contain numbers up to 254 characters, including a decimal point, but they can be only one line high.

A *Date* field can be only one line high and can contain only one date. The date must be entered in a date format ClarisWorks recognizes, such as MM/DD/YY. If you try to enter a date in an invalid format, you'll see an error message

A *Time* field can be only one line high and can contain only one time, which must be entered in a valid time format such as HH:MM:SS. You can add AM or PM to times if you like; or enter them in 24-hour format. If you try to enter an invalid time, you'll see an error message.

A *Calculation* field contains a formula that automatically calculates data from other fields in the same record and displays the result of that calculation. You can't enter data into a calculation field because the data in it is created automatically. A calculation field's length is determined by the data type of the calculated result; you can make number, date, time, or text calculations in the database. See *Defining calculation fields* on p. 199 for more information.

A *Summary* field contains a formula that calculates data from a whole group of records and displays the result of that calculation. Like a calculation field, you can't type data manually into a summary field. You typically use summary fields when you create reports that produce averages, subtotals, or other summarized calculations. See *Defining summary fields* on p. 201.

Setting entry options

Once you've created a text, number, date, or time field, you can set various options to control the type of data entered into it. Select the field in the list at the top of the Define Fields dialog box and then click the Options... button or press (Return). You'll see the Entry Options dialog box, like this:

The options you have depend on whether you've selected a text, number, date, or time field. (You can't set any of these options for calculation or summary fields.)

The Auto Entry options set the database to enter data into a field automatically.

- When you click the Data button and type text, a number, date, or time in the box at the right, ClarisWorks enters that data in the field automatically.

- Clicking the Variable button sets the database to enter the creation or modification date, creation or modification time, or creator or modifier name (as shown in the Chooser control panel on the Mac at the time the record is created or changed), depending on which option you choose from the pop-up menu at the right.

- Clicking the Serial Number button inserts a serial number in a text or number field. When you click this button, you can specify the next value and the increment value in the two boxes below.

The Verification options tell the database to check that the field is filled in, that it contains a unique text string, number, date, or time, or that it contains a certain type of data. The Range check-box is only active in numeric fields. When you check this box, you can enter a specific numeric range within which data in the field must fall. If you set one of these options and then try to enter data that doesn't meet the criteria you set, the database displays a warning message.

Finally, the Input List option lets you create a list of text, numbers, dates, or times that pops up when you select the field in Browse mode. (You can then double-click on one of the values on the list to enter it into the field.) When you check the Pre-defined List box, you see a dialog box in which you can enter a list of values, like the one at the top of the next page:

```
┌─────────────────────────────────────────────┐
│ Values for "Text" field "State"        ⬆    │
│ ┌───────────────────────────────────────┐    │
│ │                                        │    │
│ │                                        │    │
│ │                                        │    │
│ │                                   ⬇    │    │
│ └───────────────────────────────────────┘    │
│ │Enter values here                       │    │
│         ┌─────────────┐  ┌──────────┐         │
│         │   Create    │  │ Modify   │         │
│         └─────────────┘  └──────────┘         │
│ ┌──────────┐ ┌──────────┐ ┌──────────┐        │
│ │  Cancel  │ │  Delete  │ │   Done   │        │
│ └──────────┘ └──────────┘ └──────────┘        │
└─────────────────────────────────────────────┘
```

Just type each of the values you want on the list, clicking the Create button or pressing ⌜Return⌟ after each one, and then click the Done button to put the list away and return to the Entry Options dialog box. (To edit values in this list later, click the Edit List... button to display the list again.)

The Only Values From List checkbox tells the database not to accept any values other than those on the list. If you don't check this box, the field accepts data that's typed into it.

Defining calculation fields

To define a calculation field, you enter a formula specifying the calculation you want to make. After you type a field name, choose the Calculation field type in the Define Fields dialog box and then click the Create button. You see the Calculation dialog box, like the one at the top of the next page:

```
┌─────────────────────────────────────────────────────────────┐
│ Enter Formula for Field "Cost"                                │
│ ─────────────────────────────────────────────────────────────│
│ Fields            Operators    Function                       │
│ ┌──────────────┐┌─┐ ┌───┐┌─┐ ┌─────────────────────────────┐┌─┐│
│ │FirstName     ││⇧│ │ + ││⇧│ │ABS(number)                  ││⇧││
│ │LastName      │└─┘ │ - │├≡┤ │ACOS(number)                 │├≡┤│
│ │Street        │    │ * │└─┘ │AND(logical1,logical2,...)   │└─┘│
│ │City          │    │ / │    │ASIN(number)                 │   │
│ │State         │    │ = │    │ATAN(number)                 │   │
│ │Zip           │    │ > │    │ATAN2(x-number,y-number)     │   │
│ │Phone       ⬇ │    │ < │⬇   │AVERAGE(number1,number2,...)⬇│   │
│ └──────────────┘    └───┘    └─────────────────────────────┘   │
│ Formula                                                        │
│ ┌───────────────────────────────────────────────────────────┐│
│ │▏                                                           ││
│ └───────────────────────────────────────────────────────────┘│
│                                                               │
│ Format result as  [Number ▼]          [ Cancel ]  (  OK  )    │
└─────────────────────────────────────────────────────────────┘
```

You use this dialog box to specify the field's formula. Notice that the name of the calculation field you've defined is shown at the top, and the insertion point is blinking in the Formula box.

You can create a formula by typing or by choosing field names, operators, and function names from the lists. For example, here's how we would multiply the contents of a field called Price by the contents of a field called Quantity to produce an extended cost in the Cost field above:

1. Scroll the Fields list until you see the Price field's name, and click it to enter it in the formula box.

2. Click the multiplication operator (*) in the Operators list to enter it in the formula box.

3. Scroll the Fields list to display the Quantity field's name and click on it to enter it into the formula box. The formula now looks like this:

```
┌─────────────────────────────────────────────────────────────┐
│ Formula                                                        │
├─────────────────────────────────────────────────────────────┤
│ 'Price'*'Quantity'                                             │
│                                                                │
└─────────────────────────────────────────────────────────────┘
```

Notice that the field names in the formula are inside single quote marks. If you type field names from the keyboard, you must put single quotes around them so ClarisWorks knows you're specifying field names. Otherwise, it treats the text as a function name. To enter text in a formula, you must put it inside double quote marks ("").

4. Choose the data type for the field's result from the pop-up menu below the Formula box. (It's preset to Number, which is what we want here, so we don't need to change it in this example).

5. Click the OK button to complete the formula and return to the Define Fields dialog box.

Once you've defined a calculation field, ClarisWorks automatically calculates the formula in each record of your database file. Whenever you change a value in one of the fields referred to in the formula, the formula recalculates and the calculation field shows the new result.

To format the results in calculation fields with specific fonts, sizes, styles, date, time, or number formats, select the field in Layout mode and use the options in the Format menu. See *Changing field and text formats* on p. 220.

Defining summary fields

When you want to calculate numbers across a group of records, you use a summary field. Once you type a field name, click the Summary field type, and click the Create button, you see the same Calculation dialog box you see when you define a calculation field.

In the Calculation dialog box, create a formula that makes the summary calculation you want. To produce a total of all the Price field's values in a file, for example, you would use the Sum function in the formula =*Sum('Price')*. This formula tells ClarisWorks to sum all the values in the Price field from every record you're currently viewing in the database file.

You can only use a summary field in a sub-summary or grand summary part of a layout. See *Creating reports* on p. 223. For more about using functions, see Chapter 11.

Changing field definitions

Once you've defined a field, you can change its definition at any time.

1. Choose *Define Fields...* from the Layout menu.

2. Select the field whose definition you want to change.

3. Change the field name, type, entry options, or calculation or summary formula.

4. Click the Modify button and then click the Done button.

There are some considerations involved when you change field definitions, however.

• When you change a field's name, the field name is changed in every layout on which the field appears, and in every calculation formula that refers to that field name.

• When you change a field's formula, the formula is recalculated for each record in your file.

• When you change a field's type, any existing data in that field is converted to the new type. If ClarisWorks is unable to convert the data to the new field type, however, the data is deleted. You see a warning message when changing a field's type will cause data to be deleted.

Deleting fields

To delete a field, choose the *Define Fields...* command, select the field name, and click the Delete button. When you delete a field, all the field's data is deleted as well.

You can delete a field from a layout without removing it from the file. See *Adding and deleting fields* on p. 218.

If you delete a field that's referred to in a calculation formula, the formula won't calculate properly anymore, but you *won't* see a warning message. However, if you choose the affected calculation field in the Define Fields dialog box and click the Options… button to look at its formula, the name of the field you deleted will have been replaced by the name *BADFIELD* in the formula.

Viewing selected groups of records

When you first create a database file and add records, you're working with all the records in the file. But sometimes you'll want to separate a group of records from the others and view or print just that group. The database gives you three different ways to view a subset of records from a file: hiding records; using Find mode; and matching records.

Hiding records

The *Hide Selected* and *Hide Unselected* commands on the Organize menu let you hide certain records from view, depending on which records are currently selected. After you hide some records, you're working with only the visible ones; if you browse the file you'll see only the visible records, and you can print only the visible records as well. To hide a group of records:

1. Select the group of records you want hidden. (See *Selecting, copying, pasting, and deleting records* on p. 195.)

2. Choose *Hide Selected* from the Organize menu. The group of records you selected will be hidden. If you choose the *Hide Unselected* command instead, you hide all the records you didn't select.

    To work with all the file's records again, choose *Show All Records* from the Organize menu.

Using Find mode

The problem with hiding records is that you have to select the ones you want hidden (or not hidden), so you have to select a continuous group of records. For example, you couldn't select record number 1 and record number 5 without selecting records 2, 3, and 4 between them. With Find mode, however, you can isolate a group of records based on the data they contain, rather than by selecting them with the pointer.

To use Find mode, you display the Find screen and then create one or more sets of search criteria, or *find requests*. For example, suppose we wanted to find all the address records with the zip code 94111. This would involve creating one find request:

1. Choose *Find* from the Layout menu. You see the Find mode screen, like this:

2. Type *94111* in the Zip field. This is the only criterion on which we want to search, so the request is complete.

3. Press ⌈Return⌉ or click the All button at the left to search all the file's records for those matching this criterion. Claris-Works locates the records that have *94111* in the Zip field and displays only these on the screen in Browse mode.

This subgroup of records is called the *found set.* The total record number at the left of the screen indicates that you're viewing a subset of records, like this:

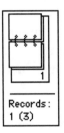

Here, the found set contains one record and the file contains three records.

To display all the file's records again, choose *Show All Records* from the Organize menu.

Finding records within a subset

Clicking the All button to execute a Find request tells ClarisWorks to search all the records in the file. However, if you've already limited the records you're working with by using a previous Find request or by using the *Hide Selected* or *Hide Unselected* command, you can tell ClarisWorks to search only among the records that are currently visible by clicking the Visible button at the left of the Find mode screen.

Using multiple find criteria and multiple requests

Our first Find mode example showed how to search for records based on one criterion in one find request. But you can enter criteria into more than one field on the Find screen to locate records more specifically, and you can also create multiple requests.

When you enter more than one criterion in a request, records found must match all of the criteria. For example, to find only the people named Jones who live in the 94111 zip code area, you would type *94111* in the Zip field and *Jones* in the LastName field.

Sometimes you need to find records that match either one set of criteria or another. For example, you might need to find people named Jones who live in San Francisco, or people named Jones who live in New York. You couldn't enter *San Francisco* and *New York* in the City field of one Find screen, because then ClarisWorks would try to find records that contained both city names in the same field, and it probably wouldn't find any. To find records based on one criterion or another, you create multiple find requests:

1. Choose *Find* from the Layout menu and enter a set of criteria.

2. Choose *New Request* from the Edit menu to display a second blank Find screen, and enter more criteria there to create a second request.

3. Repeat step 2 to create other requests, if necessary.

4. Click the All or Visible button to execute the requests you've created.

You can create as many find requests as you like. When you create more than one find request, ClarisWorks looks for records that match any one of the requests.

If you create a complex find request and you want to create a second request that contains many of the same criteria, you can duplicate the current request and then edit only the fields whose criteria you want to change in the duplicate. Just choose the *Duplicate Request* command from the Edit menu.

Using conditional operators in a request

Along with typing exact-match criteria into fields of a find request, you can also use conditional operators to search for records containing data above or below a certain range. For example, to select only records in which the zip code is greater than 94000, you could enter *>94000* in the Zip field of a request.

The conditional operators you can use are:

equal to (=)

greater than (>)

less than (<)

greater than or equal to (≥)

less than or equal to (≤)

You enter the ≥ and ≤ symbols by pressing Option . and Option , respectively, but these symbols aren't available in every font. To see if these symbols are available in the font you're using, choose *Keycaps* from the ⌘ menu, hold down the Option key, and look for these two symbols.

Omitting records

You can invert a Find operation so that ClarisWorks selects records that *don't* match the requests you've created. Just click the Omit checkbox at the left of the Find screen before clicking the All or Visible button.

Matching records

Creating find requests will take care of most of your data-selection needs, but you can also select records by entering formulas with the *Match Records…* command. You can match records directly from Browse mode rather than going into Find mode first.

Unlike using a find request, using *Match Records…* doesn't cause ClarisWorks to display a subset of records from your file.

Instead, it makes ClarisWorks select the records that match the formula—the other records are still visible, they're just not selected. (Of course, you can always hide the records that aren't selected in a match operation by choosing *Hide Unselected* from the Organize menu.)

To create a matching formula:

1. Choose *Match Records...* from the Organize menu. You see a dialog box like this:

```
┌──────────────────────────────────────────────────────────────┐
│ ┌────────────────────────────────────────────────────────────┐ │
│ │                                                            │ │
│ │  Enter Match Records Condition                             │ │
│ │                                                            │ │
│ │  Fields              Operators    Function                 │ │
│ │  ┌──────────────┐    ┌──────┐    ┌──────────────────────┐  │ │
│ │  │ FirstName  ⬆ │    │ +  ⬆ │    │ ABS(number)        ⬆ │  │ │
│ │  │ LastName     │    │ –  ≡ │    │ ACOS(number)       ≡ │  │ │
│ │  │ Street       │    │ *    │    │ AND(logical1,logical2,...) │ │
│ │  │ City         │    │ /    │    │ ASIN(number)         │  │ │
│ │  │ State        │    │ =    │    │ ATAN(number)         │  │ │
│ │  │ Zip          │    │ >    │    │ ATAN2(x-number,y-number) │ │
│ │  │ Phone      ⬇ │    │ <  ⬇ │    │ AVERAGE(number1,number2,...)⬇ │ │
│ │  └──────────────┘    └──────┘    └──────────────────────┘  │ │
│ │                                                            │ │
│ │  Formula                                                   │ │
│ │  ┌────────────────────────────────────────────────────┐    │ │
│ │  │                                                    │    │ │
│ │  └────────────────────────────────────────────────────┘    │ │
│ │                                                            │ │
│ │                              ( Cancel )  [  OK  ]          │ │
│ └────────────────────────────────────────────────────────────┘ │
└──────────────────────────────────────────────────────────────┘
```

2. Type the formula or click on field names, operators, or function names from the lists above the Formula box.

3. Click the OK button. ClarisWorks selects all the records in the file that match the formula you entered.

For example, to select all records in which the zip field is greater than 94000, you would enter the formula *'Zip'>94000*. If you try to enter an invalid formula, you see a warning message.

You can create very complex formulas with the *Match Records...* command. You can include any of ClarisWorks' built-in calculation functions (although may of them won't be suitable for finding records in a database file), and you can enter field names, text strings (if you enclose them in double quote marks), or operators. Along with the five conditional operators you can type in find requests, you can use any of the mathematical, logical, or text operators available in the spreadsheet. For more information on these, see p. 123 in Chapter 5. For more information on using functions to manipulate text, numbers, dates, and times, see Chapter 11.

Sorting records

Database records are added to a file in the order in which you create them, but you can use the *Sort Records...* command to rearrange them. For example, you might want to sort address records by zip code. To sort records:

1. Switch to Browse mode and choose *Sort Records...* from the Organize menu. You see a dialog box like this:

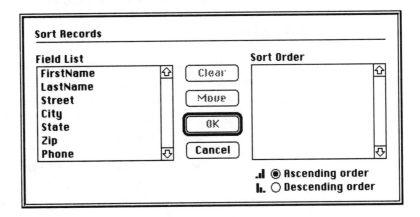

2. Double-click on the name of the field on which you want to sort the file, or click the field name and then click the Move button. The field name is added to the Sort Order list at the right, like the one at the top of the next page:

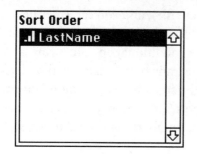

The bar graph icon next to the field name indicates that the file will be sorted in ascending order by the contents of this field.

3. Click the Descending order button at the bottom to sort on descending order on this field, if you like.

4. Repeat steps 2 and 3 to add other fields to the Sort Order list and set their sort order.

5. Click the OK button or press (Return) to sort the file.

You can always tell if a file is sorted by checking the sort status at the left of the document window in Browse mode.

Changing the sort order

You can sort on as many fields as you like by adding them to the Sort Order list. Also, you can select any field name in the Sort Order list and set ClarisWorks to sort it in ascending or descending order. For example, you could sort in ascending order on a zip code field and in descending order on a salary field.

To change the sort order, remove fields from the Sort Order list. Choose *Sort Records...* again, double-click on the field name you want to remove from the Sort Order list (or select it and click the Move button), and then click the OK button. To clear the whole Sort Order list and start over, click the Clear button.

A sort is automatically canceled when you add a new record to the file. There's no Unsort command in the database.

Working with layouts

ClarisWorks automatically arranges fields in a *standard layout* when you create a new database file, but you can create other layouts to suit other purposes. A data entry layout might contain all the fields in your file arranged like a paper form, while a label layout might contain name and address information that fits a particular label stock number. You can make a new layout whenever you're in Browse or Layout mode. To add, change, or delete fields, text, or graphics on a layout once you've created it, however, you must be in Layout mode. (See *Customizing layouts in Layout mode* on p. 215.)

Making a new layout

To make a new layout:

1. Choose *New Layout...* from the Layout menu. You see a dialog box like this:

```
┌─────────────────────────────────────┐
│  New Layout                          │
│  ─────────────────────────────────   │
│                                       │
│  Name  [Layout 2              ]       │
│  ┌Type──────────────────────────┐    │
│  │ ◉ Standard    ○ Columnar report│   │
│  │ ○ Duplicate   ○ Labels         │   │
│  │ ○ Blank        [Custom ▼]      │   │
│  └──────────────────────────────┘    │
│                                       │
│              [ Cancel ]  [  OK  ]     │
└─────────────────────────────────────┘
```

2. Type a name for the layout in the Name box. It's best to give each layout a descriptive name.

3. Click a Type button to choose the kind of layout you want.

4. Click the OK button or press [Return]. The new layout is displayed on the screen, and its name is added to the bottom of the Layout menu.

About layout types

As you can see in the New Layout dialog box, there are five different types of layouts you can create.

A *standard* layout is like the one ClarisWorks automatically creates when you first define fields for a new file. It contains all the fields defined for the file, stacked on top of one another in the order in which the fields were defined. A standard layout is as tall as it needs to be to contain all the fields in your file.

A *duplicate* layout is a duplicate of the layout that's currently showing on the screen. This option is handy when you have a complex layout and you want to create another one that's much the same, since it's easier to duplicate a complex layout and make a few changes than to re-create it from scratch.

A *blank* layout doesn't contain any fields—you start with an empty space and then add fields or graphics to it. See *Adding and deleting fields* on p. 218.

A *columnar report* layout arranges fields side by side across the screen, like this:

To create a columnar layout, you must tell the database which fields you want included in it. When you click the Columnar Report button and then click the OK button, you see a dialog box like this:

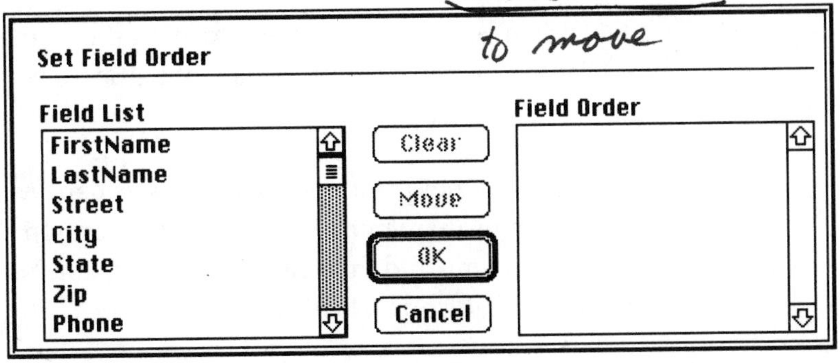

double click ! ! !

to move

Set Field Order

Field List   **Field Order**

FirstName
LastName   Clear
Street
City   Move
State
Zip   OK
Phone
                  Cancel

Here you select the names of the fields you want to add to the layout, one at a time. Double-click on a field name or select it and click the Move button to add it to the Field Order list. When you've added all the field names you want to the Field Order list, click the OK button and you see the columnar layout.

A *labels* layout usually contains names and addresses and looks like this:

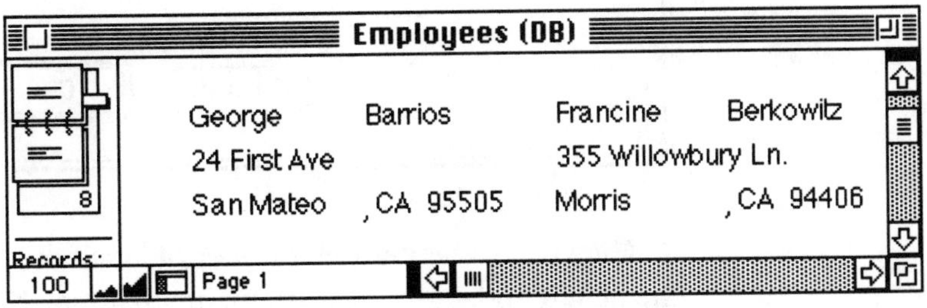

Employees (DB)

George   Barrios   Francine   Berkowitz
24 First Ave   355 Willowbury Ln.
San Mateo , CA 95505   Morris   , CA 94406

8

Records:
100   Page 1

(Although the first name, last name, city, and state data in this example are separated by spaces, the spaces will automatically be closed up when the label is printed.)

When you click the Labels option, the pop-up menu below it becomes active. ClarisWorks comes with predefined label formats for about fifty Avery mailing label formats, and if you're using one of these you can choose it by its stock number from the menu and have the database automatically set up a layout of the proper size.

When you choose an Avery format, the format's number is automatically used as the layout name, so you don't have to type one in.

If you're not printing labels on a standard Avery format listed on the pop-up menu, leave the Custom option showing on the pop-up menu and then click the OK button. You see the Label Layout dialog box, like this:

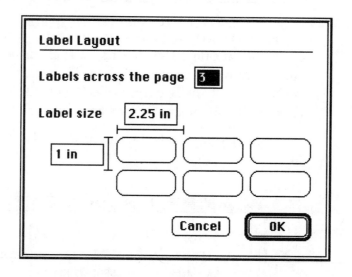

Here you can enter the number of labels across the page, and the height and width measurements that match the label stock you're printing on. Notice that the height and width measurements include the space between one label and another—be sure to include this space. Click the OK button when you're done.

Once you choose a predefined label format or specify one in the Label Layout dialog box, you see the Field Order dialog box in which you can select the names of the fields you want included on the label.

When a new label layout appears in Browse mode, you'll need to rearrange the fields on it so the data is formatted like a typical address. (See *Moving and resizing objects* on page 216.)

Switching layouts

Each time you create a layout, its name is added to the bottom of the Layout menu. Layout names appear on the Layout menu in the order in which the layouts were created. To switch from one layout to another, just choose a different layout name from the bottom of the Layout menu. You can tell which layout you're using at any time because that layout's name is checked on the Layout menu.

 If you can't find a particular field when you want to enter data in Browse mode or a find criterion in Find mode, you're probably viewing a layout that doesn't contain that field. Choose a different layout from the Layout menu.

Renaming a layout

To change the name of a layout, choose *Layout Info...* from the Layout menu to display the Layout Info dialog box. Then type a new name in the *Name* box and click the OK button.

Customizing layouts in Layout mode

Once you've created a layout, you can rearrange or resize fields; add or delete fields; change the way data is presented in fields; or add graphics or text to the layout. To accomplish any of these, you work in Layout mode.

To select Layout mode, choose *Layout* from the top of the Layout menu. The layout mode screen in a standard layout looks like this:

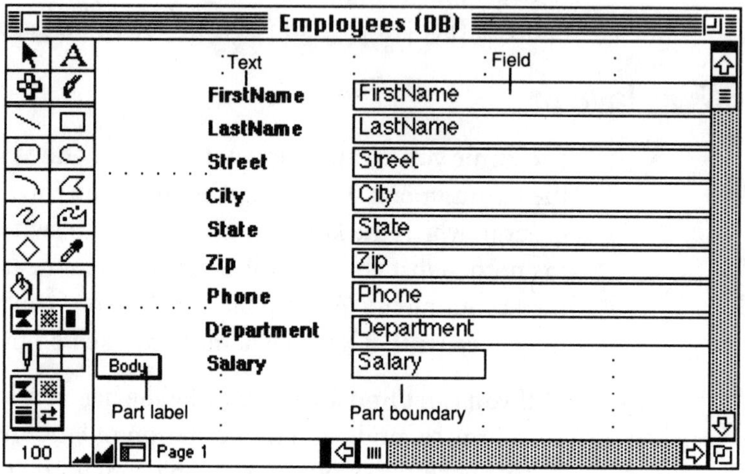

As you can see, switching to Layout mode automatically switches you to the draw environment. In Layout mode you work with fields, text, and graphics as draw objects—you can't enter or view data in Layout mode.

The layout itself contains *fields, text,* and *parts* which are identified with *part labels* and *part boundaries.* The fields are where your file's data will appear in Browse mode, and the text can be field names as shown above or other information. (For more on parts, see *About layout parts* on the next page.)

Moving and resizing objects

Each field, string of text, or graphic on the layout is an individual object that can be selected and modified with the draw tools.

- To move an object, choose the pointer tool and drag the object.

- To resize an object, select it and drag one of its selection handles.

- To edit text, double-click on it to select the text tool and then edit it as you would any text.

Since the draw tools in Layout mode work the same way as they do in draw documents, we'll cover them in Chapter 8. For now, it's important to know that everything inside a layout is a graphic object, and that you manipulate them just as you do in draw documents. This means you can move or change each object independently, and you can draw objects on top of other objects.

About layout parts

In the sample layout above, the boundary line and label at the bottom of the window identify the layout part as the Body. Each layout you create can have four different types of parts.

The *body* is the part that contains fields from the records in your file. Every layout contains a body, because that's where the data from your records is placed.

When you print or view a report, data from each record in the file or found set is shown in the Body. There's only one set of fields in the body of a layout because those fields are the same for every record in the file. However, the body is repeated as many times as will fit on your screen or printed page, so you'll see as many records on the screen or on a page as will fit.

For example, a columnar report's body contains one set of fields, like this:

But when records are displayed in Browse mode the body is repeated so you see several records listed down the screen, as shown on p. 212.

The *header* and *footer* are parts that appear at the top and bottom of each printed page, respectively. Headers and footers usually contain text such as the page number, date, report title, or field names. Of the different layouts you create, only columnar reports start out with a header part. When you add fields to a columnar report, the field names are automatically placed in the header, as shown above.

Summary parts contain summary fields, which display values calculated from a group of records. You can place summary parts before or after the records whose data they summarize. You can add *grand summary* parts that produce calculations for all the records in a file or *sub-summary* parts that produce calculations for only the sorted group of records above. For more on summaries, see *Creating reports* on p. 223.

Adding parts

To add a part to your layout, choose *Insert Part...* from the Layout menu. You see a dialog box in which you can choose the type of part you want to insert. You can only have one body, header and footer on a layout, so if you choose *Insert Part...* when you're viewing a layout that already has these parts, the options for these aren't available.

Adding and deleting fields

You can add or delete fields in a layout any time. Adding or deleting fields in a layout does *not* add or delete fields in the entire file—to do this, you use the *Define Fields...* command. (See *More about defining fields* on p. 196.)

To add a field, choose *Insert Field...* from the Layout menu. You see the Insert Field dialog box, like the one at the top of the next page:

```
┌─────────────────────────────────────┐
│                                       │
│  Insert Field                         │
│  ───────────────────────────────     │
│  ┌─────────────────────────────┐ ⬆️  │
│  │ Street                       │ ▤  │
│  │ City                         │    │
│  │ State                        │    │
│  │ Zip                          │    │
│  │ Hire Date                    │    │
│  │ Salary                       │    │
│  │ Total                        │ ⬇️  │
│  └─────────────────────────────┘    │
│                                       │
│              ( Cancel )  [  OK  ]     │
│                                       │
└─────────────────────────────────────┘
```

You can never place more than one copy of a field in a layout, so this dialog box shows only the names of fields that don't currently appear in the layout you're working with. To add a field, just double-click on it in the list, or select it and click the OK button. The field is added to the bottom of the current layout, below the other fields in the body. If necessary, ClarisWorks makes the body of the layout longer to accommodate the new field. To put the field in a different part of the layout, select it and drag it there.

To delete a field, just select it and press the (Delete) key, or choose *Clear* or *Cut* from the Edit menu. Since everything is a separate object in Layout mode, you have to select and delete the field name (which is a text object) separately.

Resizing parts

All the blank space around fields, text, or graphics in a part becomes blank space on your screen or on paper. To eliminate blank space or create more of it, you can move objects or resize a part. To change a part's size, just drag the boundary line up or down. However, ClarisWorks won't let you drag a part boundary past an object inside the part, so you may have to move objects first.

Changing field and text formats

In a new layout, ClarisWorks displays field data in a plain format. Using formatting commands in Layout mode, however, you can alter the data format or style of any field you choose. When you change a field's format, you change it only for the field or fields you have selected at the time, and only in the layout you are working in at the time.

Changing text formats

To change the font, size, style, or color of the data in a field or the text in a text object, select the field or object (or Shift-click to select several of them) and then choose an option from the Font, Size, Style, or Color submenu off the Format menu.

Changing data formats in fields

In fields that are set to number, date, or time type (or calculation or summary fields that display number, date, or time results), you can also change the data format. To do this:

1. Double-click on the field, or select it and choose *Field Format...* from the Options menu. You see a dialog box that lets you set a different number, date, or time format. The dialog box you see depends on the type of field you've selected.

2. Click a button in the dialog box to select the format you want (specify the number of decimal places in a number format if you like).

3. Click the OK button or press the Return key.

Adding borders around fields

The borders you see around fields in Layout mode are only there so you can see the exact size of each field—they don't print when you print your file. To create a field border that will print, select the field and choose an option from the line width palette in the tool panel. (See Chapter 8 for more on using the line width palette.)

Rearranging records on a layout

In all but labels layouts, records are normally displayed vertically, one on top of another. (Label layouts often arrange records in two or three columns, depending on which label format you use.) But if you're using a standard layout and the data in your records isn't very wide, you can often make better use of space on your screen or on paper by arranging the records in columns.

To rearrange a layout so the records are displayed in columns:

1. Choose the *Layout Info...* command from the Layout menu. You'll see the Layout Info dialog box, like this:

```
┌─────────────────────────────────────────────────────┐
│  Layout Info                                          │
│                               ┌─Slide Objects─────────│
│  Name  ▊Data Entry▊           │ Select to remove space│
│  ┌─Columns ────────┐          │ between objects when  │
│  │ Number of   [1] │          │ printing.             │
│  │ ○ Across first  │          │ ☐ Slide objects left  │
│  │ ◉ Down first    │          │ ☐ Slide objects up    │
│  └─────────────────┘                                  │
│                              ┌──────────┐ ┌──────────┐│
│                              │  Cancel  │ │    OK    ││
│                              └──────────┘ └──────────┘│
└─────────────────────────────────────────────────────┘
```

2. Type the number of columns you want displayed in the Number Of box.

3. Click either the Across First or the Down First button to set the order in which records are placed. (Down First is the default option, so records are arranged down the first column, then down the second column, and so on. Across

First places records first across one row, then across a second row, and so on.)

4. Click the OK button or press ⟨Return⟩ to put the dialog box away.

Sliding objects

When you create a layout, the space between one object and the next is determined by the size of each object and the amount of space between them. In some cases, however, fields in the body of your layout will be much wider or taller than the data in them, so there will be lots of extra space between a field and the one next to it.

For example, suppose a company telephone directory looks like this in Browse mode:

The body of this layout contains three fields (Last Name, First Name, and Phone). Each of the name fields has been made wide enough to accommodate particularly long first or last names, but because the Last Name field is so wide, there's a lot of space between the last names and the first names.

You can set the database to slide objects to the left or up on a layout when the layout is printed. The objects still look the same in Browse mode, but when you print the layout they slide together so any extra space that isn't used in each field is eliminated.

To slide objects:

1. Choose *Layout Info...* from the Layout menu. You see the Layout Info dialog box as shown on p. 221.

2. Click the Slide Objects Left or Slide Objects Up checkbox (or both) to make the layout's objects slide when printed.

3. Click the OK button.

Unfortunately, setting the slide objects options tells Claris-Works to slide *every object* in the body of a layout. In the directory above, for example, the phone numbers would also slide to the left against the first name data, so they wouldn't be in a neat column anymore.

To prevent an object from sliding, make it slightly larger than the object above or to the left. Objects won't slide toward objects that are smaller than they are. For example, to keep the Phone field in the above layout from sliding, make it slightly taller than the First Name field on its left. To keep a field from sliding up, make it slightly wider than the field above it.

· ·

Creating reports

Any layout you create can be printed on paper, but reports usually contain titles, page numbers, and summary calculations. In this section, we'll take a closer look at using different parts in a layout to produce reports.

For example, at the top of the next page is part of the first page of a salary report shown in Browse mode:

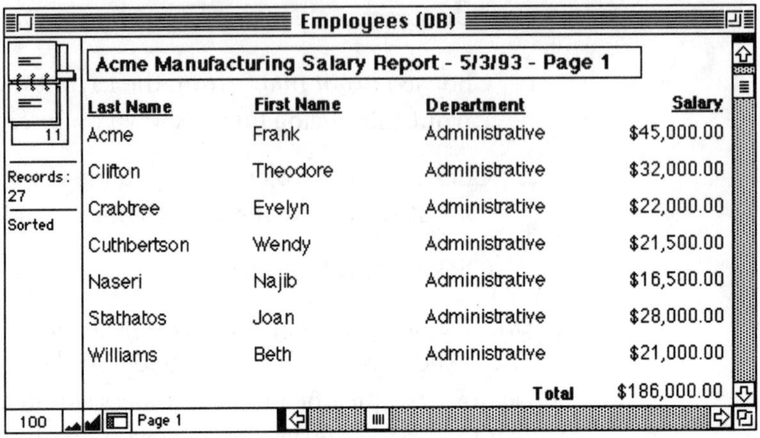

```
┌─────────────────────────── Employees (DB) ─────────────────────────┐
│ ┌───┐ ┌─────────────────────────────────────────────────────────┐ │
│ │ ≡ │ │ Acme Manufacturing Salary Report - 5/3/93 - Page 1      │ │
│ └───┘ └─────────────────────────────────────────────────────────┘ │
│ ┌───┐   Last Name      First Name      Department        Salary     │
│ │ 11│   Acme           Frank           Administrative    $45,000.00  │
│ └───┘   Clifton        Theodore        Administrative    $32,000.00  │
│ Records: Crabtree      Evelyn          Administrative    $22,000.00  │
│ 27       Cuthbertson   Wendy           Administrative    $21,500.00  │
│ Sorted                                                               │
│          Naseri        Najib           Administrative    $16,500.00  │
│          Stathatos     Joan            Administrative    $28,000.00  │
│          Williams      Beth            Administrative    $21,000.00  │
│                                               Total     $186,000.00  │
│  100  ▄▟▐□▌ Page 1                                                   │
└──────────────────────────────────────────────────────────────────┘
```

This is a columnar report layout, and the body contains four fields in four columns. The field names, report title, date, and page number are all in a header part. This report is sorted on the Department field, and then on the Last Name field, so employee names are alphabetical within each department. At the bottom, the Total field is in a sub-summary part, and it shows the total salaries for this department.

Here's the second and final page of the report:

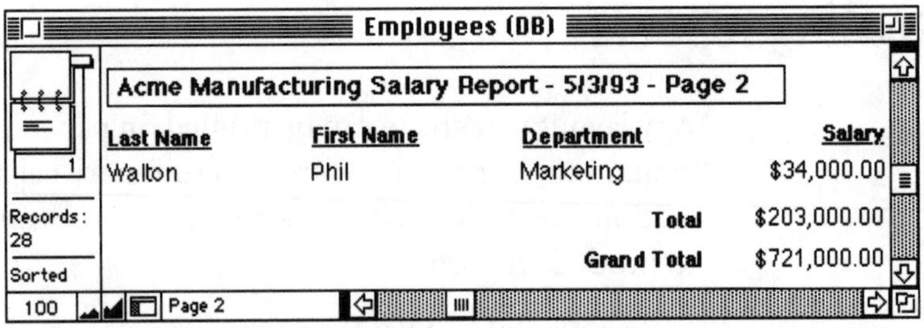

```
┌─────────────────────────── Employees (DB) ─────────────────────────┐
│ ┌───┐ ┌─────────────────────────────────────────────────────────┐ │
│ │ ≡ │ │ Acme Manufacturing Salary Report - 5/3/93 - Page 2      │ │
│ └───┘ └─────────────────────────────────────────────────────────┘ │
│ ┌───┐   Last Name      First Name      Department        Salary     │
│ │  1│   Walton         Phil            Marketing         $34,000.00  │
│ └───┘                                                                │
│ Records:                                      Total     $203,000.00  │
│ 28                                      Grand Total     $721,000.00  │
│ Sorted                                                               │
│  100  ▄▟▐□▌ Page 2                                                   │
└──────────────────────────────────────────────────────────────────┘
```

The Marketing Department's total is shown below the last record, and the Grand Total field, which is in a grand summary part, shows the total salaries for the whole company. Notice that the same header information appears at the top of this page, but that the page number has changed.

Here's how this report looks in Layout mode:

```
▤☐▤▤▤▤▤▤▤▤▤ Employees (DB) ▤▤▤▤▤▤▤▤▤▤▤
┌──┬──┬──────────────────────────────────────────────────┐
│ ↖│ A │  Acme Manufacturing Salary Report - 5/3/93 - Page 1 │  ⇧
│ ✛│ ℓ │                                                      │  ▤
├──┼──┤ ┌─────────┐                                          │
│ ╲│ ☐ │ │Header │ne    First Name    Department     Salary│  ▲
├──┼──┤ └─────────┘                                          │
│ ◯│ ○ │ ┌────┐ame   FirstName    Department    Salary │
│  │  │ │Body│                                             │
├──┼──┤ └────┘                                              │
│ ╲│ ◠ │                                                    │
├──┼──┤ Sub-summary by Department         Total      Total │
│ ↻│ ᗺ │                                                    │
├──┼──┤ Grand Summary                  Grand Total   GrTotal│  ⇩
│ ◇│ 🖊 │                                                    │
├──┴──┼────────────────────────────────────────────────────┤
│ 100 │ ▢▢ ☐ Page 1      ◁ ▥                           ⇨ ◪│
└─────┴────────────────────────────────────────────────────┘
```

Here you can see each of the parts in this report. Now let's see how to build a report like this.

Adding text in headers or footers

Because this is a columnar report, ClarisWorks automatically included a header part with the field names in it when the layout was created. If you're working with a standard or label layout, you can add a header or footer with the *Insert Part...* command on the Layout menu. See *Adding parts* on p. 218.

Header and footer parts in a database layout aren't the same as document headers and footers, as described in Chapter 2. You can add a document header or footer to your database file by choosing *Insert Header* or *Insert Footer* from the Format menu when you're in Browse mode. If you add a document header or footer, however, it will appear on every layout in your file. Header and footer parts appear on individual layouts.

The report title, date, and page number in this header are text. To add this text, we need to make the header part tall enough to accommodate it, move the field labels down so the extra blank space in the part is above them, and then add the text and the box around it. We'll go through the basic procedure here, but if you need help using the draw tools, see Chapter 8.

1. Drag the header part boundary down about half an inch.

2. Shift -click on the field labels and drag them down so they're just above the header part boundary. (Selecting them as a group allows you to move them all at once so they stay lined up with each other.)

3. Select the text tool and draw a text box about 5 inches wide above the field labels. (If you just click in the blank space, ClarisWorks creates a text box about an inch wide, and you'll have to resize the box afterwards to stretch the text out on one line.)

4. Type *Acme Manufacturing Salary Report* followed by the space, the dash, and the space after the dash.

5. Choose *Insert Date* from the Format menu. Since you're working in a text box, you have the word processor's extra formatting features available, including inserting automatic dates and page numbers.

6. Type a space, a dash, and another space, then type *Page* and a space.

7. Choose *Insert Page #* from the Edit menu.

8. Choose the rectangle tool from the panel, select the no-fill pattern from the fill pattern palette, and draw a rectangle around the text.

Adding report totals

The department salary totals and the grand total in this report are created by summary fields in two different parts. When you add each part, you must decide where the part goes in relation to the body (which contains the records it summarizes), and in the case of a sub-summary part, you must specify which field the file is sorted on to produce the subtotal. Let's look more closely at this process.

Adding summary parts

To add the sub-summary part:

1. Choose *Insert Part...* from the Layout menu. You'll see a dialog box like this:

Insert Part

○ Header
○ **Leading grand summary**
◉ **Sub-summary when sorted by**
○ **Trailing grand summary**
○ **Footer**

| FirstName |
| LastName |
| Street |
| City |
| State |
| Zip |

[Cancel] [OK]

The sub-summary part option is already selected, but you need to choose a field on which the file is sorted to produce the summary you want. We want the sub-summary totals by department, so the file will be sorted on the Department field to produce the groups of records we need for these totals.

2. Select the Department field from the list and click the OK button. ClarisWorks now needs to know whether you want the part placed above or below the records being summarized (the body part), so it presents a dialog box like this:

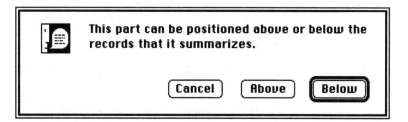

This part can be positioned above or below the records that it summarizes.

[Cancel] [Above] [Below]

3. Click the Below button or press ⟨Return⟩ to place the part below the body in the layout. ClarisWorks adds the new, empty part to the layout. The part's label indicates "by Department," so you can easily see which is the sort field for this summary.

To add the second summary part for the grand total on the second page of the report, just choose *Insert Part...* again, click on the Trailing Grand Summary option, then click the OK button. Since this is a trailing summary, ClarisWorks automatically places it after all sub-summary parts and above the footer part (if any) in the layout.

Creating summary fields

The layout now contains empty summary parts, and we need to add summary fields to them in order to produce the report totals. The calculation we want to make is a sum of the Salary field, but although this is the same calculation we need for both parts, we must create separate fields for each part because database layouts can't contain more than one copy of any field. We'll call these fields STotal and GrTotal, for subtotal and grand total. Here's how to create them:

1. Choose *Define Fields...* from the Layout menu.

2. Type *STotal* in the Name box, click the Summary type button, then click the Create button. You see the Calculation dialog box, as shown on p. 200.

3. Scroll the Function list until you see the Sum function, then click on it to add it to the formula box, like this:

```
Formula
SUM(number1,number2,...)
```

Notice that ClarisWorks automatically includes text after a function to help you remember the kinds of values the function requires. See Chapter 11 for more information.

4. Select all the text between the parentheses and press the Delete key to remove it.

5. Scroll the Fields list until you see the Salary field, then click on it to add it inside the parentheses in the formula.

6. Click the OK button to enter the formula. ClarisWorks returns to the Define Fields dialog box, and the new summary field STotal now appears in the list of defined fields.

7. Type *GrTotal* in the Name box, click the Summary type button below, and then click the Create button.

8. Repeat steps 3 through 6 to define the formula for the GrTotal field exactly as it was for the STotal field.

9. Click the Done button to put the Define Fields dialog box away and return to the layout.

Adding fields to a layout

With the summary fields defined, we can add them to the layout.

1. Choose *Insert Field...* from the Layout menu to display the Insert Field dialog box.

2. Scroll to the bottom of the field list and double-click on the STotal field name. ClarisWorks adds it to the layout, like this:

Unfortunately, ClarisWorks adds every field you insert to the body of a layout, no matter what. New fields are added below any others on the layout, and the layout part is lengthened to make room for them. We'll have to drag the new field and field name to their proper location in the sub-summary part. Since we know this will happen again when we insert the GrTotal summary field, we might as well insert both fields now and then move them afterwards.

3. Repeat steps 1 and 2 to insert the GrTotal field in the body of the layout.

4. (Shift)-click to select the STotal field and field name, and then drag them into the sub-summary part below the Salary field, as shown in the layout on p. 225.

5. Repeat step 4 with the GrTotal field and field name, but drag these into the Grand Summary part.

6. Drag the body part's boundary line up to eliminate the blank space left where the two summary fields were originally placed. (If you leave this blank space in the layout, each record in the body will be separated by about half an inch of blank space.)

7. Drag the sub-summary and grand summary part boundaries up to eliminate extra space above or below the fields you placed in them.

Editing field names

The only remaining task in creating this layout is to edit the summary field names so they read "Total" and "Grand Total."

1. Double-click on the STotal field name. The text tool is automatically selected and the insertion point is blinking inside the STotal text.

2. Delete the S from the beginning of the field name.

3. Click on the GrTotal field name and edit it so it reads "Grand Total."

When a report contains summary calculations, you can copy the summary values to the Clipboard for use in another document. Just display the report in Browse mode and sort it, if necessary, to calculate the summary values, and then choose *Copy Summaries* from the Edit menu. You can then paste the summary totals into a spreadsheet, word processor document, or anywhere else you might want to use them.

Exploring reports on your own

The example above barely scratches the surface of what you can do with database reports. You can print reports in standard layouts that contain one record per page, print standard layout reports in columns, or print dozens of mailing label formats. Using the draw tools and formatting options, you can add all kinds of graphics and visual enhancements to database layouts. For tips on how to manipulate objects in layouts more effectively, see Chapter 8. Also, check out the sample documents that came with your copy of ClarisWorks for some more ideas about database reporting.

Printing

The basic procedure for printing a database document is the same as for other ClarisWorks documents, and is covered on pp. 41–45 in Chapter 2. In the database, however, you can select which of your file's records you want to print.

To print the data from records in your database file, you must be in Browse mode. ClarisWorks allows you to print all the currently visible records from Browse mode, or just the record that's currently selected. Here are the steps to select and print the records you want:

1. Display the records you want to print in Browse mode by hiding records you don't want or by using Find mode to isolate a group of records.

2. Switch to the layout you want by choosing its name from the bottom of the Layout menu. If you want to print just one record, select it on the layout.

3. Choose *Print...* from the File menu.

4. Click the Visible Records or Current Record button at the bottom of the Print dialog box, select any other options you want (see Chapter 2 for more information), then click OK or press Return to print your data.

Troubleshooting

There's more data in a field than you can see in Browse mode. Switch to Layout mode and make the field wider or taller.

You can't find a field in Browse mode. Scroll the window to view more of the record, or switch layouts. You may be using a layout that doesn't include the field you want.

You see parts of two records in Browse mode. Choose *List View* from the Layout menu.

You can't find a record in Browse mode. You're probably viewing a found set that doesn't contain that record. Choose *Show All Records* from the Organize menu and try browsing for the record again. If you still can't find it, switch to Find mode and create a find request to locate the record you want.

You want to enter a find criterion in Find mode, but you can't see the field you want to enter it in. You're probably viewing a layout that doesn't contain that field. Try scrolling the layout to reveal fields that aren't on the screen. If you still can't find the field, switch to a layout that includes it.

A field's top or bottom is chopped off in Browse mode. The field's top or bottom edge is overlapping the boundary between the body and another part. Switch to Layout mode, zoom the layout in to magnify it, and make sure the field's boundary isn't touching a part boundary.

You can't duplicate or copy and paste a field in Layout mode. You can't have more than one copy of each field in any one layout, so ClarisWorks won't let you duplicate or copy and paste a field in the same layout.

Sub-summaries don't appear in Browse mode or in a printed report. Sub summaries can't be calculated or displayed unless you sort the file on the proper field. Check the sub-summary part label in Layout mode to see which field you need to sort on to make the summary appear.

There's a zero in a calculation field. Check the field's formula. Either the fields referred to in the formula are empty, or they contain text (which evaluates to zero), or one of the fields referred to has been deleted from the file.

You get a Bad Formula message when you try to complete a calculation or summary formula. There's something wrong with the formula's syntax. See *Troubleshooting* on p. 366 in Chapter 11.

Your data overlaps the edges of labels when you print it. Label stock can slip slightly in your printer, so it's best to design labels layouts so that the fields or text on them is as far as possible from each edge of the layout. Switch to Layout mode and drag fields farther away from the top, bottom, left, and right edges of the layout to create more space there. Use a smaller font size for the label's text or data, if necessary; or make fields smaller to create more space at the label's edges.

CHAPTER

8

The drawing program

The drawing program in ClarisWorks lets you draw objects and arrange them precisely on a page. You can use it to create floor plans, page layouts, and other documents in which you want complete control over the sizes and positions of elements on a page. In this chapter, we'll see how the ClarisWorks drawing program works. And, because the same draw tools are available in most other types of ClarisWorks documents, this chapter is where you'll learn how to draw anything anywhere in ClarisWorks. ➤➤

235

Basic drawing concepts

ClarisWorks has separate programs for drawing and painting, because drawing and painting are different ways to create artwork on a computer.

When you draw, you create an *object*, which is a pattern of dots identified by its end points on the screen. You can use the drawing program to create lines, rectangles, polygons, ovals, arcs, and free-hand lines. For example, a rectangle is identified by the points at its corners, like this:

After you draw an object, you can select it and change its size by dragging one of its points or sides. You can fill the whole object with a pattern or color or change its line thickness by choosing an option from the tool panel.

Each object in a draw document exists in its own layer, so when you draw one object on top of another, the upper object doesn't erase the one under it—it just covers it up. Objects are layered, or stacked, in the order in which you create them, but you can change the stacking order easily to uncover one object that's hidden by others.

When you paint, on the other hand, you create a bitmapped *image*, which is made up of the pixels or dots on your screen. As you draw a line or a box with the painting program, you turn a series of pixels on or off. Painted images aren't identified by points at their corners or ends, and you can't resize a painted object by dragging one of its sides. And, since images aren't objects, you can't change the pattern or line thickness of an image by selecting it and choosing an option from the tool panel—you must change individual pixels within the image. Also, painted images don't exist in separate layers: if you paint one image on top of another, you replace the old image.

The draw document window

When you choose the *New...* command from the File menu and then double-click on the Drawing document type in the New Document dialog box, a new draw document appears, like this:

The work area at the right is where you create objects, using the tools in the tool panel at the left. In the work area, the grid of dotted lines helps you align objects precisely with each other. The grid spacing is determined by the unit of measurement and number of divisions you set with the *Rulers...* command on the Format menu (see p. 18 in Chapter 2).

Tip New documents don't open with the rulers showing. Choose *Show Rulers* from the View menu to display them.

The draw tools

Before we get into drawing objects, let's look at the different tools in the tool panel. Each one creates a different type of object.

The *pointer* is the tool you use to select, move, or resize objects. You can click anywhere inside or on an object's borders to select it. The pointer is automatically selected whenever you open a draw document or when you finish drawing any object.

The *text* tool lets you create text frames or edit the text inside a text frame.

The *spreadsheet* tool lets you create spreadsheet frames or work with data inside existing spreadsheet frames.

The *paint* tool lets you create paint frames or edit images inside them.

The *line* tool draws straight lines in any direction.

The *rectangle* tool draws rectangles or squares.

The *rounded rectangle* tool draws rectangles or squares with rounded corners.

The *circle* tool draws circles or ovals.

The *arc* tool draws arcs, and the area under the arc is filled with the current fill pattern.

The *polygon* tool draws polygons.

The *freehand* tool is like a pencil. It draws lines of any shape.

 The *bezigon* tool draws shapes that are made up of points connected by Bezier curves.

 The *regular polygon* tool draws hexagons with sides of equal length, and the polygon rotates to different positions as you move the pointer.

 The *eyedropper* tool picks up the color you point to and changes the fill tool to that color.

 The *fill* tool fills an object with a color and pattern or gradient. The *fill indicator* next to the paint can icon shows the currently selected color, pattern, or gradient. The three palettes below are (from left to right) color, pattern, and gradient. The preset fill color is white.

 The *pen* tool sets the color, pattern, thickness, and style of the lines in an object's border. The *pen indicator* next to the pen icon shows the current pen color, pattern, thickness, and style. The four palettes below are (clockwise from the upper left) pen color, pattern, style, and thickness. Object lines are preset as plain, black, and 1 point thick.

 Each of the fill and pen tool palettes can be displayed as a separate window. To do this, click on the palette to display it, drag it away from the tool panel, and release the mouse button. Palette windows also have the gravity zoom feature—see p. 23 in Chapter 2.

Drawing objects

To draw an object, just click on the tool for the type of object you want to draw, point to the place where you want the object to begin, hold down the mouse button, and drag to the point where you want the object to end. When you draw an object, the pointer is a crosshair, and you see a dotted outline of the object as you drag it so you can tell how big the object is, like this:

When you release the mouse button, the object is selected, like this:

Each object you draw has the color, fill pattern, gradient, and line attributes that are currently set with the fill and line tools. See *Changing object colors, patterns, and borders* on p. 255 for more information.

If you want a tool to remain selected after you draw an object (so you can draw several of the same object without having to reselect the tool each time), you can lock it. Double-click on the tool when you choose it from the panel.

You use the same click-and-drag method to draw lines, rectangles, circles, and arcs, and you'll quickly get the hang of it. However, the technique is slightly different with polygons and freehand lines.

Drawing polygons

Since a polygon doesn't have a predetermined shape, you can't simply draw one on the screen. Instead you click at different places to indicate the length of each polygon side. This way, you can create polygons with as many sides as you like.

1. Click where you want the first side to begin, then move the pointer to that side's end point. As you move the pointer, the side appears as a dotted line.

2. Click to indicate the end point of the first side.

3. Move the pointer and click to indicate each polygon side after that.

4. Click on the original starting point to complete the last side.

If you want to create an open polygon (such as a u-shape), double-click to indicate the end point of the last side.

You can set ClarisWorks to close polygons automatically, completing the last side from wherever you double-click. Choose the *Preferences...* command from the Edit menu and click the Automatic option in the *Polygon Closing* area of the Graphics preferences dialog box.

Drawing bezigons

Bezigons are polygons whose click points are connected by Bezier curves instead of straight lines. You create a bezigon the same way you create a polygon, but the result is much different:

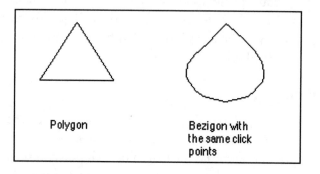

Polygon

Bezigon with the same click points

Rather than having sharp angles at its corners, a bezigon has curves. When you select a bezigon and drag one of its handles, you can change the angle of the curve.

Drawing regular polygons

Unlike polygons and bezigons, you draw a regular polygon as if you're drawing a circle: you click at the center of the polygon and then drag outward to indicate the size of the polygon. As you drag outward to set the polygon size, a dotted outline appears so you can see how big it is, like this:

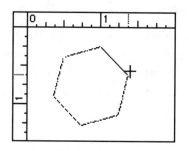

Before you release the mouse button to fix the polygon's size, you can also change its angle of rotation by dragging up, down, left, or right. If you hold down the Shift key while you drag the pointer, you'll constrain the polygon's angle of rotation to 45 degree intervals. Try it and see.

You can constrain a polygon's angle of rotation to any value between 0 and 45 by changing the shift constraint value. Choose the *Preferences...* command from the Edit menu and type a new value in the *Shift constraint* box in the Graphics preferences dialog box.

The regular polygon tool is preset to create a hexagon, but you can create regular polygons with from 3 to 40 sides. Here's how:

1. Select the regular polygon tool.

2. Choose *Polygon Sides...* from the Options menu. You see a dialog box where you can specify the number of polygon sides.

3. Enter a value between 3 and 40 in the dialog box and then click the OK button. The polygon will have the number of sides you specified.

Once you change the number of regular polygon sides, all regular polygons in the current draw document will have that many sides until you change the value again.

Drawing freehand lines

When you use the freehand tool, a line appears wherever you move the pointer, just as if the pointer had a pencil attached to it. Rather than specifying end points, as you do in a straight line, the line follows every movement of the pointer.

Constraining objects

If you hold down the Shift key before you begin drawing an object with a particular tool, you constrain the object to a specific shape or angle. The type of constraint depends on the type of object you draw. When you hold down (Shift) to constrain an object:

- The line tool creates lines of 0, 45, or 90 degrees;

- The rectangle and rounded rectangle tools create perfect squares or rounded squares;

- The circle tool creates perfect circles (rather than ovals);

- The arc tool creates 90-degree arcs, or quarter circles;

- The regular polygon tool rotates the hexagon at 45-degree intervals.

You can adjust the constraint angle of lines and regular polygon rotation to any angle between 0 and 45 degrees with the *Preferences...* command.

Placing objects precisely

ClarisWorks will put an object anywhere you want in the work area, but the drawing program has a couple of built-in features that help you put them exactly where you want them.

Using ruler guides

When the document rulers are showing, dotted ruler guides appear in them to indicate the position of the pointer. The guides are circled in the example below:

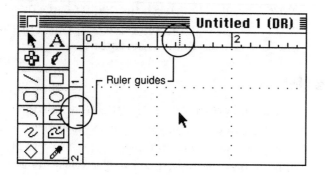

By watching for the ruler guides, you can always tell exactly where the pointer is on a page.

Using the autogrid

The grid of dotted lines in the work area helps you see each object's position because each dot in the grid is a division in the ruler. But the grid in the drawing program also acts like a magnet: objects you draw "snap to" points on the grid automatically. Thanks to the autogrid, you don't have to put the pointer exactly on a grid point to put an object there: as long as the pointer is closer to that grid point than to any others, the object will align on that grid point.

The autogrid helps a lot when you want to place objects according to divisions on the ruler, but when it's on you can't place objects between grid points. When you don't want objects snapping to the grid, choose *Turn Autogrid Off* from the Options menu.

Aligning objects with each other

Another way to position objects precisely is to align them with each other. To do this:

1. Select the objects you want to align with each other.

2. Choose the *Align Objects...* command from the Arrange menu. You see a dialog box like the one at the top of the next page:

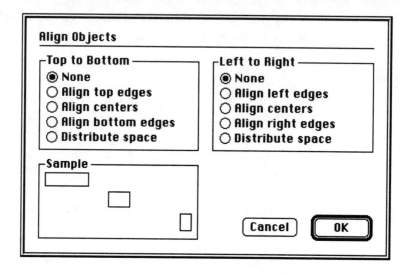

3. Click a button in each of the two areas to align objects with each other along their top, bottom, left, or right edges or their centers. As you click different options, the Sample area shows how the objects will align. (The Distribute Space option isn't shown in the Sample area—this option equalizes the space between each of the selected objects.)

4. Click the OK button or press [Return] to confirm your choices.

Selecting, moving, and resizing objects

To select an object, just click its border. If the object is filled, you can also select it by clicking anywhere inside its border. To select more than one object or to remove one object from a group of selected objects, [Shift]-click.

When you select an object, handles appear at each of the object's ends (if it's a line) or corners. If the object is an oval, arc, or polygon, ClarisWorks places selection handles at each corner of an invisible rectangle that encloses the object.

You can have ClarisWorks display extra handles between each of an object's corners by choosing *Preferences...* from the Edit menu and clicking the option for extra handles in the Object Selection area of the Graphics preferences dialog box.

Dragging to select groups of objects

You can also drag a selection rectangle around a group of objects to select them all. Just choose the pointer tool and drag a rectangle around the objects. When you release the mouse button, all the objects that are completely inside the rectangle are selected.

Grouping objects

Sometimes you'll draw several objects to make up one complex object, like this:

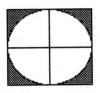

This object is really four separate objects: a rectangle, an oval, and two straight lines. Once you've completed a complex object, however, you can group all its components as one so they can't be individually moved or changed anymore. Grouping prevents you or others from accidentally selecting and moving one component in the future.

To group a complex object, select all the objects in the group and then choose the *Group* command from the Arrange menu.

If you need to work with one of the component objects in a group later, you can ungroup the objects by choosing *Ungroup* from the Arrange menu.

Managing objects in layers

Each object you draw is in a transparent layer of your document. Objects are placed in layers from the bottom-most layer up, in the order in which you draw them. Since a drawing (like the logo above) can consist of several objects arranged on top of each other, it's important to be able to choose which layer an object is in. For example, the gray square in the logo example above has to be in the bottom layer; otherwise it would cover up the other objects.

You can change an object's layer position by selecting it and choosing one of the four commands at the top of the Arrange menu.

- *Move Forward* moves an object forward one layer, so it's on top of the object it used to be underneath.

- *Move To Front* moves an object to the top-most layer, in front of everything else.

- *Move Backward* moves an object back one layer.

- *Move To Back* moves an object to the bottom-most layer, behind every other object.

Locking objects

When you've drawn an object and then want to protect it from being moved, changed, or deleted, you can lock it. Once locked, the object is automatically moved to the bottom-most layer of the document and its selection handles turn gray, which means it can't be selected or changed.

To lock an object, select it and choose *Lock* from the Arrange menu. To unlock an object, select it and choose *Unlock*.

When one object is so close to another that you can't select the object you want—you keep selecting the other one instead—lock the object that's always getting selected. Then you'll be able to select the other one.

Moving and resizing objects

Once you've drawn an object, you can change its size, shape, or position in various ways. The simplest way to move or resize an object is to drag the object (to move it) or drag one of its selection handles (to resize it).

If the autogrid is on, the object will snap to grid points as you move or resize it. If you're dragging a handle on a circle, rectangle, arc, or polygon, you can constrain it to certain sizes or shapes when you resize it by holding down the ⌈Shift⌋ key as you drag a selection handle.

Beyond dragging, however, there are other ways to change an object's size, shape, or position.

Moving or resizing objects precisely

When you know the exact dimensions or position of an object, you can move or resize it by entering them. To do this:

1. Select the object and then choose *Resize...* from the Options menu. You see a Size window on the screen, like this:

	Size	
←	1 in	
↑	0.24 in	
→	2.01 in	
↓	1.13 in	
↔	1.01 in	
↕	0.89 in	

The top four boxes show the object's distance from the left, top, right, and bottom of the document page, respectively. The bottom two boxes show the object's width and height.

2. Click in the box whose measurement you want to change and type the new value. (You don't have to include the *in* after a value—ClarisWorks automatically uses the unit of measurement you currently have specified for the rulers.)

3. Edit other measurements as necessary.

4. Press the [Return] key. The object will be moved or resized to those measurements.

Like the floating palette windows, the Size window has a gravity zoom box. See p. 21 in Chapter 2 for more on this feature.

Scaling objects

Another way to precisely resize an object or group of objects is to scale it.

1. Select the object(s) and choose the *Scale Selection...* command from the Options menu. You see a dialog box like this:

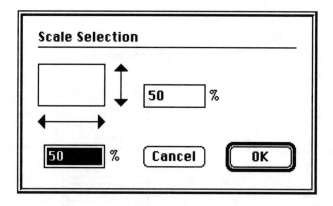

2. Select either the vertical or horizontal dimension box and type a new value in it.

3. Click the OK button or press [Return].

To return a previously scaled object to its original size, enter *100* in both dimension boxes in the Scale Selection dialog box.

Flipping and rotating objects

Another way to change an object's position is to flip or rotate it. Just select the object and choose the *Rotate, Flip Horizontal,* or *Flip Vertical* command from the Arrange menu. When you rotate an object, it rotates 90 degrees each time.

Reshaping objects

Another way to change an object is to reshape it or smooth it. Reshaping lets you make small changes to an object's shape rather than having to redraw it. You can reshape polygons, bezigons, arcs, and freehand lines. Smoothing eliminates sharp angles on polygons, bezigons, or freehand shapes. You can also change the angle of the corners on rounded rectangles.

To reshape an object:

1. Choose *Reshape* from the Edit menu. The pointer changes to the reshape cursor:

2. Click on the object you want to reshape. Its selection handles appear, but they're hollow squares instead of filled ones.

3. Drag one or more selection handles to change the object's shape.

4. Choose the *Reshape* command again to exit reshape mode.

Reshaping lets you change the range of an arc. Arcs are
normally 90 degrees, but with the *Reshape* command you can
make an arc any angle from 0 to 360 degrees.

Modifying arcs

Instead of using the *Reshape* command and dragging one of an
arc's endpoints to change its angle, you can use the *Modify Arc...*
command on the Options menu. This method lets you specify
precise values for an arc's *start angle* and *arc angle*. The start angle
is the angle of the arc's starting point—straight up (like 12:00 on a
clock face) is 0 degrees. The arc angle specifies the range of the
arc—a quarter-circle would be 90 degrees, for example.

To modify an arc:

1. Select the arc you want to modify and choose the *Modify
    Arc...* command. You see a dialog box like the one at the
    top of the next page:

```
┌─────────────────────────────────────────┐
│                                           │
│   Modify Arc                              │
│   ─────────────────────────────          │
│   ⦿ Normal    ○ Frame Edges              │
│                                           │
│   Start angle      ▐ 180 ▌               │
│   Arc angle        │ 90  │               │
│                                           │
│        ( Cancel )   (   OK   )           │
│                                           │
└─────────────────────────────────────────┘
```

2. Type the start angle and the arc angle you want. Click the
    Frame Edges option if you want a border line to appear
    across the arc's open side, so it looks like a pie slice.

3. Click the OK button.

Smoothing objects

When you *smooth* an object, you eliminate any sharp angles from it. For example, smoothing a polygon replaces its sharp angles with gentler curves, like this:

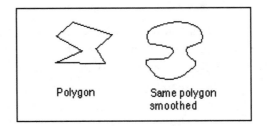

To smooth an object, just select it and choose *Smooth* from the Edit menu. To unsmooth an object, select it and choose *Unsmooth* from the Edit menu.

You can combine the Reshape command and the Smooth command to smooth only part of a polygon or freehand shape:

1. Select the object and choose the *Reshape* command.

2. Shift-click on the selection handles for the part of the object you want to smooth.

3. Choose the *Smooth* command. That part of the object will be smoothed and its selection handles will become filled circles, like this:

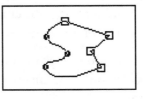

You can create lots of interesting effects with the *Smooth* and *Reshape* commands.

You can set ClarisWorks to smooth freehand shapes automatically as you draw them. Choose *Preferences…* from the Edit menu and click the Automatically Smooth Freehand checkbox in the Polygon Closing area under the Graphics preferences.

Adjusting rounded corners

When you draw a rounded rectangle, ClarisWorks automatically rounds the corners to a certain radius, but you can change the radius value to round corners more or less gradually. You can also select regular rectangles or squares and round their corners. Here's how:

1. Select the rounded rectangle or rectangle.

2. Choose the *Round Corners…* command from the Options menu. You see a dialog box like this:

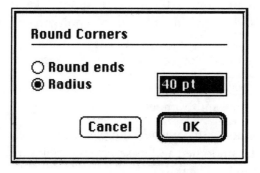

3. Type a different value (in points) for the size of the radius used for the object's rounded corners, then click the OK button to complete the change.

Once you change the value in the Round Corners dialog box, all rounded rectangles from then on will have corners with that radius.

The Round Ends option in the Round Corners dialog box does what it says: it rounds the sides of a rectangle, which turns it into more of a circle or oval shape.

Changing object colors, patterns, and borders

Every object you draw has the color, fill pattern, and borders (or *pen attributes*) that are in effect at the time you draw it. You can tell which color, pattern, and pen attributes are in effect by looking at the fill and pen tools. Next to each tool is a box that shows the current setting, like this:

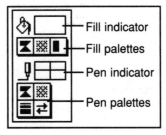

To change any of these, select the object and choose a different option from one of the fill or pen palettes. When you click on one of the palettes, the palette pops open, and you can then drag the pointer to select the option you want.

Changing the default settings

When you select an object and change its color, pattern, or pen attributes, you change the settings for that one object, but the default color, pattern, and pen attributes remain unchanged. To change the default color, pattern, or pen attributes, choose an option when none of the objects in your document is selected.

About fill colors, patterns, and gradients

You choose fill colors, patterns, and gradients from one of the palettes below the fill tool:

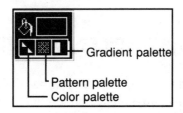

The color palette can look different, depending on which Mac you're using. On a monochrome Mac the palette lists eight colors by name; on a color Mac it shows the actual colors.

If your Mac can display 256 colors, you can select a 256-color palette by clicking the Palettes icon in the *Preferences...* command's dialog box and then clicking the Editable 256 Color Palette button. By clicking the Load Palette and Save Palette buttons, you can create and store different 256 color palettes for different purposes.

An object can have only one color and either one pattern or one gradient—you can't choose a pattern and then apply a gradient on top of that pattern, for example. When you choose a pattern, it has the color that is currently selected on the color palette. Gradients, however, aren't affected by the color on the color palette—you can set gradient colors by editing the gradient. See *Editing gradients* on page 259.

Gradients are complex and the gradient palette can take a long time to display. To speed up gradient displays a little, choose *Preferences...* from the Edit menu and click the Faster Gradients checkbox at the bottom of the Graphics preferences dialog box.

Transparent vs. opaque settings

The pattern palettes in both the fill and pen tools have transparent and opaque options:

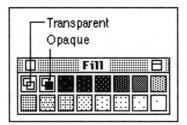

The transparent option means that objects will have no fill pattern or color—you can overlay such objects on others and see through them to the objects underneath. The opaque option means that the object is filled with a color, pattern, or gradient. The default fill setting for shapes is white and opaque, except for freehand shapes, which are preset to be transparent.

When you select a fill pattern, color or gradient, any object automatically becomes opaque; when you set the transparent option, an object automatically loses whatever fill pattern, color, or gradient it had before.

The fill indicator next to the fill tool looks the same when you have a white fill color selected as it does when you have the transparent pattern option selected. If you can see through the object, you have the transparent option set. The only way to select a transparent object is to click on its border.

Editing patterns

If you can't find a pattern you like from among the 62 offered on the pattern palette, you can edit any pattern to customize it. With some clever pattern editing, you can create patterns with logos, monograms and other cool stuff. To do this:

1. Choose the *Patterns...* command from the Options menu. The fill palette window opens, along with the Pattern Editor. The Pattern Editor looks like this:

 If the fill palette window is already open—you have to drag the fill palette away from the tool panel to display it as a window by itself—you can also display the Pattern Editor by double-clicking on the pattern you want to edit.

2. Select the pattern you want to change in the fill palette. That pattern appears in the Pattern Editor window.

3. Click or drag in the editing area at the left of the Pattern Editor window to change which dots are on or off. The changes are reflected in the sample area. To invert the pattern (swapping black or colored dots for white ones), click the Invert button.

4. Click OK or press Return to confirm the changes, or click Cancel to forget the whole thing and keep the original pattern

 The Pattern Editor is a window, so you can drag it around to see objects in your document.

Editing gradients

You can also edit any of the gradients on the gradient palette. Just choose *Gradients...* from the Options menu to display the Gradient Editor and the gradient palette window, or double-click on the gradient you want to edit if the gradient palette window is already open. The Gradient Editor looks like this:

```
┌──────────────────────────────────────────┐
│ ≣≣≣≣≣≣   Gradient Editor   ≣≣≣≣≣≣          │
│ ┌────────────────────────────────────────┐│
│ │                                         ││
│ │  Angle    [ 90 ]   Sample               ││
│ │   ┌─────────┐   ┌───────────┐           ││
│ │   │    ●    │   │███████████│           ││
│ │   │  ╱ │    │   │           │           ││
│ │   │ │  │ │  │   │           │           ││
│ │   │  ╲ │    │   │···········│           ││
│ │   │    ●    │   │███████████│           ││
│ │   └─────────┘   └───────────┘           ││
│ │                                         ││
│ │   Sweep   [Directional ▼]               ││
│ │   Colors  [ 2 ▼]  ■  □                  ││
│ │                                         ││
│ │  (Revert)  (Cancel)  [ OK ]             ││
│ └────────────────────────────────────────┘│
└──────────────────────────────────────────┘
```

This editor can look different, depending on the gradient you choose to edit. We won't go into all the possibilities here, but these are the options you can use to edit a gradient:

- Type an angle in the Angle box or drag the point on the perimeter of the circle to set the direction for a Directional or Circular sweep gradient. (Circular gradients have two different points you can drag.)

- Choose Directional, Circular, or Shape Burst style from the Sweep menu.

- Choose the number of colors from the Colors number pop-up menu.

- Choose the specific colors you want from one of the pop-up palettes to the right of the Colors number pop-up menu.

Try playing with this editor to see the range of gradient effects you can create. You can always see what you've done by checking the Sample area. Click the Revert button to return to the original gradient you began with.

About pen attributes

Pen attributes control the color, pattern, width, and style of the lines that make up objects. There are four palettes you can use to set pen attributes:

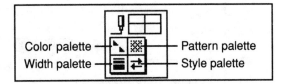

The default pen attribute is an opaque black line that's 1 point thick.

The color and pattern palettes are the same as they are in the fill tool. The width palette contains settings for line widths of from 1 to 8 points, or you can choose an *Other…* command from the palette to set any width up to 255 points. Finally, you can set a thickness of *None*, which is the same as a transparent pattern setting, or *Hairline*, which is thinner than 1 point.

The style palette lets you add arrow points to one or both ends of your lines, like this:

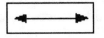

Arrow sizes are proportional to the width of the line, so changing the line width changes the height of arrow points as well. The standard arrow setting is *Plain Line,* or no arrow points. You can also choose to have an arrow point at the starting point of a

line, an arrow at the end of a line, or arrows at both ends, as
shown above.

 Unlike other settings, arrow options are not shown in the pen
indicator box—the indicator shows plain lines even if you have
an arrow option set.

Working with multipage documents

Every draw document starts out as a single page, but you can
create multipage documents to produce posters, architectural
plans, and other large drawings. To add pages to your document:

1. Choose the *Document...* command from the Format menu.
   You see the Document dialog box, like this:

   Document

   ┌─Margins─────────────┐ ┌─Size──────────────┐
   Top   `0.43 in`   Pages across `1`
   Bottom `0.43 in`   Pages down   `1`
   Left   `0.42 in`
   Right `0.42 in`   ┌─Display─────────┐
                               ☒ Show margins
   Starting page # `1`   ☒ Show page guides

                               (Cancel) (OK)

2. Click in the Pages Across or Pages Down box and enter the
   number of pages you want. You can add pages in both
   directions if you like.

3. Click the OK button to put the dialog box away.

The other options in this dialog box are the same in every ClarisWorks document, and are covered on p. 39 in Chapter 2.

Once you have a multipage document, you can create objects that span more than one page. Choose *Page View* from the View menu to show the page edges, then just draw or move an object so it spans the border between two pages.

. . . .

Using a master page

A master page is an independent, transparent layer of a draw document that displays the same text or graphics on every page. For example, you might want to have "Proof Only" appear underneath each page of a document, like this:

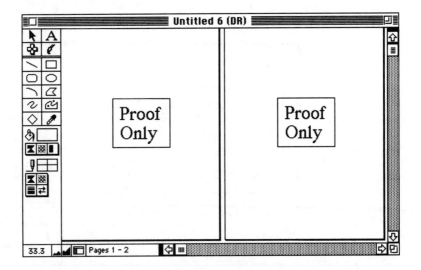

Then you can draw whatever you like on each page, and when you print the document the "Proof Only" designation will appear on each page.

Creating or changing a master page

To create a master page:

1. Choose *Edit Master Page* from the Options menu. The work area becomes blank, and you see *Master Page* instead of the document page number in the box at the lower left corner of the document window. (Any work you had showing in the document is still there, it's just temporarily hidden.)

2. Add the text or graphics you want to appear on the master page.

3. Choose *Edit Master Page* again to switch back to normal drawing mode.

When you're not in Page View, master page elements are hidden so you can concentrate on the other contents of each page. To display the master page elements, choose *Page View* from the View menu.

Troubleshooting

An object covers up the grid lines or another object in a document. Objects normally have a white fill pattern, so they cover up anything under them. Select the object and choose the transparent fill pattern from the fill pattern palette, or choose *Send To Back* from the Arrange menu to put the object behind others.

A polygon won't close. If the autogrid is off, you have to click *exactly* on the starting point for the first polygon side to complete a polygon, and that's not so easy sometimes. Zoom the layout to see the starting point more clearly and then try again. In the future, choose Automatic Polygon Closing in the Graphics preferences dialog box, or turn on the autogrid before you begin drawing the polygon.

Some objects don't align to the autogrid. The autogrid only aligns objects when it's on. Objects you draw before the autogrid is on won't snap to the autogrid points after you turn it on. Use the *Align Objects...* command to align these objects.

Straight lines become jagged when you resize them. When you drag a line's endpoint in or out along the plane of the line, you lengthen or shorten it, but when you drag the endpoint away from the plane of the line, you change its angle. To constrain the pointer so you'll only lengthen or shorten a line without changing its angle, hold down the Shift key as you drag the endpoint.

You changed a fill or line attribute, but the next object you draw has the same old attribute. If you change an attribute while an object is selected, you only change it for that object. To change the current setting for new objects, choose the new attribute when no objects are selected.

The Gradients palette is really slow to open. It is, isn't it? Click the Faster Gradients checkbox in the Graphics preferences dialog box to speed things up a little, but don't expect miracles.

There aren't enough colors in the color palette. Choose Editable 256 Color Palette in the Palettes preferences dialog box. If this doesn't work, open the Monitors control panel in your Control Panels folder (or click the Monitors icon in your Control Panel desk accessory on the menu), and set your monitor to display more colors. Of course, if your Mac can't display more colors, you're out of luck.

CHAPTER 9

The painting program

The painting program lets you create complex images using colors, patterns, and lines, and a variety of paint tools. The techniques we'll cover in this chapter also apply to paint frames, so you can use them to create colorful images in other types of ClarisWorks documents. ➻

Basic painting concepts

Painting is different from drawing because when you paint, you create *bitmapped images* by controlling the individual dots of light, or pixels, on your screen. As you paint with a tool, you affect groups of pixels in the tool's path, turning them on or off or changing their colors. Although the painting program has tools for creating rectangles, ovals, polygons, and arcs, these shapes are images in a paint document—once you draw them the only way to change them is by changing the individual pixels that make them up.

With a draw program, on the other hand, you create objects that are defined by points at their edges, and once you draw an object you can select or work with it as a whole.

The paint document window

When you open a new paint document, the screen looks like the one at the top of the next page:

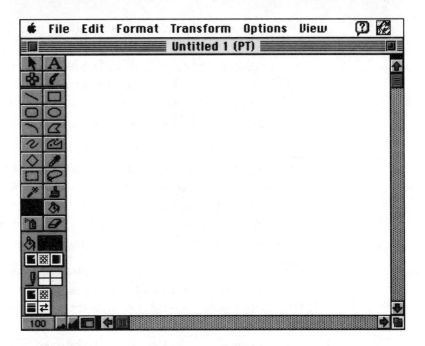

The work area at the right is blank (although you can show rulers at the top and left side by choosing the *Show Rulers* command from the View menu), and there's no grid of dotted lines as there is in a draw document.

The paint tools

A paint document's tool panel has many of the same tools as in a draw document, and all of these work the same way as they do in draw documents, except that they create images rather than objects. For more on using these tools, see p. 238 in Chapter 8. In this chapter, we'll look at the six extra tools you have available in paint documents or frames.

The *selection rectangle* selects portions of the work area. When you drag the rectangle over part of the screen, you select everything inside it. Double-click on the selection rectangle to select the entire work area. To select just the images in the work area (without the white space around them), hold down ⌃⌘ as you double-click on this tool.

 The *lasso* selects a particular image without the white space around it. When you drag the lasso tool, a freehand line appears. Draw a line around the image you want to select and release the mouse button to select just that image. You can also double-click on the lasso to select all the images in a document without selecting the white space around them.

 The *magic wand* selects only adjacent pixels of the same color. This tool is handy when you want to change a few pixels from one color to another. When you drag the magic wand over part of an image, the first pixel you select determines which color will be selected, and then any other pixels of that color in the path you drag will also be selected. Once you release the mouse button, the cursor changes to a pointer and you can move the selection or change its color.

The *brush* is one of four paint tools you use to paint free-hand images with. Just drag the brush across the work area to paint in the shape of the brush. ClarisWorks has 32 built-in brush shapes to choose from. To change the brush shape, double-click on the brush tool to display the Brush Shape dialog box, like the one at the top of the next page:

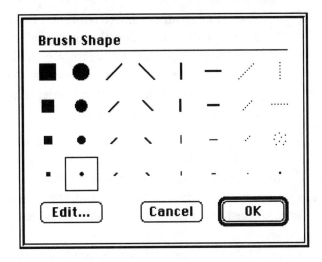

Double-click on a shape to select it. If you don't like any of the shapes you see, click on a shape you know you won't use and click the Edit... button. You see the Brush Editor, like this:

Here, you can click anywhere inside the box to add or remove dots to create different brush shapes. Click OK when you're done and you see the new brush shape in the Brush Shape dialog box.

The *pencil* creates thin freehand lines in the color shown in the pen indicator. Unlike the brush, you can't change the pattern, thickness, or style of the pencil's line. (Except for color, the pen tool settings have no effect on the pencil tool—they affect the lines that border shapes you draw. See *Creating images* on the next page.)

Use the pencil to turn individual pixels on or off when you make detailed changes to an image. First click the zoom in control at the lower left corner of the document window to magnify the work area, then click on individual pixels or drag across groups of them to make small changes in an image.

The *paint bucket* fills an enclosed image with the current fill color, pattern, or gradient. To fill an enclosed image, just select the color, pattern, or gradient you want to use, choose the paint bucket, and click inside the enclosed area—ClarisWorks fills the enclosed space. See *Using the paint bucket* on p. 278.

The *spray can* paints a round group of dots with the color, pattern, or gradient you've selected. If you hold the pointer in one place, the pattern gets thicker and thicker, just as it would with a real spray can.

You can constrain the brush, pencil, or spray can to a straight vertical or horizontal line by holding down the (Shift) key before you begin painting.

If you don't like the spray can's *dot size* (the size of the dot group) or its *flow rate* (the speed at which dots are filled when you spray), double-click on the spray can. You see an editor window, like the one at the top of the next page:

```
┌──────────────────────────────────────────┐
│ ════════════ Edit Spray Can ════════════  │
│ ┌────────────────────┐                     │
│ │                    │  Dot size   [25  ]  │
│ │                    │                     │
│ │                    │  Flow rate  [20  ]  │
│ │                    │                     │
│ │                    │  ( Clear Sample Area)│
│ │                    │                     │
│ │                    │                     │
│ │                    │  ( Cancel )  ( OK ) │
│ └────────────────────┘                     │
└──────────────────────────────────────────┘
```

The *Dot Size* box sets the diameter of the spray can's dot circle (in pixels), and the *Flow Rate* box sets the speed at which dots are filled. You can see how different values affect the tool by spray painting in the sample area at the left.

 The *eraser* clears any portion of the work area you click it on or drag it over. To erase the whole work area, double-click on the eraser.

If the eraser is too big to fit in an area you want to erase, zoom the work area to 200 or 400 percent—the image size gets bigger but the eraser size stays the same.

Creating images

With all the tools available, there are lots of ways to create images. You can create specific shapes with the draw tools or create freeform images with the pencil, spray can, or brush. Whichever tool you use, however, there's a basic procedure to follow:

1. Select a color, pattern, or gradient with the fill tool, and choose a line color, pattern and width with the pen tool.

(Because images are just groups of individual pixels, it's difficult to edit the pattern, color, or gradient of an image after you create it. Therefore you should always set the patterns first.)

2. Choose a tool and draw the image.

Tip

If your Mac can display 256 colors, you can use a 256-color palette instead of the standard 81-color palette, and you can edit the palette or save different ones. To do this, choose *Preferences...* from the Edit menu, click the Palettes icon, and click the Editable 256 Color Palette button there. Once you edit palettes for different uses, you can click the Load Palette and Save Palette buttons to save and load different ones.

Painting shapes

To paint a shape, choose one of the draw tools described in Chapter 8. The shape will have the fill pattern and pen attributes shown on the fill and pen indicators at the bottom of the tool panel. You can set the thickness or pattern of a shape's border as well as its color by using the pen tool palettes.

Painting with the brush or spray can

When you paint with the brush or the spray can, the line or pattern of dots you paint has the color, pattern, or gradient shown in the fill indicator. When you paint with the pencil, you always create a thin line in the color shown in the pen indicator.

Changing the paint mode

Paint documents are preset to *Opaque* paint mode, so when you draw one image on top of another, the new image covers up the old one, like this:

However, you can also choose Transparent or Tint mode to achieve a different effect. To change the paint mode, choose *Paint Mode...* from the Options menu and click an option in the dialog box that appears.

In *Transparent* mode, you can see through an image to one underneath it, so the patterns in the two images merge, like this:

In *Tint* mode, the color you're painting tints any objects underneath the new one.

 Use Tint mode to create different colors by overlaying one color on top of another.

Manipulating images

Once you've created images, you can edit them, delete them, move them, resize them, and reshape them.

Selecting images

Before you can move, resize, or apply special visual effects to an image, you must select it. You can use either the selection rectangle or the lasso tool to select images. And, since images are just collections of dots, you can also select any part of an image by dragging the rectangle or lasso over just that part—something you can't do in draw documents.

Drag the selection tool around the image you want to select, then release the mouse button. When an image is selected, a flashing dotted line appears to show the border of the selection. You can then delete, move, resize, or reshape the selection.

When you use the selection rectangle, you also select any white space enclosed in the rectangle, like this:

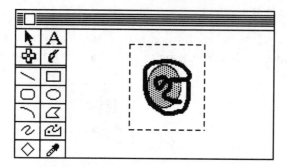

The easiest way to select only an image without the white space around it is to use the lasso tool instead. The lasso tightens up around the edges of an image to select just the image. If you're using the selection rectangle, you must drag it exactly on an image's border to select just the image without white space.

 To select the entire work area (including white space), double-click on the selection rectangle. To select all the images in the work area without selecting the white space around them, double-click on the lasso tool, or hold down the ⌘ key while double-clicking on the selection rectangle.

To deselect an image, click a different tool, or click outside the image in the work area.

Copying and duplicating an image

Once you select an image, you can use the standard *Copy*, *Cut*, and *Paste* commands to copy it or move it from one place to another. You can copy within the paint document or between the paint document and other ClarisWorks documents.

When you paste an image, it's just like painting it from scratch: it covers up anything underneath it. However, the image remains selected after you paste it so you can continue working with it.

You can also choose the *Duplicate* command from the Edit menu. When you do this, a duplicate of the selected image appears exactly on top of the original, and the duplicate is selected. You can then drag the duplicate off of the original and move it to a different location.

Editing an image

The only way to edit an image is to change the pixels that make it up. You use different methods to do this, however, depending on the type of edit you want to make.

To change only a small or irregular part of an image, use the brush, pencil, spray can, or eraser. Remember, you only change the portion of the image that's in the path of the tool you're using.

To change a larger portion of an image, it's often faster to move or draw another shape on top of the one you're changing. For example, if you want to change half of a rectangle to a different pattern or color, draw a smaller rectangle in the pattern you want on top of the half you want to edit.

 Change the paint mode to Transparent or Tint and then paint over an image to create different fill patterns or colors.

Deleting an image

To delete an image, either erase it with the eraser, or select it and press the (Delete) key. Double-click on the eraser to clear the whole work area.

Moving an image

To move an image, select it and drag it. You can drag one image onto another to combine them. To constrain the movement to a straight vertical or horizontal line, hold down the (Shift) key after you select the image but before you begin dragging it.

Remember, you can select part of an image. By doing this you can cut pieces off of an image or move part of an image from one place to another.

 If you move an image so that part of it extends past the edge of the document and then deselect the image, the portion that's off the document will be lost.

Aligning images with the autogrid

When you want to line up several images along the same vertical or horizontal line, or to create images that are precisely sized, choose the *Turn Autogrid On* command from the Options menu. When the autogrid is on, objects you draw or move snap to points on the grid.

To set the grid size, choose the *Grid Size…* command from the Options menu. You'll see a dialog box like this:

```
┌─────────────────────────────────────┐
│  Painting Grid Size                  │
│  ─────────────────────────────────   │
│  ○ 2 pixels       ○ 16 pixels        │
│  ○ 4 pixels       ○ 32 pixels        │
│  ● 8 pixels                          │
│                                      │
│          ┌──────────┐  ┌──────────┐  │
│          │  Cancel  │  │    OK    │  │
│          └──────────┘  └──────────┘  │
└─────────────────────────────────────┘
```

To line up several images on the same horizontal or vertical line, turn on the autogrid before you create any of them.

Picking up an image

The *Pick Up* command on the Transform menu lets you replace an object with one underneath it. To use this command, select the object you want to replace, drag it on top of the object you really want, and then choose *Pick Up.* The object underneath replaces the object that was covering it.

Resizing an image

To resize an image, select it and choose *Resize* from the Transform menu. Selection handles appear at the corners of the image, and you can drag one of them to resize it. To constrain the resizing so it's proportional, hold down the (Shift) key before you drag a handle.

Scaling an image

To resize an image to a precise size, select it and choose the *Scale Selection...* command from the Transform menu. You see the Scale Selection dialog box, where you can enter vertical and horizontal scaling percentages. The original image size is 100%, so 50% is half size, 200% is double size, and so on.

Rotating an image

There are two ways to rotate an image.

- Choose the *Rotate...* command to display a dialog box in which you can enter the number of degrees by which you want the object rotated.

- Choose the *Free Rotate* command to add selection handles to the image, then drag one of the handles to rotate it.

Reshaping an image

There are three different ways to reshape an image (other than editing it), depending on the visual effect you want to create. The Transform menu's *Shear, Distort,* and *Perspective* commands reshape images differently. When you select an image and choose one of these, selection handles appear at the image's corners, and you can drag one of them to reshape it. Depending on which command you've chosen, dragging a selection handle reshapes the image in different ways. At the top of the next page is a simple example:

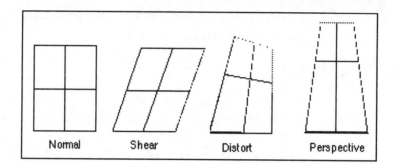

Normal   Shear   Distort   Perspective

Try these reshaping options on your own to see how they work.

Changing fills, colors, and shades

Along with changing the shape or size of images, you can also change the colors or shades that make them up. Initially, you apply a color or pattern by selecting it from one of the fill palettes before you create the image, but once an image is created you can select it and use other commands to change its color or shade.

Using the paint bucket

The paint bucket applies a fill color, pattern, or gradient to an enclosed image that is currently blank. Just choose the fill you want and then click inside the enclosed area you want to fill. If you click with the bucket inside a space that isn't completely enclosed, however, ClarisWorks will fill all the white space in the document except other, completely enclosed images, like the one at the top of the next page:

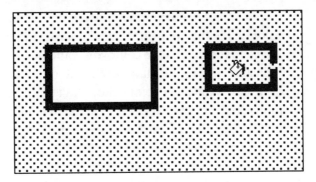

When this happens, choose *Undo Paint* from the Edit menu to cancel the fill, then close up the image you want to fill and try again. If you have trouble finding the gap in the image, zoom the document (as in the example above).

The paint bucket won't work on images that are already filled with a pattern or color.

Using the *Fill* command

Another way to change the fill in an image is the *Fill* command on the Transform menu. Unlike the paint bucket, this command lets you fill an image that already has a color or pattern. Just select the image you want to fill, then choose the *Fill* command. The selected area will be filled with the current fill color, pattern, or gradient.

Using the eyedropper to set the fill color

When you want to change the fill color to one that's already showing in your document, select the eyedropper and click the color you want.

If your image has a complex pattern or gradient with many colors, drag the eyedropper slowly across the portion of the image that contains the color you want and watch the fill indicator next to the fill tool. The fill indicator changes as you drag across different colors. Stop dragging and release the mouse button when the color you want is showing in the fill indicator. If the colors change too quickly, zoom the document and try again.

Inverting colors

If you're working with a black and white image or an image composed of any two colors, you can invert the colors. Just select the area you want to invert and choose *Invert* from the Transform menu.

Blending colors or shades

When you select an image and choose the *Blend* command from the Transform menu, ClarisWorks creates a smooth blend between colors or shades in a selection, like this:

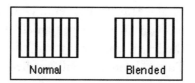

If you're working in color, ClarisWorks adds intermediate shades of the colors so the transitions between them aren't as abrupt.

Tinting an image

When you select an image and choose the *Tint* command from the Transform menu, ClarisWorks uses the current fill color to tint the color of the selection. So, for example, by choosing a red fill color with the fill tool and then applying the *Tint* command to a blue selection, you can add the red tint and change the selection to purple.

Lightening and darkening an image

Choose the *Lighter* or *Darker* command from the Transform menu when you want to lighten or darken an entire selection, like this:

Original   Lightened   Darkened

Notice, though, that darkening a selection darkens the white space in it along with everything else.

Once you darken a selection, you can't lighten it to return it to its original condition—the dark tint remains on the selection's white space, it just gets lighter. To return a darkened image to its original condition, choose *Undo Darker* immediately from the Edit menu.

Changing the document size, resolution, and depth

The work area in new paint documents is preset at 468 pixels wide and 648 pixels tall. Each paint document can have only one page. To change the size of the work area, choose *Document...* from the Format menu, type new values in the Pixels Across and Pixels Down boxes, and click the OK button. The work area size changes on the screen.

Paint document sizes are limited by the amount of available memory. If your Mac is low on memory, new documents may be smaller, and you may not be able to open some you've created before without closing other documents or quitting other programs first. Changing the margin settings in the Document dialog box has no effect on the size of the work area in a paint document.

Changing the resolution and depth

You can change the resolution of a paint document to match the resolution of the printer you're using. And, if you're using a color or grayscale monitor, you can change the number of gray shades or colors displayed in the document. To change either of these:

Choose the *Resolution & Depth...* command from the Format menu. You see a dialog box like this:

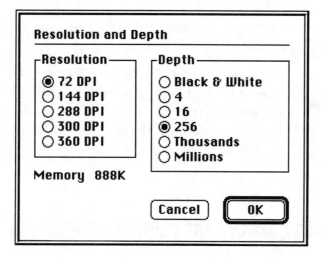

Click the option in each area to set the resolution and depth you want, then click the OK button.

The Resolution option default is 72 dots per inch (DPI), which matches the Mac screen. Other options match various printers.

The Depth options determine the number of colors or gray shades in color palettes of the fill and pen tools. The more colors or shades you select, the more memory your paint document uses, as shown below the Resolution options.

Painting Shortcuts

The best way to learn about painting is to experiment on your own, but here are a few techniques that can help you accomplish your goals more quickly.

Recycle images. There are lots of perfectly good, ready-made paint images available, and if an image is complex, it's easier to change it a little bit than to create a new one from scratch. ClarisWorks 3.0 includes dozens of ready-made clip art images, and you can copy these to paint documents or paint frames and modify them. Other collections of clip art are available from user groups and retail sources. A couple of good clip art collections can save you many hours of work, and will also give you ideas about new designs of your own.

Use Undo a lot. It's far easier to undo a painting operation than to use the eraser. Undo works on every painting, fill, resizing, and reshaping operation.

Duplicate images to try things out. To try several different fill options, first duplicate an image and arrange the copies side by side, then use the paint bucket or *Fill* command to fill each one differently.

Zoom in for details. By zooming in on the work area, you can magnify the pixels so it's easy to edit them one at a time, or to see small details in an image. By choosing the *New View* command from the View menu, you can create a second view of the same document and then zoom one of the views. This way, you can make changes in the zoomed view and at the same time see how they really look in the normal view. Arrange both views side by side on your screen so you can quickly see how your changes look.

Zoom out for perspective. To see how a whole page will look, click the zoom out control to see the whole page on your screen in a reduced size.

Troubleshooting

A message says there isn't enough memory to complete the operation.
Paint documents are real memory hogs, especially if you have the document
depth set to display lots of colors. Try closing other documents or other
programs to free up some memory. If this doesn't work, save everything and
restart your Mac. You can also increase the amount of memory ClarisWorks
itself has to work with by using the *Get Info...* command in the Finder. See
p. 431 in Appendix A.

You copy an image into a paint document, and it's too big for the window.
Any portion of an image that extends past the edge of the paint document is
lost for good, so if you paste something into a document and it doesn't fit
within the edges of the page, you won't have the whole image. Try enlarging
the document with the *Document...* command on the Format menu. Paste
the image to the Scrapbook (it's on the ❤ menu), close all your documents
and other programs, then open a new paint document and see if it's larger.
If it is, you can copy the image from the Scrapbook and paste it into the new
document.

You can't make a document bigger than one page. The painting program
uses up too much memory to permit multipage documents. Use the draw
program.

**You select a small part of an image with the lasso but then can't seem to
drag it or resize it.** After you select something with the lasso, the lasso
pointer changes back to the arrow pointer so you can move or resize the
object. But it's sometimes hard for ClarisWorks to grab a small selection
when you've used the lasso tool to select it, and the lasso cursor won't change
to the pointer. Try moving the pointer slowly across different parts of the
selection and watch for the pointer to change to an arrow. If this doesn't
work, zoom the document window and try again; or use the selection
rectangle to make the selection.

The communications program

The communications program lets you make connections with other computers and exchange data with them. Communications can be a complex business, and ClarisWorks has dozens of options that allow you to communicate with many different types of computers in various ways. However, most of us will use only a handful of ClarisWorks' most basic settings and options for our communications needs. ➤➤

In this chapter, we'll cover those basics and look only briefly at the more advanced options. If you need more information beyond what's covered here, check the ClarisWorks Help facility or the *ClarisWorks User's Guide.*

How computers communicate

There are standard methods by which computers communicate, and the ClarisWorks communications program sets up your Mac to conform to them. The communications program is also called a *terminal emulation* program, because it makes your Mac act like a communications *terminal.* In the old days, you needed a special device called a terminal to communicate with another computer, but now we use terminal emulation software to make any personal computer act like a terminal.

If you're using a standard telephone line, you need a *modem* to communicate. A modem translates the Mac's data into sounds that can be transmitted over ordinary telephone lines. Otherwise, you must be connected directly to the other computer by a cable or network.

You can communicate either with another personal computer or with a larger computer that supports an *online service.* Each connection with another computer is called a communications *session.*

Online services are set up to communicate with dozens or hundreds of personal computers at a time. They typically offer collections of information, games, electronic shopping, weather, news, and electronic mail services. You need a special subscriber account to use an online service, and there's a charge for doing so. After you connect to the computer supporting an online service, you must *log on* to (or access) the service itself with the user name and password for your subscriber account.

Computers communicate according to a set of *connection protocols* that determine the speed and format of the data being exchanged. Both computers must use the same protocol settings to communicate properly.

Once you connect to a remote computer, you can type on your screen to send data to it, or you can use a *file transfer protocol* to exchange complete files. There are several different file transfer protocols you can use to send whole files without having to monitor the transmission. Most protocols also check for errors and will resend parts of a file if they aren't received properly by the other computer.

Connecting to a remote computer

To connect with another computer, you set up your Mac's hardware to make the physical connection, and then you open a communications document to turn your Mac into a terminal, make the call, and transmit or receive data.

Setting up your hardware

You must have a physical link to the remote computer. The most common link is a telephone line (which requires you to have a modem connected to your Mac), but you can also use an Apple-Talk network or a cable that connects your Mac directly to another computer. We'll cover the modem method here, since it's the most common.

Modems transmit data at different speeds (called the *baud rate*); most of today's computers exchange data at 1200 or 2400 baud. If you don't have a modem, you can buy a 2400 baud model for as little as $100 from a mail-order catalog or computer dealer.

To set up an external modem:

1. Plug its data cable into the modem port on your Mac.

2. Plug its phone line into a telephone jack.

3. Plug its power cord into an electrical outlet.

4. Turn it on.

If your modem is an internal one that plugs into a slot inside your Mac, you need only plug in the telephone line to the modem board.

Once the modem is set up, you can open a new ClarisWorks communications document and set it up to communicate properly with the remote computer.

Opening a communications document

When you open a new Communications document, it looks like this:

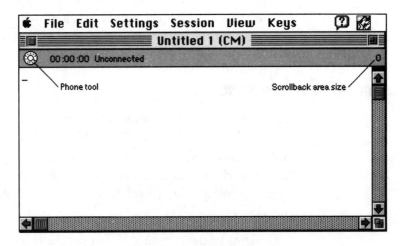

This window isn't very interesting unless you're connected and are sending or receiving data. Then the blank part of the window (the work area) displays data as it's transmitted or received.

The phone tool at the top of the window displays a pop-up menu that gives you access to the phone book (see p. 299). Next to it you can see how long you've been connected during the current session, and whether you're connected or not.

Choosing connection settings

To call another computer or receive a call from another computer, you need to set the document's connection settings.

1. Choose the *Connection...* command from the Settings menu. You see a dialog box like this:

```
┌─────────────────────────────────────────────────────────────┐
│  Connection Settings                          ┌──────────┐    │
│                                               │    OK    │    │
│      Method:      ┌ Apple Mode...  ▼ ┐        └──────────┘    │
│                   └───────────────────┘       ┌──────────┐    │
│                                               │  Cancel  │    │
│                                               └──────────┘    │
│  ──────────────────────────────────────────────────────────  │
│  Phone Settings                     Port Settings            │
│                                                               │
│   ○ Answer Phone After 2  Rings      Baud Rate :  2400  ▼    │
│   ● Dial Phone Number [          ]    Parity :    None  ▼    │
│                                       Data Bits : 8  ▼       │
│    ▦▦▦  ☒ Redial 3   Times            Stop Bits : 1  ▼       │
│    ▦▦▦    Every 10   Seconds          Handshake : None  ▼    │
│    ▦▦▦                                                        │
│           Dial : [ Tone ▼ ]          Current Port            │
│                                                               │
│  Modem Settings                                               │
│   Modem : [ Hayes-Compatible Modem  ]   ▐███▌      ┌─┐        │
│   □ Disconnect when NO CARRIER detected  Modem Port Printer Port │
│   □ Display Modem Monitor Window                              │
└─────────────────────────────────────────────────────────────┘
```

The default connection settings shown here are the ones you'll use for most of the remote computers you'll call. The Method pop-up menu at the top determines which other options you have below in this dialog box. If you're calling another computer or receiving a call over a telephone line, leave this menu on Apple Modem Tool—this tool works with most of the modems available.

2. If you're receiving a call, click the Answer Phone button under Phone Settings. If you're placing the call, click the

Dial Phone Number button and then enter the phone number in the box to its right. You can enter numbers with or without dashes between prefixes.

You can tell ClarisWorks to pause before dialing part of a number by entering a comma before that part. For example, if you need to dial 9 to get an outside line at your office, you could enter 9, and then the phone number to give your phone system time to produce an outside dial tone. Each comma you enter tells ClarisWorks to pause for a second or two.

3. Choose the brand and model of modem you're using from the Modem pop-up menu in the Modem Settings area. If you don't see your modem brand and model, leave this option as shown above.

4. Click the Disconnect When NO CARRIER Detected box. This tells ClarisWorks to automatically close the connection when the remote computer hangs up. Otherwise, you have to remember to close the connection manually (see p. 295). Don't check the Display Modem Monitor Window box— this box shows the actual commands ClarisWorks sends to your modem, and there's no point in looking at them unless you're diagnosing a modem problem.

5. Choose the Port Settings options from the pop-up menus that match the baud rate and data format options used by the other computer. These settings must match the remote computer's settings for the connection to work properly. If necessary, talk to the other computer's owner first to agree on a group of settings, or consult the manual if you're calling an online service. The settings shown above are the most common ones.

6. Make sure the correct icon is selected in the Current Port area. It should be the port where you have your modem, network, or direct-connect data cable plugged in.

7. Click OK or press (Return) to store the settings and telephone number you've entered.

There are other options in the Connection Settings dialog box, but they're fairly self-explanatory. If you have questions about them, consult the ClarisWorks Help facility.

Opening a connection

Once you've chosen the connection settings, you're ready to connect.

1. Turn on your modem.

2. Choose *Open Connection* from the Session menu. The Modem Status box appears, like this:

```
┌──────────────────────────────────────────────┐
│ ══════════════  Modem Status  ══════════════  │
│ ┌──────────────────────────────────────────┐ │
│ │  ☎                                         │ │
│ │ →▭    Initializing modem...                │ │
│ │                                            │ │
│ │                                            │ │
│ │                              ( Cancel )    │ │
│ └──────────────────────────────────────────┘ │
└──────────────────────────────────────────────┘
```

You see a series of messages in this box as ClarisWorks sets up your modem with the connection options you've chosen, dials the number, and waits for an answer. If your modem has a speaker, you also hear the modem dialing and connecting. Finally, you see a message that says you're connected.

3. Click the OK button or press [Return] to put the Modem Status box away.

If you called an online service, you see a prompt like the one at the top of the next page:

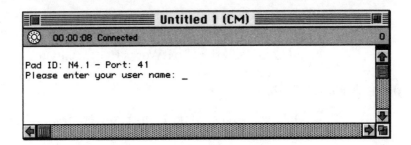

```
≣≣≣≣≣≣≣≣≣≣≣  Untitled 1 (CM)  ≣≣≣≣≣≣≣≣≣
⊙  00:00:08  Connected                              0

Pad ID: N4.1 - Port: 41
Please enter your user name: _
```

4. Type your user name and password as you're prompted
    (check your online service's user guide for specific instruc-
    tions). If you called another personal computer, you can
    type a greeting message and press Return to send it to the
    other computer's operator or simply wait to receive one on
    your screen.

If you frequently connect with an online service, you can save a
lot of keystrokes by creating a macro that enters your user name
and password automatically each time you connect. See p. 386
in Chapter 13.

Working with data during a connection

Once you're connected, you send data to the other computer by
typing it and pressing Return or by pasting it into the communications document's window. Everything you type or paste appears
on your own screen as it's sent to the other computer, and everything you receive from the remote computer also appears on
your screen.

As data appears on your screen, you can select it and copy, but
you can't edit it or delete it.

To copy a table of data, hold down the ⌘ key as you select the
data and then choose *Copy Table* from the Edit menu. This
preserves the tab stops between columns in the table.

Once your screen is filled with data, the oldest data you received scrolls off the top of the screen into the *scrollback area*, and new data scrolls in from the bottom. The scrollback area is part of the document that's saved when you save the document.

Using the scrollback pane

Normally the scrollback area is invisible, but you can divide the work area so it appears as a separate pane:

- Drag the pane marker down from the upper right corner of the window (above the scroll arrow); or

- Choose *Show Scrollback* from the Session menu.

The scrollback pane looks like this:

```
┌─────────────────────────────────────────────────────┐
│■□            Untitled 1 (CM)                        ▣│
│ ◉   00:01:50 Connected                            16 │
│ Please enter your user name: crubin               ⬆  │
│ Password:                                            │
│ COM                                                  │
│                                                      │
│ Welcome to MCI Mail!                                 │ ← Scrollback
│                                                      │    pane
│ What's happening in Washington?                      │
│ Read the White House bulletin                        │
│ boards from the convenience of your               ▤  │
│ desk.                                             ⬇  │
│─────────────────────────────────────────────────────│
│ Command: sc desk                                  ⬆  │
│                                                      │
│   1 message in DESK                                  │ ← Incoming
│                                                      │    data
│ No.  Posted       From           Subject             │
│   1  Sep 29 12:55  On Mail        On Mail Newsletter - Iss ⬇ │
│ ⬅□          ⬛⬛                              ➡□   │
└─────────────────────────────────────────────────────┘
```

When the scrollback pane is showing, you can:

- Scroll through it to review data you've received;

- Select, cut, copy, or paste data in it (choose *Save Current Screen* from the Session menu to copy the entire work area screen to the scrollback pane);

- Empty it by choosing *Clear Saved Lines* from the Session menu;

- Resize it by dragging the pane marker up or down; or

- Hide it by choosing *Hide Scrollback* from the Session menu.

New communications documents are set for a scrollback area of unlimited size, but if you receive lots of data you can run out of memory. You can limit the scrollback area's size with the *Preferences...* command on the Edit menu. See p. 302.

Capturing text to a file

When you save a communications document, you automatically save all the text in the scrollback pane and in the work area. However, you can also *capture* incoming text and save it as a separate file on your disk. When you capture a file, the incoming data isn't stored in the scrollback area at all. To capture a file:

1. Choose *Capture to File ...* from the Session menu. You see a dialog box in which you can name the captured file and select a folder or disk location for it.

2. Type a name for the file, choose a location for it, and click the Save button in the dialog box. ClarisWorks saves everything that appears in your document's work area from that point on.

ClarisWorks won't capture any text already showing in the work area when you begin capturing a file, so make sure to begin the capture before receiving any text you want to save.

To stop capturing text, choose *Stop Capture* from the Session menu. Once you've saved a captured text file, you can open it with the word processing program.

Printing a communications document

You can print a communications document whenever you're connected to a remote computer or after you've disconnected from it. See p. 41 in Chapter 2 for the basic printing procedure.

Ending a communications session

To end your communications session, choose *Close Connection* from the Session menu. This hangs up the telephone line and resets your modem (if you're using one).

If you're connected to an online service, you should log off from it with the service's command (usually *exit, off,* or something like that) before closing the connection. Logging off tells the service you're disconnecting so it knows when to stop charging you.

Transferring files

So far we've covered the basics of connecting and sending or receiving data in the work area. When you send or receive data in the work area or capture incoming data to a file, however, you're working only with text information—characters you see on your screen. This information doesn't have all the formatting it had originally, and you must usually open and reformat the text in the word processing program.

However, ClarisWorks also has specific file transfer capabilities that let you send or receive files of all types—not just text—using special error-checking options. With the file transfer methods, you can send or receive fully formatted spreadsheet, database, graphics, and other types of files.

Choosing a file transfer method

Before you can send or receive a file, you must set ClarisWorks to use the same file transfer protocol and method as will be used by the remote computer. You can set the transfer protocol and method before you connect or while you're connected as described in the steps beginning on p. 298.

File transfer settings

Here's a quick rundown on the options in the File Transfer Settings dialog box on p. 298. Not all of these options are available at all times—it depends on which protocol and method you have selected. See the *ClarisWorks User's Guide* for more information.

The Protocol menu

The two protocols are the XMODEM Tool and the Text Tool. The XMO-DEM Tool is the default—it checks for errors as portions (or blocks) of the file are sent or received. If an error occurs, that block of data is sent again.

XMODEM Tool options

When you have the *XMODEM Tool* selected, the Method menu has four options.

- *MacBinary* is for sending a complete Mac file to another Mac if the remote Mac doesn't support MacTerminal 1.1.

- *MacTerminal* 1.1 is like MacBinary, but it allows automatic file reception. This is the preferred Mac-to-Mac transfer option.

- *Straight XMODEM* sends only the data from a Mac file without the creator ID or other resource information. Use this when you're sending data to non-Mac computers that don't support XMODEM binary transfers.

- *XMODEM Text* is like Straight XMODEM, except that it converts return characters at the end of each line to return/line feed characters. Use this option when the other computer uses return/line feed characters instead of return characters only.

The *Timing options* tell ClarisWorks when to *timeout*, or stop sending data if it doesn't receive a signal from the other computer for a specific number of seconds; and how many times to *retry*, or retransmit a block of data when the block isn't received accurately.

The *Transfer Options* menu has four choices.

- *Standard* sends data in 128-byte blocks without extra error checking.

- *CRC-16* sends data in 128-byte blocks with CRC-16 error-checking. This method is more reliable.

- *1K Blocks* also uses CRC-16 error-checking, but transmits data in larger, 1024-byte (1K) blocks.

- *CleanLink* is like 1K Blocks, but it disconnects if it detects an error. Don't use this unless you know you have a very error-free connection with the remote computer.

The *Received File options* aren't available at all times; their availability depends on which method you've chosen.

- *Creator ID* lets you choose the ID type for received files. The ID is shown in the Creator ID window. Click the button below it to display a dialog box in which you can select the application whose creator ID you want the received file to have. By setting the creator ID, you set the file's "native" format and determine which program launches when you double-click on the file's icon in the Finder.

- *Use Filename Sent By Remote Computer* tells ClarisWorks to save received files with the same name they had on the remote computer. This box is normally checked.

- *Enable Auto Receive* tells ClarisWorks to automatically receive a file from the remote computer without your choosing *Receive File...* from the Session menu.

Text Tool options

The *Text Tool* options let you set timing delays (in 60ths of a second) for each character or line you send or receive; choose the character inserted at the end of each line (return or linefeed and return); or set the number of characters on a line before the line is wrapped (the default is 80).

1. Choose *File Transfer...* from the Settings menu. You see the File Transfer Settings dialog box, like this:

2. Choose a protocol from the Protocol pop-up menu.

3. Choose a method from the Method pop-up menu.

4. Choose any other options, as necessary, then click the OK button. See *File transfer settings* for more on these options.

Once you've set the transfer protocol, method, and options, you're ready to send or receive a file.

Sending a file

To send a file:

1. Open a connection with the remote computer.

2. Choose *Send File...* from the Session menu. You see a dialog box in which you can select the file you want to send.

3. Double-click on the name of the file you want to send (or select it and click the Send button). You see a progress dialog box on the screen as the file is transmitted. When the transfer is complete, your Mac beeps.

You can switch to other ClarisWorks documents and work on something else while a long file transfer is underway. Because the Mac beeps when the transfer is complete, you'll know when to switch back to your communications document and go on to the next procedure there.

Receiving a file

To receive a file, choose *Receive File...* from the Session menu. ClarisWorks begins waiting for the other computer to send the file, and you see a progress dialog box on the screen, like this:

```
┌─────────────────────────────────────────────────────────────┐
│         File Transfer Status for "Untitled 1 (CM)"           │
├─────────────────────────────────────────────────────────────┤
│ Downloading...                                                │
│                                                               │
│   ┌──┐         ┌──┐      Method:        MacBinary             │
│   │  │ ◄──────  │  │      Option In Use: Standard              │
│   └──┘         └──┘                                           │
│ ............................................................. │
│ File Size:            36K                                     │
│ Blocks Transferred:   15                                      │
│ Bytes Transferred:    1920                                    │
│ Time Remaining:       3 minutes                               │
│ Status:               Receiving.                              │
│                                                               │
│ ████▌                                           ┌──────────┐ │
│ 0  10  20  30  40  50  60  70  80  90  100%     │  Cancel  │ │
│                                                 └──────────┘ │
└─────────────────────────────────────────────────────────────┘
```

As with sending a file, your Mac beeps when the transfer is complete.

· ·
Using the phone book

Each communications document can store only one set of connection, terminal, and file transfer settings, so if you regularly communicate with other computers that use different settings, you must create and save a separate document for each one.

However, many computers use the same settings, and it would be a shame if you had to store a separate communications document for each of these just because each had a different phone number. Although you can store only one phone number in the Connection Settings dialog box, you can use the Phone Book feature to store others.

To add entries to the phone book:

1. Choose *Phone Book...* from the Settings menu, or click the Phone tool above the document work area and then choose *Edit Phone Book...* from the pop-up menu. You see a dialog box like this:

```
┌─────────────────────────────────────────────┐
│  ┌───────────────────────────────────────┐   │
│  │                                       │   │
│  │  Edit Phone Book Entry                │   │
│  │  ──────────────────────────────────   │   │
│  │                                       │   │
│  │  Name    ┌─────────────────────────┐  │   │
│  │          │                         │  │   │
│  │  Number  ┌─────────────────────────┐  │   │
│  │          │                         │  │   │
│  │  Type    │ PhoneNumber             │  │   │
│  │          └─────────────────────────┘  │   │
│  │                                       │   │
│  │           ( Cancel )   (( OK ))       │   │
│  │                                       │   │
│  └───────────────────────────────────────┘   │
└─────────────────────────────────────────────┘
```

2. Type a name to identify whose phone number you're entering.

3. Click in the Number box and type the phone number.

4. Click OK or press [Return]. You see the Phone Book dialog box, like the one at the top of the next page:

```
┌──────────────────────────────────────────────┐
│  Phone Book                                    │
│  ──────────────────────────────────────────   │
│  ┌──────────────────────────────────────┬──┐  │
│  │ MCI Mail                             │⬆ │  │
│  │                                      ├──┤  │
│  │                                      │  │  │
│  │                                      │  │  │
│  │                                      │  │  │
│  │                                      ├──┤  │
│  │                                      │⬇ │  │
│  └──────────────────────────────────────┴──┘  │
│                                                │
│  ┌─────────┐ ┌─────────┐    ┌─────────┐        │
│  │ Delete  │ │  New    │    │  Done   │        │
│  └─────────┘ └─────────┘    └─────────┘        │
│            ┌─────────┐    ┌───────────┐        │
│            │  Edit   │    │  Connect  │        │
│            └─────────┘    └───────────┘        │
└──────────────────────────────────────────────┘
```

The name you just entered appears in the list, and also on the phone tool's pop-up menu.

5. Click Done to put the Phone Book dialog box away.

Once you've entered a number in the phone book, the Phone Book dialog box appears whenever you choose the *Phone Book...* command or choose *Edit Phone Book...* from the phone tool's pop-up menu. Then you can add other phone numbers (click the New button), delete or edit the selected entry, or dial a number.

Dialing a number

To dial a number stored in the phone book, either choose the entry name from the phone tool's pop-up menu, or choose the *Phone Book...* command and double-click on the entry name in the Phone Book dialog box. ClarisWorks dials the number stored with that name and uses the settings that are currently stored in the Connection, Terminal, and File Transfer dialog boxes.

. . . .

Setting communications preferences

There are lots of general options you can set in communications documents that help automate or improve your connections. To set them, choose the *Preferences...* command from the Edit menu. You see the Preferences dialog box, like this:

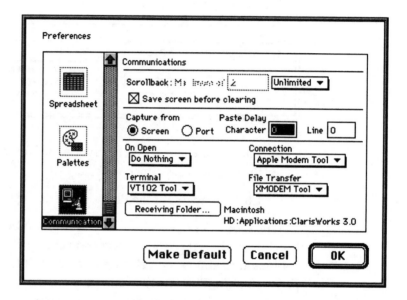

If you have a communications document open when you set these preferences, they'll apply to that document only. If you want the preferences to apply to all communications documents, either:

- Click the Make Default button at the bottom of the dialog box before clicking OK to save the preferences; or

- Set the preferences when no communications documents are open.

Here's what the options do.

The *Scrollback* pop-up menu lets you set the size of the scroll-back area. *Unlimited* is the default, but you can choose *Lines,*

Kilobytes, or *Screens* from the pop-up menu and then type a number in the box to set a limit.

Save Screen Before Clearing tells ClarisWorks to save the contents of the work area before clearing it. Some online services send a whole screen at a time and clear the old screen before sending a new one. Checking this box tells ClarisWorks to save the old screen in the scrollback area before clearing it.

The *Capture From* buttons determine the format of text as it's saved to a captured text file. *Port,* the default, captures data along with any tab, return, or linefeed characters. For example, a group of spreadsheet columns will be captured as columns because the tabs are saved with them. The *Screen* option saves text as an unbroken stream without tabs.

The *Paste Delay* options slow down the transmission of data you paste into a communications document. Normally Claris-Works sends the data as fast as it can, but if the remote computer can't receive data as fast as it's transmitted when you paste it, you can enter values here to insert delays after each character or line to slow things down. Values in these boxes are in 60ths of a second.

The *On Open* menu tells ClarisWorks to perform tasks automatically when this communications document is opened. The options are *Do Nothing* (the default), *Automatically Connect,* and *Wait For Connection* (which sets ClarisWorks to answer the phone).

The *Connection, Terminal,* and *File Transfer* menus let you set the default choices from these dialog boxes. See *Choosing connection settings* on p. 289, *Terminal settings,* next, and *File transfer settings* on p. 296 for more information.

The *Receiving Folder...* button lets you specify a folder in which incoming files are stored when you use the *Receive Files...* command. This option does not set a default folder for captured text files—you must choose one of those each time you use the *Capture To File...* command.

Terminal settings

The terminal settings control how your Mac emulates a communications terminal and how it displays data on your screen. The preset terminal settings should work in all communications you have with online services or other personal computers. Of all the terminal settings, only a handful will be of use for these types of communications, and we'll focus on those few options in this section.

Most of the terminal options are only useful when you're connecting to a mainframe or minicomputer system. If you need to do this, your mainframe or minicomputer system administrator can explain all these options to you. If you simply can't contain your curiosity about options not discussed in this section, check the *ClarisWorks User's Guide* or the ClarisWorks Help facility.

Displaying the terminal settings

To display the Terminal Settings dialog box, choose *Terminal...* from the Settings menu. The options you see depend on which terminal emulation tool you're using.

VT102 Tool settings

When you have the VT102 Tool selected on the Emulation menu in the Terminal Settings dialog box, the dialog box looks like the one at the top of the next page:

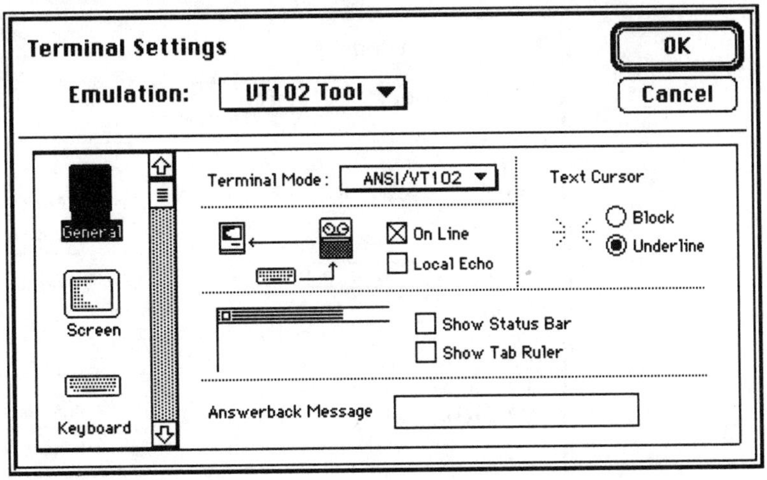

The options you see depend on which of the four icons is selected in the scrolling list at the left. Among the General settings shown above, the two important ones in most cases are the On Line and Local Echo checkboxes.

The *On Line* box should always be checked. If it isn't, you can connect to the remote computer but you can't send or receive data from it.

The *Local Echo* box is normally unchecked. If you can't see characters on your screen when you type, check this box.

None of the other options for the VT102 tool should ever have to be changed if you're communicating with another personal computer or an online service.

TTY Tool settings

When you're using the TTY terminal emulation tool, the Terminal Settings dialog box looks like the one at the top of the next page:

```
┌─────────────────────────────────────────────────────────────┐
│  Terminal Settings                    ┌─────────────────┐     │
│                                       │       OK        │     │
│  Emulation:   [ TTY Tool      ▼ ]     └─────────────────┘     │
│                                       ( Cancel )              │
│  ┌──────────────────────────────────────────────────────┐   │
│                                        Text Cursor            │
│   ▯  ←─────  ▤    ☒ On Line          ⊃ ⊂   ○ Block           │
│   ▭  ─┐      ┌    ☐ Local Echo        ⊃ ⊂   ● Underline       │
│                                                               │
│   Width: [ 80 Columns  ▼ ]            Scroll Text             │
│   Size:  [ 9 point  ▼ ]              ● Jump   ○ Smooth        │
│                                                               │
│   Characters                          1              80       │
│    ☐ Show Control Characters                                  │
│    ☐ Auto Wrap to Next Line          ┌──────────────────┐    │
│                                      │This is a sample of T│   │
│   Holding Down Keys Will             │This is a sample of T│   │
│    ☒ Auto Repeat Keys                │This is a sample of T│   │
│    ☐ Repeat Control Keys             └──────────────────┘    │
│                                      ☐ Swap 'Backspace' and 'Delete'│
│                                      ☐ New Line on a Return   │
└─────────────────────────────────────────────────────────────┘
```

You'll see many of the same options here that you'll find among the VT102 tool's General, Screen, and Keyboard options. Again, the two important options for general communications are the On Line and Local Echo checkboxes.

Troubleshooting

You can't connect. Make sure your modem or data cable is connected to the right port on your Macintosh, that the modem's telephone line is plugged into a working jack, and that the modem's power is on. If all this is okay, you should at least be able to make your modem dial a number (and you should hear a dial tone when the call begins) when you choose *Open Connection* from the Session menu. If you can do all this, then the remote computer isn't answering.

You can connect, but then you're disconnected right away, or you see lots of meaningless characters on your screen. Your connection settings don't match those of the remote computer. Call the other computer's operator or check the online service's manual to make sure your settings are correct.

You can see recognizable characters, but there are still some meaningless characters thrown in once in awhile. You have a noisy telephone connection. Try disconnecting and dialing again.

You're connected, but you can't see anything you type or paste into the work area. Display the Terminal Settings dialog box, click the Local Echo checkbox, then click OK.

Every character appears twice on your screen, instead of once. Display the Terminal Settings dialog box, click the Local Echo checkbox to uncheck it, then click OK.

You can't type in the work area or paste data into it. You're not connected to another computer. You can't do anything in the work area unless you're connected.

You get a low memory or out-of-memory message. Try reducing the size of the scrollback area with the *Preferences...* command. If this doesn't work, close other documents and other programs you're using. If that doesn't work, try increasing ClarisWorks' memory size or reducing your Mac's RAM cache size (see Appendix A).

P A R T

3

Advanced techniques

Spreadsheet and database functions

Functions are predefined calculations that you can use in spreadsheet and database formulas. ClarisWorks has a hundred different functions that can deliver all sorts of useful information automatically. Chapters 5 and 7 explain the mechanics of using functions in the spreadsheet and database. In this chapter, we'll learn specifically what each function does. ➤➤

311

Functions fall into eight categories:

- Financial

- Date and Time

- Information

- Logical

- Numeric

- Statistical

- Text

- Trigonometric

We'll look at each category in general with examples of how this group of functions can work in the spreadsheet and database, and then we'll follow up with brief descriptions of each function. First, though, we'll learn more about the structure of functions and how they're used in formulas.

Note: Not all functions can be used in database calculations. When a function can be used only in the spreadsheet, you'll see an icon in the margin next to the function name, like this:

$\boxed{\$}$.

About functions and arguments

Every function has a name, and most functions have one or more *arguments*, which are numbers, cell references, or other data upon which the function's calculation is made. Arguments are always enclosed in parentheses.

Using functions in formulas

To use a function in a formula, you can:

- Paste it into the formula with the *Paste Function...* command in the spreadsheet (see p. 127 in Chapter 5);

- Choose the function name from the list in the Calculation dialog box when you define the calculation field in the database (see p. 199 in Chapter 7); or

- Type the function name and argument into the spreadsheet cell or the Calculation dialog box.

You can enter function names with any combination of upper- and lowercase letters.

Some functions don't have arguments, so the parentheses after the function name are empty. Nevertheless, you must always type a set of parentheses after a function name. Here are some examples:

=SUM(number1,number2,...)

=DATE(year,month,day)

=CONCAT(text1,text2,...)

=PI()

When you paste a function or choose its name from a list, the parentheses contain abbreviations like those above to help you understand the arguments required. You have to replace the abbreviations with the real arguments (cell references, numbers, text, or other data). When you replace the abbreviations, however, the commas that separate the abbreviations must be used to separate the arguments from one another. See *Using the* Paste Function... *command* on p. 127 in Chapter 5 and *Defining calculation fields* on p. 199 in Chapter 7 for more about entering functions in the spreadsheet and database.

When there's an ellipsis (...) inside the parentheses (as in the SUM and CONCAT functions above), it means you can add more arguments. (For example, you could enter more than two arguments in the SUM formula to sum several different values.)

Some arguments are optional. These are indicated inside curly brackets ({}).

Nesting functions

You can perform more complex calculations by nesting functions in a formula. For example, if you knew a value calculated with the AVERAGE function would contain a long decimal fraction, you could round it off with the ROUND function in a formula like this:

$$=ROUND((AVERAGE(B2..E2)),2).$$

This formula tells ClarisWorks to round off the result of the AVERAGE function's calculation (the average of the values in the spreadsheet range B2..E2) to two decimal places. Lots of functions beg to be nested because they're not all that useful by themselves, as we'll see.

Formula limits

With optional arguments, nested functions, and the like, individual formulas can get to be pretty long. But no matter what, a formula can't contain more than 255 characters in all, including the function name and parentheses.

Syntax counts

When you enter a function name and arguments, it's important to enter the name exactly as it is spelled, and to follow the syntax of the argument (commas and parentheses) exactly as shown in the example. Any extra commas must be enclosed in single or double quote marks so ClarisWorks doesn't mistake them for divisions between one argument and another, for example. The syntax can get complicated in long formulas that contain several functions (each of which has its own arguments enclosed in parentheses).

When you nest functions, make sure you use the same number of parentheses on each side of the formula. If you don't, you'll get a "Bad Formula" error message when you try to enter the formula. See *Troubleshooting* at the end of this chapter.

Financial functions

Financial functions are for calculating the income and outgo of investments over periods of time. ClarisWorks has eight financial functions, and all of them require numeric values in their arguments.

Argument abbreviations

Each financial function uses special abbreviations in its argument.

fv is the future value of an investment.

nper is the number of periods in a loan payback or investment payout. This value must agree with the rate value (see below).

pmt is the amount of a loan payment.

pv is the present value of an investment.

rate is the interest rate on a loan or investment. This value must agree with the nper value—if the number of loan periods is in months (36 for a 3-year loan, for example), the rate must be a monthly rate.

type is the payback type, which determines whether a loan or investment's first payment occurs at the beginning (type 1) or end of the first period (type 0). The type argument is an optional one; if you don't enter a type value, ClarisWorks enters type 0 for you.

When you specify values in financial function arguments, positive numbers indicate cash received (income from investments or loans made to you) and negative numbers indicate cash paid out (investments or loan payments you make). Financial functions also display their results the same way: if an amount represents outgoing cash, it's displayed as a negative number.

 Use the ABS function to convert negative numbers into positive numbers in a formula's result. See p. 344.

Financial functions in the database

Most financial functions work in either the spreadsheet or the database. The nice thing about using them in the database is that you can make a new record to calculate each of several different financial scenarios.

For example, you can use the PMT function in a calculation field to calculate a loan payment, and use other fields in the record to supply the interest rate, number of periods, and loan amount for the function's argument, like this:

```
┌──────────────────── Loans (DB) ────────────────────┐
│                                                     │
│              Loan Amount   $5000.00            ⇧    │
│              Interest Rate  0.83%              ≡    │
│              No. of Payments 36                     │
│              Monthly Payment -$161.33          ⇩    │
│   100                                          ⇨    │
└─────────────────────────────────────────────────────┘
```

The Monthly Payment field here is a calculation field that contains the following formula:

=PMT('Interest Rate','No. of Payments','Loan Amount').

Once this field is defined, you simply fill in the loan amount, interest rate, and number of payments in the fields above to calculate the loan payment in this record. You can easily add new records and enter different loan amounts, interest rates, or pay-back periods to calculate payments for different loan scenarios. Once you have several different records, you can produce a columnar report that lists all the different loans for easy comparison.

Financial functions in the spreadsheet

In the spreadsheet, you can type numbers in financial function arguments, or you can use cell references instead. The advantage of using cell references, of course, is that you can recalculate the formula for different future values, present values, rates, payments, or numbers of periods by simply changing entries in the cells referred to in the formula. On the other hand, you should use numbers to specify constants that you don't expect to change.

When a function's argument contains a range of numbers, it makes more sense to make the calculation in the spreadsheet. For example, here's a formula that calculates the effect of inflation on an investment's value:

D2	× ✓	=NPV(A2,C2..C6)	
	A	**B**	**C**	**D**
1	Inflation	Cash Flows		Net Present Value
2	5.00%	Year 1	-$5000	$5163.56
3		Year 2	$1500	
4		Year 3	$2500	
5		Year 4	$3500	
6		Year 5	$4500	
7				

The formula in cell D2 uses the NPV (Net Present Value) function, and the argument refers to the range C2..C6, which contains the initial investment (-$5,000) and the income it generates over the next four years. To make this calculation in a database record, you would need individual fields named Year 1, Year 2, and so on.

Note: If you use a range of cells and any of them is empty, the formula treats the empty cell as the value 0.

Now let's look at the functions themselves.

FV(rate,nper,pmt{,pv}{,type})

FV, or Future Value, calculates the future value of an investment based on a certain interest rate (rate), a certain number of payment periods (nper), and a certain payment amount (pmt). Optional arguments are the present value (ClarisWorks assumes 0 if you don't specify one) and the type (ClarisWorks assumes type 0).

For example, to calculate the size of a retirement nest egg if you invest $200 per month at 10 percent annual interest for 10 years, the formula would be =FV((.10/12),120,200). Notice that the rate amount is specified with the expression (.10/12) so the annual interest rate (.10) is converted to a monthly rate.

Warning

Always indicate interest rates as percentages or decimal fractions. Enter *.10* or *10%* (not *10*) to indicate ten percent.

$ IRR(range{,guess})

IRR (Internal Rate of Return) calculates the interest rate you receive on an investment that's paid back over a period of time. Use this function when you know how much cash you'll receive in repayment of an investment over time, and you want to determine the rate of interest those repayments represent. The optional *guess* argument lets you enter your guess for what the rate of return will be. If you don't enter one, ClarisWorks assumes a 10 percent rate of return.

Here's an example. Suppose your Aunt Tillie left you $15,000 and you want to decide whether to invest in a chinchilla farm or buy a savings bond. In the spreadsheet, the chinchilla farm investment and the cash flows you project from it might look like this:

G2	×✓	=IRR(A2..F2)				
	A	**B**	**C**	**D**	**E**	**F**	**G**
1	Investment	Yr. 1	Yr. 2	Yr. 3	Yr. 4	Yr. 5	Return
2	-$15,000	$3,000	$4,000	$5,000	$6,000	$7,000	17.01%
3							

The initial investment is a negative number, because it's outgoing cash flow. The internal rate of return is calculated at 17.01 percent. The formula that produces this rate is shown in the text box.

IRR is an *iterative* calculation. ClarisWorks uses the *guess* interest rate and then adjusts it, recalculating each time, until the rate (when applied to the original investment) produces the series of cash flows in the range argument. If, after 20 recalculations, ClarisWorks can't produce the cash flows you've specified in the range, you'll see the #NUM! error message.

MIRR(safe,risk,values,...)

MIRR(Modified Internal Rate of Return) also calculates the overall rate of return on an investment, except it assumes you borrowed the money for the investment and you plan to reinvest the cash flows from the investment as they come in. It takes into account the rate of interest you're paying on the money you borrowed (the *risk* rate) and the rate at which you can safely reinvest the cash flows as they come in later (the *safe* rate).

For example, suppose you borrow $15,000 at 12 percent interest, and you expect to reinvest the annual cash flows from this investment at 10 percent. The spreadsheet might look like this:

12	×✓ =MIRR(A2,B2,C2..H2)							
	A	B	C	D	E	F	G	H	I
1	Safe	Risk	Invest.	Yr. 1	Yr. 2	Yr. 3	Yr. 4	Yr. 5	Return
2	10%	12%	-$15,000	$3,000	$4,000	$5,000	$6,000	$7,000	15.12%
3									

NPER(rate,pmt,pv{,fv}{,type})

NPER (Number of Periods) calculates the number of payments needed to pay off a loan (pv) at a specific interest rate (rate) with payments of a certain amount (pmt). For example, suppose you can borrow $15,000 from your Aunt Tillie at 10 percent interest, and you know you can pay her back $200 per month. To figure out the number of months it would take to repay the loan, you'd use the following formula:

=NPER(10000,(.10/12),-200).

The rate argument here is the expression *(.10/12)* to convert an annual 10 percent rate into a monthly rate, since the payments are monthly.

NPV(interest-rate,payment1,payment2,...)

NPV (Net Present Value) calculates the current value of a series of uneven future cash flows (payment1, etc.), assuming a certain rate of inflation (interest-rate). Use this function to determine whether the total value of an investment's payback will (at the end of the payback period) be more than the initial investment. This assumes that the value of money declines over time due to a certain inflation rate, and that paybacks you receive in the future are made in cheaper dollars than those in the original investment.

For an example of how this function might be used in a spreadsheet formula, see p. 317. In that example, the negative cash flow in Year 1 is the original $5,000 investment. Despite the apparently generous paybacks in years 2 through 5, you can see that even a modest inflation rate takes its toll on the total payback, so the net present value at the end of Year 5 is only slightly more than the original investment.

PMT(rate,nper,pv{,fv}{,type})

The PMT (Payment) function calculates the periodic payment on a loan of a certain amount (pv) at a certain fixed rate of interest (rate) over a certain number of periods (nper). If you don't plan to pay off the loan completely—an auto lease with a residual value, for example—you can enter the future value (fv) as an option. ClarisWorks assumes that the future value is 0 (the loan is paid back in full) if you don't enter one. See p. 316 for an example of this function at work in a database file. In the spreadsheet, it might be used like the one at the top of the next page:

B5	×✓	=ABS(PMT(B3,B4,B1))	
	A	**B**	**C**
1	Loan Amount	$15000.00	
2	Annual Rate	11.50%	
3	Monthly Rate	0.96%	
4	Term (months)	36	
5	Monthly Payment	$494.64	
6			

This formula uses the ABS function to convert the monthly payment amount from a negative to a positive number. Cell B2 shows the annual interest rate so we can see it at a glance, but since we want to calculate the monthly payment, the loan term is expressed in months (cell B4) and we need to convert the annual interest rate into a monthly rate in cell B3. Cell B3 contains the formula =B2/12. The optional arguments for future value and loan type are missing, so ClarisWorks assumes a future value of 0 and a type of 0.

PV(rate,nper,pmt{,fv}{,type})

PV (Present Value) calculates the current value of a series of even future cash flows based on a fixed rate of interest for a certain number of periods. Use this function to determine whether the payoff of an investment will keep up with a certain inflation rate when the paybacks are equal payments over a certain period of time. For example, suppose your Aunt Tillie is thinking of loaning you $10,000, to be paid back at $200 per month for five years. She wants to know if this payback scheme will preserve the value of her money, assuming a 5 percent inflation rate. The spreadsheet might look like the one at the top of the next page:

B6	×✓ =PV(B5,B3,B2)		
	A	**B**	**C**
1	Loan Amount	$10,000.00	
2	Monthly Payment	–$200.00	
3	Number of Payments	60	
4	Annual Inflation Rate	5.00%	
5	Monthly Inflation Rate	0.42%	
6	Present Value	$10,598.14	
7			

The present value formula in cell B6 shows that the initial loan will be worth slightly more at the end of the payback period. The loan value in cell B1 is just there for reference, as is the annual inflation rate amount in cell B4.

RATE(fv,pv,term)

The Rate function calculates the interest rate required to increase an initial investment (pv) to a future amount (fv) when compounded over a specific number of payments (term). The rate value produced can be monthly or yearly, depending on whether you specify a number of months or a number of years for the term. For example, suppose you have $5,000 to invest for a child's college fund, and you'd like to increase that amount to $20,000 over ten years, with interest compounded monthly. The spreadsheet might look like this:

B4	×✓ =RATE(B2,B1,B3)		
	A	**B**	**C**
1	Initial Amount	$5,000.00	
2	Future Amount	$20,000.00	
3	Number of Months	120	
4	Monthly Rate	1.16%	
5	Annual Rate	13.94%	
6			

The formula in cell B4 calculates a monthly interest rate, because the term is expressed as a number of months. The annual rate in cell B5 is there for reference; it's calculated with the formula =B4*12.

Date and Time functions

Dates and times are stored in ClarisWorks as serial numbers so it's easy to calculate them. For dates, day 0 is January 1, 1904. Each date after that is a positive number, and each date before that is a negative number. For example, May 1, 1995, is stored as 33358.

For times, 0 is 12:00:00 midnight, and a full day equals 1, so the time is represented by a decimal fraction that represents part of a day. For example, 12:00:00 noon is stored as .5.

You can combine dates and times in a single value by specifying the date number to the left of a decimal point and the time number to the right. For example, 33358.5 would equal 12:00:00 noon on May 1, 1995.

Calculating dates and times

When you calculate with dates and times, remember that later dates and times are represented by larger numbers than earlier ones. Therefore it's best to subtract an earlier date or time from a later one so you produce a positive number. For example, suppose you give your customers 30 days to pay invoices, and after that you consider the bill past due. To calculate the number of days an invoice is past due, you could create a database layout like the one at the top of the next page:

Past Due Invoices	
Customer Name	Verde Valley Ceramics
Cust. No.	V86337
Invoice Date	11/1/94
Amount	$213.50
Current Date	2/1/95

Days Past Due: 62

Here's how this layout uses dates and date calculations:

- The *Invoice Date* field's data is entered by hand, and it's formatted to show the date you see here. Internally, ClarisWorks stores this date as the serial number 33177.

- The *Current Date* field is a calculation field that's set for a Date result type. It contains the formula *=NOW()*, which reads the current date from the Mac's internal calendar. The date is displayed in the MM/DD/YY format, but it's stored as 33269.

- The *Days Past Due* field is a calculation field containing the formula, =TRUNC('Current Date'-('Invoice Date'+30)).

The Days Past Due calculation in this particular record is 33269–33207. This calculation adds 30 days to the Invoice Date field's data and then subtracts that date from the current date to arrive at the number of days past due.

The NOW function supplies both the date and the time in the Current Date field, so the Days Past Due field can contain the wrong number because of rounding. Times after noon are rounded to the next day, so if this record is viewed after noon, the Days Past Due field shows 63. To solve the rounding problem, the Days Past Due field's formula uses the TRUNC function to eliminate the decimal fraction without rounding. See *Now* on p. 329 and *Trunc* on p. 348.

Optional format arguments

Some date and time functions have an optional *format number* argument that specifies the particular date or time format. Here are the numbers and formats:

Format Number	Date Format
0	12/30/94
1	Dec 30, 1994
2	December 30, 1994
3	Fri, Dec 30, 1994
4	Friday, December 30, 1994

Format Number	Time Format
0	1:15 PM
1	1:15:30 PM
2	13:15
3	13:15:30

For both date and time formats, the default format number is 0 unless you specify otherwise.

In looking at the individual date and time functions, we'll group some of them together because they perform very similar calculations.

DATE(year,month,day)

This function lets you specify a date in YYYY/MM/DD format and then converts it to the corresponding serial number. You can use cell or field references to supply the arguments for this function. For example, if you had three fields in the database named Year, Month, and Day, you could combine this information and produce a date serial number with a calculation field containing the formula =DATE('Year','Month','Day').

When you use numbers for each argument, the year can be any number between 0 and 29941. If you enter only two digits for the year (91, say), ClarisWorks assumes you mean the year 0091. Month numbers must be between 1 and 12.

You can also use expressions for each argument to increase dates by a certain number, as with *DATE(('Year'+1),'Month','Day')*.

DATETOTEXT(serial-number{,format-number})

TIMETOTEXT(serial-number{,format-number})

These functions convert a date or time serial number into a formatted date or time and change the data type to text. For example:

Formula	Result
=DATETOTEXT(33258)	1/21/95
=TIMETOTEXT(.678)	4:16 PM

The optional format argument lets you specify the date or time format by entering a number, as explained in the previous section.

Once you convert a date or time to text information, you can use it as part of a text string in a text calculation. For example, suppose you want to send a notice about a past-due invoice. Using text operators and the DATETOTEXT function, you could create a database calculation field that produces a line in a form letter like this:

```
Dear Valued Customer:

Your invoice dated November 1, 1994 is 52 days past due.
```

Here the date and number of days past due are merged, or *concatenated*, into the text sentence, and the entire sentence is a calculation field. Here's the formula for this field:

="Your invoice dated "&DATETOTEXT('Invoice Date',2)&" is "&NUMTOTEXT('Days Past Due')&" days past due."

The DATETOTEXT function takes the date from the Invoice Date field in the database and converts it to text with format number 2 to produce the "November 1, 1994" you see in the sentence. For more information about using text calculations to create sentences like this, see *Text functions* on p. 354.

DAY(serial-number)

WEEKDAY(serial-number)

MONTH(serial-number)

YEAR(serial-number)

These four functions convert a date's serial number into the day, weekday, month, or year number from that date. For example, for day number 33258 (January 21, 1995), this is what you'd get with each formula:

Formula	Result
=DAY(33258)	21
=WEEKDAY(33258)	7
=MONTH(33258)	1
=YEAR(33258)	1995

DAYNAME(number)

MONTHNAME(number)

The DAYNAME and MONTHNAME functions convert a number into a day's or month's name. Days of the week are numbered 1 through 7, where 1 equals Sunday; months are numbered 1 through 12. For example:

Formula	Result
=Dayname(5)	Thursday
=Monthname(5)	May

DAYOFYEAR(serial-number)

WEEKOFYEAR(serial-number)

The DAYOFYEAR function converts a date's serial number into a number between 1 and 365. The WEEKOFYEAR function converts a serial number into a number between 1 and 52. For example:

Formula	Result
=DAYOFYEAR(33705)	103
=WEEKOFYEAR(33705)	15

HOUR(serial-number)

MINUTE(serial-number)

SECOND(serial-number)

These functions display the hour, minute, or second indicated by the serial number in the argument. Hour values returned can be from 0 to 23; minute and second values returned can be from 0 to 59. For example, the number .678 represents the time 16:16:19, so with this value in their arguments, these formulas would produce the following results:

Formula	Result
=HOUR(.678)	16
=MINUTE(.678)	16
=SECOND(.678)	19

NOW()

The Now function has no argument. It simply reads the current date and time from your Mac's internal clock/calendar and displays its value. Instead of the date/time value, you can display a formatted date or time if you choose a date or time format for the cell or the calculation field's result. See p. 143 in Chapter 5 or p. 220 in Chapter 7 for more on formatting.

When you use the NOW function in a larger calculation, make sure you don't get the wrong result due to rounding. For example, the formula =ROUND(NOW(),0) will be rounded up to the next day if this calculation is made after noon.

TEXTTODATE(date-text)

TEXTTOTIME(time-text)

These two functions convert dates or times expressed as text into date or time serial numbers. For example:

Formula	Result
=TEXTTODATE(1/21/95)	33258
=TEXTTOTIME(4:16 PM)	.678

The date or time text supplied in the argument can be in any of the formats supported by ClarisWorks. For times, seconds are optional and you can use AM and PM designations if you like. Dates can have month names spelled out, or they can be in MM/DD/YY format. See p. 325 for date and time format options.

TIME(hour,minute,second)

This function returns a serial number that represents the time of day indicated by the three values specified in its arguments. For example, =TIME(12,0,0) returns .5.

. . . .

Information functions

Information functions search for values, produce messages or beeps, and perform other general data-manipulation tasks. Most of the arguments specify *values*, which can be a number, a cell reference, or a logical number or expression.

Some of these functions are grouped together because they perform similar tasks.

$ ALERT(value)

This function displays the argument's value in an alert box on your screen. In most cases, you'll use this function as part of a larger formula so that an alert is displayed when certain conditions exist in your spreadsheet. To guard against keyboard errors in a payroll file, for example, you might display a warning if someone enters a value in the wrong range in a particular spreadsheet cell. The formula might read =IF(C32>500,ALERT("Check FICA amount!"),"").

In this case, the spreadsheet displays an alert that says "Check FICA amount!" whenever an amount greater than 500 is entered in cell C32. If the amount is less than 500, the cell containing this formula is left empty. See *Logical functions* on p. 337 for more about using the IF function to have ClarisWorks make decisions like this.

BEEP()

The BEEP function just makes your Mac beep. As with the ALERT function, you use this as part of a larger formula to produce a beep sound under certain conditions.

CHOOSE(index,value1,value2,...)

The CHOOSE function displays one of the value arguments, depending on the number in the index argument. The index argument specifies which of the values to display. For example,

=CHOOSE(1,B4,B5,B6) would return the value in cell B4, because it's the first value in the group and the index number is 1. If the index number were 2, the formula would return the value in cell B5.

$ COLUMN({cell})

$ ROW({cell})

These functions return the column or row number of the cell where the function is used, or, optionally, of the cell reference in the argument. For example, if the formula =ROW() is used in cell A24, the cell will display the number 24. If the formula =COLUMN(G32) is used in any cell, it displays the letter G.

ERROR()

The ERROR Function displays *#ERROR!* in the cell where it's used. Typically, you use this function as part of a larger formula to display the error message if a certain logical condition is met. For example, the formula =IF(B4>500,ERROR(),"OK") in cell B6 would display the error message in cell B6 whenever cell B4 contains a value higher than 500. If the value in cell B4 is less than 500, cell B6 displays the text *OK*.

$ HLOOKUP(lookup-value,compare-range,index{,method})

$ LOOKUP(lookup-value,compare-range,result-range{,method})

$ VLOOKUP(lookup-value,compare-range,index{,method})

Lookup functions all return a certain value from a range of spreadsheet cells based on the position of another value in that same range. The range is a group of cells containing more than one row and column, like the one at the top of the next page:

	A	B	C	D	E
1	Product	Cost	Price	Markup	
2	Squegeez	$5.00	$9.00	$4.00	
3	Foamit	$6.00	$10.80	$4.80	
4	Solderall	$7.00	$12.60	$5.60	
5	Grabomatic	$8.00	$14.40	$6.40	
6	Musclebind	$9.00	$16.20	$7.20	
7	Maxwrench	$10.00	$18.00	$8.00	
8					
9					

Use one of these lookup functions when you have values stored in a spreadsheet and you want to be able to select one of them based on the position of another one. In these functions:

- The *lookup-value* is a number or text you want to search for.

- The *compare-range* is the range of cells you want searched.

- The *index* tells ClarisWorks where to find the value you want returned. It tells ClarisWorks how many rows down or columns over to move to select the value you want.

- The *method* is an optional argument that tells ClarisWorks how to search for the lookup value. When the values in your compare-range row or column are in ascending order, method 1 finds the first number less than or equal to the lookup value. When values in your row or column are in descending order, method -1 finds the first number that is greater than or equal to the lookup value. If the values in your range aren't in any particular order, method 0 looks for an exact match to the lookup value.

There are three different lookup functions to give you flexibility about how a range is searched and which value is returned. Let's look at some examples.

The HLOOKUP function tells ClarisWorks to search across the top row of the *compare-range* you specify, searching for the *lookup-value,* and then returning the value from the same column in one of the rows below it, depending on the index number you specify. In the product table on the previous page, for example, =HLOOKUP(9,B2..C7,1,0) would return the value $10.80. This formula looks for the value 9 in the top row of the range (row 2) and then returns the number from the same column one row below, because the index number in the formula is 1. The method argument here is 0 because the values in row 2 aren't in ascending or descending order, so we need ClarisWorks to find an exact match.

The VLOOKUP function tells ClarisWorks to search down the left-most column of the *compare-range* you specify, searching for the *lookup-value* and then returning the value from the same row in a column to the right, depending on the *index-value* you specify. For example, to return the markup amount for the Musclebind wrench from the sample worksheet on p. 314, you'd use the formula =VLOOKUP("Musclebind",A1..D7,3,0). This formula looks for the value "Musclebind" in the left-most column of the range (column A) and then returns the value from the same row, three columns to the right, because the index value is 3. The method argument is also 0 because we're searching for an exact match for our lookup value. Notice that the lookup-value is text here.

The LOOKUP function uses a *result-range* argument instead of an index number. It finds the lookup value and then returns a value in the corresponding position from the result-range. For example, suppose you had a bean-counting contest and the guesses and corresponding ticket numbers were stored in adjacent groups of cells, like the one at the top of the next page:

	A	B	C	D	E	F
1	Guesses			Ticket Number		
2	1000	1025	1090	100	101	102
3	1099	1100	1105	103	104	105
4	1151	1190	1201	106	107	108
5	1251	1320	1330	109	110	111
6	1385	1400	1425	112	113	114
7	1450	1500	2000	115	116	117
8						
9	Actual Count	1410				
10	Winning Ticket	113				

To find the winning ticket, the formula in cell B10 is
=LOOKUP(B9,A2..C7,D2..F7). This tells ClarisWorks to look in
the compare range A2..C7 for the lookup value in cell B9 (1410,
the actual bean count). ClarisWorks finds the highest number less
than or equal to 1410 (which is 1400, in cell B6) and then returns
the value from the corresponding position in the range D2..F7.
Since cell B6 is the middle column of the fifth row of the compare
range, ClarisWorks returns the value from the middle column of
the fifth row in the result range, or 113.

The LOOKUP function is preset to scan across the rows in the
compare-range, moving from left to right and from top to
bottom. Because the values in this table are in ascending order
from left to right and top to bottom, it wasn't necessary to include
a *method* argument. However, we could have used a -1 method
value if the values had been in descending order (to find the
lowest number greater than or equal to the lookup value), or a 0
method value (to find an exact match if the values weren't in any
order at all).

$\boxed{\$}$ INDEX(range,row,column)

The INDEX function is like the index value supplied in a lookup function's argument (see *LOOKUP* above). It tells ClarisWorks which value to return, based on the range of cells and the row and column position of the value within that range.

	A	B	C	D
1		Small	Med.	Large
2	Widgets	33	324	249
3	Gizmos	45	200	125
4	Whatnots	150	75	10
5	Whozits	35	4	89

For example, in the above spreadsheet, the formula =INDEX(B2..D5,3,2) would return the value 75, the value from the cell in the third row and the second column of the range.

MACRO(text)

The MACRO function executes the macro whose name appears in the argument. The macro name must be entered in quotation marks. For example, =MACRO("Make Chart") would play the macro named Make Chart.

Macros can automate any ClarisWorks operation. In the spreadsheet, you can use the MACRO function to automatically select, copy, or chart certain ranges of data. In the database, you can use the MACRO function in a calculation field to select and copy data in another field, switch layouts, perform a Find operation, or open other files and copy data from them. The possibilities are staggering. See Chapter 13 for information on how to create macros.

$ MATCH(lookup-value,compare-range{,type})

The MATCH function returns the position of the lookup value within the compare range specified. The optional type argument specifies whether the values in the range are in ascending order (type 1, the default), in descending order (type -1), or in no particular order (type 0).

	A	B	C	D
1		Small	Med.	Large
2	Widgets	33	324	249
3	Gizmos	45	200	125
4	Whatnots	150	75	10
5	Whozits	35	4	89

For example, the formula =MATCH(200,B2..D5,0) returns 5, because the value 200 is the fifth value in the compare range. ClarisWorks searches the compare range from left to right and then from top to bottom: cell C3 (which contains the value 200) is the fifth cell in the search. We use the 0 type argument here because the values aren't in ascending or descending order.

$ NA()

Like the ERROR function, the NA function tells the spreadsheet to display an error message, in this case, *#NA!*. Use this function as part of a larger formula to display the #NA! message when a certain condition isn't met. For example, the formula =IF(ISBLANK(B4),NA(),B4) displays the #NA! error message if cell B4 is blank; otherwise it displays the contents of cell B4.

TYPE(value)

The TYPE function returns a number from 1 to 4, indicating the type of data in its argument.

- Type 1 means the cell is blank.

- Type 2 means the cell contains logical data (TRUE, FALSE, etc.).

- Type 3 means the cell contains a number.

- Type 4 means the cell contains text.

Typically, you'll use a cell reference or field name in the argument. Fields or cells that contain dates and times are identified as type 3, since dates and times are stored as numbers.

The words TRUE and FALSE are identified as logical data only if they're entered by themselves, in all capital letters, in a cell or field. You can type them this way or have a logical function insert them automatically. If you type *"TRUE,"* 'TRUE,' or *True,* for example, the data is treated as text.

Logical functions

With logical functions, you can create formulas that make decisions based on logical comparisons of two or more variables. The basic decision-making function is IF, and the other functions qualify the IF function's decision or the data being evaluated.

The IF function makes decisions based on Boolean logic (named after George Boole, the nineteenth-century English mathematician who dreamed it up). Boolean logic uses comparison operators such as = (equal) or > (greater than) to evaluate expressions as true or false. For example, *5=4* is false, while *(3+2)>4* is true. Boolean logic can also evaluate individual numbers: any nonzero number is true, while zero is false.

Along with mathematical expressions, however, Boolean logic can also be used to evaluate text, date, numeric, or even financial expressions when you combine the IF function with other functions in the same formula. For example, you could use the IF and ALERT functions together to see whether a spreadsheet cell or database field contains a certain value, and then produce an alert dialog box if it doesn't. (See *ALERT()* on p. 330.) We'll see examples of how you can evaluate text strings with logical functions in the *Text Functions* section that begins on p. 354.

For now, let's look at the logical functions by themselves. Since the IF function is the key to this whole situation, we'll look at it first.

IF(logical,true-value,false-value)

The IF function evaluates a *logical* argument and then returns one of two different results (the *true-value* or the *false-value*), depending on whether the logical argument proves true or false. This function is incredibly powerful and has millions of uses. Here are a couple of simple examples.

C2	×✓	=IF(B2>60000,2000,1000)	
	A	**B**	**C**	**D**
1	**Name**	**Sales**	**Bonus**	
2	Brown	54200	1000	
3	Jones	35235	1000	
4	Smith	79400	2000	
5	Wong	66950	2000	

Suppose you want to pay a $1,000 bonus to employees whose total sales are $60,000 or less and a $2,000 bonus to employees whose sales are more than $60,000. The spreadsheet above determines the amount of each person's bonus, depending on the volume of his or her sales. The formula in cell C2 is shown in the text box. The logical argument B2>60000 evaluates whether the number in cell B2 is greater than 60,000 and then returns either the *true-value* 2000 or the *false-value* 1000, accordingly.

Note: There aren't any comma separators in the argument values (such as "60,000" or "2,000"), because ClarisWorks treats commas as argument separators. Inserting commas in these numbers would cause a Bad Formula message. (See *Troubleshooting* on p. 366.)

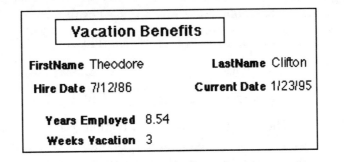

This database layout automatically assigns three weeks of vacation to employees with five years or more employment, and gives two weeks of vacation to those with less than five years. The Weeks Vacation field is a calculation field containing the formula =IF('Years Employed'>=5,3,2). The IF function looks at the value in the Years Employed field, and if the value is greater than or equal to 5, it returns 3. Otherwise, it returns 2.

The Years Employed field is a calculation field that subtracts the Hire Date from the Current Date and converts the number of days to years with the formula =('Current Date'-'Hire Date')/365.

AND(logical1,logical2,...)

OR(logical1,logical2,...)

The AND and OR functions allow you to evaluate more than one logical argument at a time.

- The AND function evaluates two or more logical expressions and returns TRUE if they're all true and FALSE if any of them proves false.

- The OR function evaluates two or more logical expressions and returns TRUE if any of them proves true, and FALSE only if they all prove false. At the top of the next page, for example:

Formula	Result
=AND(5+1=6, 2+2=4)	TRUE
=AND(5+1=6, 2+2=5)	FALSE
=OR(5+1=6, 2+2=5)	TRUE

The real purpose of these functions is to extend an IF formula so that it can evaluate more than one logical argument. By itself, the IF function's argument allows only one logical condition, but when you use the AND or OR function in place of the *logical* argument in an IF formula, you tell the IF function to evaluate more than one logical condition.

For example, suppose you wanted to grant a $2,000 bonus only to workers whose sales were greater than $60,000 and whose expenses were less than $3,000. A spreadsheet might look like this:

D5	×✓	=IF(AND(B5>60000,C5<3000),2000,1000)		
	A	**B**	**C**	**D**	**E**
1	Name	Sales	Expenses	Bonus	
2	Brown	54200	2200	1000	
3	Jones	35235	1500	1000	
4	Smith	79400	3250	1000	
5	Wong	66950	2875	2000	
6					

The logical formula in cells D2 through D5 is as shown in the text box. As you can see, only salesperson Wong's numbers satisfy both conditions of the formula, so Wong is the only person to receive a larger bonus. On the other hand, if the AND function above was replaced by the OR function with the same logical arguments, then every employee would receive the higher bonus, because everybody has either expenses below $3000 or sales higher than $60,000.

ISBLANK(value)

The ISBLANK function determines whether the argument's value (usually a cell reference or field name) is blank. It returns FALSE if the cell or field contains a number or text, and TRUE if the cell or field is empty. In order to return a FALSE result, the cell or field must be completely empty; if it contains a zero, that's counted as a number, so the function returns TRUE.

By combining this function with the IF function, you can check for a blank cell or database field. For example, suppose you want to make sure the State field in your employee database is always filled in when new records are created. You might create a layout like this:

FirstName	Evelyn
LastName	Crabtree
Street	345 Sutter St.
City	Daly City
State	
Zip	94022
Phone	415-555-2273

Fill in State information!

Here the message in the box at the bottom is supplied by a calculation field containing the following formula:

=IF(ISBLANK('State'),"Fill in State information!","")

The text appears because the logical condition is true (the State field is blank). If the State field wasn't blank, the box would be empty, because there's no text between the quote marks in the false-value argument of the formula. (See *Text functions* on p. 354 for more on using text strings in formulas.)

ISERROR(value{,error-type})

This function determines whether an error has occurred in a particular cell or database calculation field. It returns a TRUE if there is an error and FALSE if not. By using the optional *error-type* argument, you can have this function display one of ClarisWorks' built-in calculation error messages. You can use any built-in error message for the error-type argument except #PRECISION! and ##### (see *Calculation error messages* on p. 367).

You'll probably combine this function with the IF function in a formula that takes a specific action if an error exists. In a large spreadsheet, for example, there might be a calculation error in a distant cell that you don't normally view on your screen. Claris-Works will display an error message in the cell itself, but if you seldom view that area of the spreadsheet you may not discover the problem. Instead, you could use the IF and ISERROR functions to display a message someplace else in the spreadsheet where you're more likely to see it, like this:

A1	×✓	=IF(ISERROR(AH177),"Check Expense Values!","")		
	A	**B**	**C**	**D**
1	**Check Expense Values!**			
2				
3	**Grand Summary**	**Jan**	**Feb**	**Mar**

Here, the formula in cell A1 displays the message because it uses the ISERROR and IF functions to check for error messages in cell AH177.

ISLOGICAL(value)

This function determines whether the expression in the argument is a true (or valid) Boolean expression. For example:

Formula	Result
=ISLOGICAL(2+2=4)	TRUE
=ISLOGICAL(2+2=5)	FALSE

Use this function to check for the presence of logical errors, much as you'd use the ISERROR or ISNA function to check for error messages or the #NA! message in a database field or spreadsheet cell. See the example under *ISERROR* above.

$ ISNA(value)

The ISNA function looks specifically for the #NA! error message in a spreadsheet cell and returns TRUE if it finds it. Use this function like the ISERROR function. See p. 341.

ISNUMBER(value)

ISTEXT(value)

These functions determine whether a spreadsheet cell or database field contains a number (ISNUMBER) or text (ISTEXT), and return TRUE if they do. You can use one of these functions to have ClarisWorks determine whether the proper type of information has been entered in a cell or field, and then display a message if not. For example:

A1	× ✓	=IF(ISTEXT(AH177!),"Number required in AH177!","")			
	A	**B**	**C**	**D**	**E**
1	Number required in AH177!				
2					
3	Grand Summary	Jan	Feb	Mar	Apr

This function (combined with the IF function) is also handy for displaying text messages when the proper type of data isn't entered in database fields.

Error messages aren't evaluated as text or numbers by the ISNUMBER and ISTEXT functions. If the cell or field being checked contains an error message, ClarisWorks returns the #ARG! error message.

NOT(logical)

This function inverts the sense of the logical expression in its argument, changing a true expression to a false one, and vice versa. For example, =NOT(5+3=8) returns FALSE, because 5+3=8 is a true Boolean expression.

You can use this function to reverse the sense of a logical test when you use the IF function or other logical functions. For example:

=IF(NOT(B2>60000),1000,2000).

However, in most cases, you can duplicate the action of the NOT function by reversing the *true-value* and *false-value* arguments in an IF formula, or by using a different logical operator. For example, compare the formula above with the one on p. 338. Both formulas produce the same result (awarding a $2000 bonus to employees with sales over $60,000). Switching the logical operator also does the trick. For example:

=(NOT(B2>60000) returns the same result as =B2≤60000.

Numeric functions

Numeric functions perform standard mathematical calculations on numbers. Arguments for these functions must either be numbers, references to cells or fields that contain numbers, or mathematical expressions that evaluate to numbers.

ABS(number)

The ABS (Absolute Value) function returns the non-negative version of its argument. This function is useful when a calculation produces a negative result but you want to view it as positive. For example, =ABS(-$453.05) returns $453.05.

All of ClarisWorks' financial functions show outgoing cash flows as negative numbers, so you can use the ABS function to convert the result into a positive number, as shown on p. 321.

FACT(number)

The FACT (Factorial) function calculates the factorial of a number, which is the number multiplied by every other number between itself and zero. For example, =FACT(6) returns 720, because the factorial of 6 is 6*5*4*3*2*1.

FRAC(number)

The FRAC (Fraction) function returns only the decimal fraction portion of a number. For example:

Formula	Result
=FRAC(3.14159)	0.14159
=FRAC(-357.7896)	0.7896

This function always produces a positive fraction as a result, even if the original number is negative.

INT(number)

The INT (Integer) function returns the integer (or whole number) portion of a number, eliminating any decimal fraction. If the argument is a positive number, INT eliminates the fraction. If the argument is a negative number, INT rounds it down, no matter what the fraction is. For example:

Formula	Result
=INT(45.9897)	45
=INT(-45.372)	-46

MOD(number,divisor-number)

The MOD (Modulo) function returns the remainder of the *number* argument after dividing it by the *divisor-number* argument. For example, =MOD(8,3) returns 2, because when 8 is divided by 3 the remainder is 2.

C2	×✓	=MOD(A2,B2)		
	A	B	C	D
1	Floor size	Tiles per box	Tiles left	
2	260	50	10	
3				

In the example above, the MOD function calculates the number of floor tiles remaining to complete a floor. Knowing this, you might decide to buy the tiles individually rather than buying a whole extra box.

RAND({number})

The RAND (Random) function randomly generates a decimal fraction between 0 and 1. Use this function when you want Claris-Works to pick a number at random. When you include a number in the optional argument, RAND produces only whole numbers between 0 and the number in the argument.

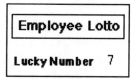

Employee Lotto

Lucky Number   7

In this database layout, for example, the Lucky Number field contains the formula =RAND(15). Each time you create a new record, ClarisWorks randomly calculates a whole number between 0 and 15 in this field. If you want ClarisWorks to return a decimal fraction greater than 1, multiply the RAND function's result by another number. For example, =RAND()*15 might return 8.7185.

ROUND(number,num-digits)

The ROUND function rounds off its *number* argument to the number of digits in its *num-digits* argument. You can use positive or negative values for the *num-digits* argument. Negative *num-digits* arguments round off numbers to the left of a decimal point. For example:

Formula	Result
=ROUND(453.7864152,2)	453.79
=ROUND(453.78493,2)	453.78
=ROUND(453.7864162,0)	454
=ROUND(453.7864152,-1)	450
=ROUND(453.7864152,-2)	500

SIGN(number)

This function returns a number to indicate whether the number in its argument is positive or negative. It returns 1 if the number is positive, 0 if the number is 0, and -1 if the number is negative. You might use this function to evaluate a spreadsheet cell or database field and report on the sign of the number it contains, and then do something with that information. For example, in a corporate budget spreadsheet the SIGN function could be used along with the IF and ALERT functions to display a message if a certain cell that reports cash flow dips below zero, like this:

=IF(SIGN(C32)=-1,ALERT("Cash flow headed south!"),"").

However, you could eliminate the SIGN function from this formula by simply using the <, >, ≤, or ≥ operator. For example:

=IF(C32≤0,ALERT("Cash flow headed south!"),"").

SQRT(number)

The SQRT (Square Root) function calculates the square root of the number in its argument. The argument must be a positive number. For example, =SQRT(81) returns 9, but =SQRT(-81) returns the message #NUM!, because you can't calculate the square root of a negative number.

TRUNC(number)

The TRUNC (Truncate) function removes the fractional part of a number, leaving just the integer. Unlike the INT and ROUND functions, however, TRUNC doesn't round the integer up or down; it just chops off everything to the right of the decimal point. For example:

Formula	Result
=TRUNC(459.64282)	459
=TRUNC(-85.2685)	-85

. . . .

Statistical functions

Statistical functions can be used in the spreadsheet or database to characterize or evaluate groups of numbers. All of these functions can calculate more than one argument. Numeric arguments can be a number, expression, range, or individual cell or field reference.

AVERAGE(number1,number2,...)

This function calculates the average of the values in its arguments. In a budget spreadsheet, for example, you might specify a range of cells in the argument to calculate the average monthly cost in an expense category, like this:

O2	× ✓	=AVERAGE(B2..M2)		
	A	**M**	**N**	**O**	**P**
1	Expenses	December	Total	Average	
2	Salaries	$11300.00	$137800.00	$11483.33	
3	Benefits	2000	37650	$3137.50	
4	Materials	300	25350	$2112.50	

Here the range B2..M2 in the formula contains salary expense values for the months January through December.

In the database you could use the AVERAGE function to produce an average of values in a summary field. For example, in a salary report you could calculate the average salary with the formula =AVERAGE('SALARY') and then insert that field in a summary part to produce the calculation.

 When you specify a range of cells and any of the cells in the range is blank or contains text, ClarisWorks supplies a value of 0 for that cell when determining the average.

COUNT(value1,value2,...)

The COUNT function counts the number of values in the arguments you specify. Arguments can be text strings, numbers, cell or field references, ranges, or expressions. For example, you could use this function to quickly determine the number of cells in a spreadsheet range, like this:

B13	×	✓	=COUNT(A2..A10)
	A	**B**	**C**
8	Utilities	225	230
9	Insurance	200	200
10	Telephone	550	575
11			
12	**Total**	28175	30905
13	**Categories**	9	

Here the formula in cell B13 counts the cells in the range that contains all the expense category labels, so it reports the number of expense categories. When you specify a range in the argument, COUNT includes every cell in the range, empty or not.

In the database, you could use COUNT in a summary field to display the number of employees in a corporate salary report, like the one at the top of the next page:

```
┌─────────────────────────────────────────────────────────────┐
│ Acme Manufacturing Salary Report - 5/5/95 - Page 2           │
│                                                               │
│ Last Name      First Name      Department              Salary │
│ Nicholson,     Janice          Marketing          $19,000.00  │
│                                                               │
│ Robertson,     Maxine          Marketing          $40,000.00  │
│                                                               │
│                               Marketing Total    $169,000.00  │
│                                                               │
│            Total Employees    27    Grand Total  $687,000.00  │
└─────────────────────────────────────────────────────────────┘
```

Here the Total Employees field is a summary field that contains the formula =COUNT('Last Name'). This formula is in the Grand Summary part of this layout. Since the Last Name field in each record is filled in and there's a record for each employee, the Total Employees field accurately reports the total number of employees in the company.

> *Tip*
>
> When you use COUNT in the database, ClarisWorks only counts fields that contain data, so you can use it to report how many records have that field filled in. For example, in a database of student test results, you could count the Last Name field and the Grade field separately and then compare them to see how many students took the test: every record would have the Last Name field filled in, but only records for students who took the test would have the Grade field filled in.

COUNT2(search-value,value1,...)

The COUNT2 function counts the number of occurrences of the *search-value* argument in the other arguments. Use this function when you want to count the number of times a specific value occurs in a particular range of cells or in a database field. For example, if you wanted to count the number of months during a year in which you spent exactly $25 in the Phone category of your budget, and the Phone expense cells were in the range B4..M4, the formula would be =COUNT2(25,B4..M4). ClarisWorks would search those cells for the value 25 and would return the number of times that value occurred.

MAX(number1,number2,...)

MIN(number1,number2,...)

The MAX (Maximum) and MIN (Minimum) functions return the maximum and minimum values from their arguments. For each function, you can supply several numbers, cell or field references, or expressions and have ClarisWorks find the lowest value.

P2	×|✓	=MIN(B2..M2)		
	M	**N**	**O**	**P**	**Q**
	December	Total	Average	Lowest	Highest
1	December	Total	Average	Lowest	Highest
2	$11300.00	$137800.00	$11483.33	10200	12400
3	2000	37650	$3137.50	2000	4850

In the above example, the Lowest and Highest columns show the minimum and maximum monthly expense values from columns B through M. The MIN formula for cell P2 is shown in the text box.

In the database, you could use MIN or MAX in a summary field calculation to show the lowest or highest salary in a summary part of a salary report layout, or show the lowest or highest quantity in an inventory report, for example.

PRODUCT(number1,number2,...)

The PRODUCT function returns the product of all its arguments, which means it multiplies all the arguments and returns the total. For example, =PRODUCT(35,2,3) equals 35*2*3, or 210.

You can accomplish the same thing by simply multiplying the arguments without the PRODUCT function. For example, to find the product of cells B2, B3, and B4, you could enter =(B2*B3*B4). When you want to multiply lots of values, however, the PRODUCT function is faster because you can specify a range in its argument: instead of =B2*B3*B4*B5, you could enter =PRODUCT(B2..B5).

STDEV(number1,number2,...)

The STDEV (Standard Deviation) function calculates the average amount by which a group of values diverges from the group's arithmetic mean, or average. Use this function when you want to know the typical variance of a group of numbers from the average.

Customer Name	Cust. No.	Amount	Days Late
Arlon Sheetrock	AS008	1253.07	8
Intermountain	IP023	441.95	56
Jonas Paving	JP001	353.07	45
Lough Associates	LA033	650	73
New Moon	NM012	1475.6	51
Sicard Heating &	SH007	37.5	56
Verde Valley	VV024	213.5	56

Avg. Age 49   **Age Variance** 20

In this database layout from an invoicing file, for example, the Avg. Age field in the summary part at the bottom calculates the average of the Days Late field. The Age Variance field calculates the standard deviation from this average. By the standard deviation, we know that invoices less than 29 days late (49-20) or more than 69 days late (49+20) are outside the standard deviation range.

Tip This is a very limited presentation of the standard deviation concept. To learn more, consult a statistics textbook.

SUM(number1,number2,...)

The trusty SUM function is the workhorse of every spreadsheet and of many database reports. It sums the values in its argument, and the values can be numbers, cell or field references, or ranges. In the spreadsheet, you can use SUM to add up the values in a column or row of spreadsheet cells to produce category totals or monthly totals in a budget, like the one at the top of the next page:

N2	× ✓	=SUM(B2..M2)		
	K	**L**	**M**	**N**
1	October	November	December	Total
2	$11300.00	$11300.00	$11300.00	$137800.00
3	2000	2000	2000	37650

The SUM formula in cell N2 adds up the values in cells B2 through M2 to produce a total for the expenses in this row.

In the database, use SUM in summary fields to produce totals in summary parts of reports, like this:

Manufacturing	$21,000.00
Administrative	$28,000.00
Administrative	$21,000.00
Grand Total	$687,000.00

Here the Grand Total field is a summary field that sums all the salary fields with the formula =SUM('Grand Total').

When you use SUM or other statistical functions (such as COUNT and AVERAGE) that operate on multiple values in the database, you must use them in a summary field to calculate values from more than one record. If you use SUM in a calculation field, it sums only values from one record at a time.

VAR(number1,number2,...)

The VAR (Variance) function calculates the variance of a population, based on sample numbers from that population that are supplied in its arguments. For example, =VAR(32,45,67,21) returns 390.91.

A population's variance has a specific statistical meaning, an explanation of which is beyond the scope of this book. For more information, consult a statistics textbook.

Text functions

Text functions let you manipulate or evaluate strings of text in various ways. Using these functions, you can determine the length, position, or case of text in a spreadsheet cell or database field; you can combine strings of text with text results from other functions; and you can search for, replace, or convert text. When a function argument calls for text, you can type text directly in the formula (following the right rules—see below), or you can use a cell or database field reference, as long as the cell or field referred to contains text.

Using text in calculations

Before we get into the functions, let's go over the rules for using text in calculation formulas. Like other functions, text functions have arguments inside parentheses, and when there are multiple arguments, each one is separated by a comma. Since most text function arguments consist of text instead of numbers, however, you must differentiate strings of text from function or field names. To do this, you must:

- Enter text strings enclosed in double quote marks ("");

- Enter field names enclosed in single quote marks (''); and

- Enter function names without any quote marks around them.

To enter text that itself contains quotation marks, you have to add an extra set of them. For example, suppose you want a field to display the quotation, "To err is human, to forgive divine." In this case, you would type, ""To err is human, to forgive divine.""

Also, be careful about apostrophes, commas, and spaces. Any of these enclosed inside the double-quote marks that mark the beginning and end of a text string are treated as text. For example, the CONCAT function's argument format is (text1,text2), so to join two text strings with the CONCAT function, you would type

=CONCAT("I'm joining this text"," with this text.")

Notice that the comma separating the two arguments is outside the double-quote that ends the first text string. If it were inside the double-quote mark, the comma would be treated as text and the formula would be invalid, because there would be no comma separating the two arguments. (The function requires two arguments, and without the comma it would look like there was only one.)

Also, notice the space before *with* at the beginning of the second argument. We want the words *text* and *with* to have a space between them, so we must include that space in one of the two text strings.

ClarisWorks can't wrap text in calculation fields, so even if you create a calculation field that's several lines high, text inside that field can only be one line high. Any text that doesn't fit on one line is chopped off.

CHAR(number)

The CHAR (Character) function returns the alphanumeric character that corresponds to the ASCII code number in its argument. Each uppercase and lowercase letter and symbol on your keyboard has its own ASCII code number. (ASCII stands for American Standard Code for Information Interchange, by the way.) If you know the ASCII code number for the character you want to produce, you can make ClarisWorks display it with this function. ASCII codes are all whole numbers, so if you enter the code number with a decimal fraction, the fraction is ignored. So, for example, =CHAR(72) returns H, because 72 is the ASCII code for H (capital H); but =CHAR(72.456) also returns H.

CODE(text)

The CODE function is the opposite of the CHAR function: it returns the ASCII code number for the first character in its argument. Use this function to find out the ASCII code of any character. For example, =CODE("m") returns 109; and =CODE("M") returns 77.

Since this argument requires text, the text has been entered inside double quote marks. Without the quote marks, you'd get a Bad Formula message. The argument for the CODE function can contain more than one character, but the function only returns the code number for the first character in the argument.

CONCAT(text1,text2,...)

The CONCAT (Concatenate) function joins two strings of text together. ("Concatenate" is a fancy word for "join.") We saw an example of this function at work on p. 337. Actually, however, you can concatenate two strings of text by simply placing the & operator between them. For example, =CONCAT("Join this text"," with this text.") produces the same result as ="Join this text"&" with this text.").

EXACT(text1,text2)

The EXACT function compares two text strings and returns TRUE if they're the same and FALSE if they're not. The EXACT function won't return a TRUE value unless the two strings in its argument are precisely the same, with the same letters, spaces, capitalization, and punctuation. For example, =EXACT("The same","THE SAME") returns FALSE, while =EXACT("The same","The same") returns TRUE.

Typically you'll use this function with the IF function to compare two text strings and then take different actions depending on the result.

C3	×✓	=IF(EXACT(B3,B4),"","Wrong text in B4!")		
	B	**C**	**D**	**E**
3	Widget	Wrong text in B4!		
4	widget			
5				

Here, for example, the EXACT function is used in an IF formula to test for correct capitalization and display an error message if the two strings don't match.

FIND(find-text,in-text{,start-offset})

The FIND function locates a particular string of text (the *find-text*) within a larger string (the *in-text*) and returns the position number of the first character of the found string. If the *find-text* string isn't found, the function returns 0. This function is case-sensitive, and spaces count when the position is determined. For example, =FIND("Dog","Hound Dog Blues") returns 7, because the first character in "Dog" is the seventh character in the *in-text* string. However, =FIND("DOG","Hound Dog Blues") returns 0, because "DOG" isn't found (it's not the same as "Dog").

LEFT(text,number-of-characters)

MID(text,start-position,number-of-characters)

RIGHT(text,number-of-characters)

The LEFT, MID, and RIGHT functions return a portion of the *text* argument, depending on the value in the *number-of-characters* argument (and on the value in the *start-position* argument in the MID function). The LEFT function returns characters by counting from the left end of the *text* string, and the RIGHT function returns characters by counting from the right end of the *text* string. The MID function counts from the *start-position* and returns the number of characters. For example:

Formula	Result
=LEFT("Sam Jones",3)	Sam
=RIGHT("Sam Jones",3)	nes
=MID("Samantha",3,3)	man

Using these functions, you can extract part of the text in one field and use it someplace else.

Customer Info	
Customer Name	Arlon Sheetrock
Address	123 Forthview St.
City	Camp Verde
State	AZ
Zip Code	86337-1150
Cust. No.	Arlo86337

In the layout above, for example, the Cust. No. field is a calculation field containing the formula =LEFT('Customer Name',4)&LEFT('Zip Code',5). This formula creates the customer number automatically by extracting the first four letters from the left of the Customer Name field and combining them with the first five numbers from the left in the Zip Code field.

The Zip Code field must be set to the Text (not Numeric) data type if you want to use zip codes in text calculations. You'll want zip code fields to be text data anyway, because in numeric fields the leading zero of a number is automatically dropped, and that screws up zip codes like 01241.

LEN(text)

The LEN (Length) function counts the number of characters in the string of text in its argument. For example, =LEN("Antidisestablishmentarianism") returns 28.

You might want to use the LEN function in an IF formula to produce an error message if text in a database field is too long. For example, if you know your mailing labels can't hold a customer name longer than 25 characters, you could create a calculation field that displays a warning message like this:

```
Customer Name    Apex Drywall Fabricators of Southern
    Address      1150 Alameda Blvd., #455
     City        Los Angeles
     State        CA
   Zip Code      91052
   Cust. No.     Apex91052
```

> **Customer name too long!**

Here the box at the bottom contains a calculation field with the formula =IF(LEN('Customer Name')>25,"Customer name too long!","").

LOWER(text)

UPPER(text)

PROPER(text)

The LOWER, UPPER, and PROPER functions all change the case of the text in their arguments. LOWER changes all characters to lowercase; UPPER changes all characters to uppercase; and PROPER capitalizes the first letter of each word and leaves the rest lowercase. For example:

Formula	Result
LOWER("HapHazard")	haphazard
UPPER("clarisworks")	CLARISWORKS
PROPER("amerigo vespucci")	Amerigo Vespucci

These functions are a good way to standardize entries in a database field. For example, if entries in the State field have been entered as "CA," "ca," and "Ca," you can standardize them as all uppercase with the formula *UPPER('State')*. Of course, to do this you'd have to create a new field (called New State, for example) which would calculate all the standardized information. Once the

New State field had completed its calculations, you could delete the State field and rename the New State field State.

 You can also use the UPPER, LOWER, and PROPER functions to modify the EXACT function. Normally, EXACT is case-sensitive, so it would return FALSE when matching "Text" with "text", for example. With the UPPER or LOWER function, though, you could change both strings to the same case so they'd match. For example, =EXACT(UPPER("Text"),(UPPER("text") would return TRUE, because the text in both arguments has been converted to uppercase.

NUMTOTEXT(number)

This function converts a numeric value into text-type data. The data won't look much different in a spreadsheet or database (except that it will be aligned differently in a field or cell), but it will be treated differently by other ClarisWorks functions. Use this function when you want to make use of a number in a text string. See *TIMETOTEXT* on p. 326 for an example of this function at work.

REPLACE(old-text,start-num,num-characters,new-text)

The REPLACE function replaces a certain number of characters in a text string with new text that you specify.

- The *old-text* argument identifies the text string (or the spreadsheet cell or database field that contains it).

- The *start-num* value is the position in the string where you want the replacement to begin.

- The *num-characters* argument is the number of characters you want replaced.

- The *new-text* argument is the text string you want inserted in place of the replaced text. (The replacement text doesn't have to be the same length as the *num-characters* of text being replaced.)

You can use the Find/Change command on the Edit menu to search for text and replace it, but this command isn't specific about the location of text found or replaced. With the REPLACE command, on the other hand, you can be specific about the field or cell (as well as the position within a string) where text is replaced.

For example, suppose the area code used by some of your customers has been changed to a different one. You could use the REPLACE function to test for the old area code and then replace it with the new one, like this:

| Phone | 213-849-2750 |
| New Phone | 310-849-2750 |

Here the formula in the New Phone field is:

=IF(LEFT('Phone',7)="213-849",REPLACE('Phone',1,4,"310-"),"").

If you used the Find/Change command to perform this replacement and used the Change All option, you would replace the string "213-849" anywhere else it occurred (as in a Zip Code or Part Number field), as well as in the Phone field.

REPT(text,num-times)

The REPT (Repeat) function repeats a string of text a certain number of times. For example, =REPT("Ha",3) returns HaHaHa.

The REPT function repeats any text string or character, so you could use it to put a row of dashes in a cell or field, like this:

=REPT("—-",4).

TEXTTONUM(text)

This function converts text data to numeric data so you can perform math calculations with it. This function is useful when you've combined text and numbers in a spreadsheet cell or database field (which automatically makes the data text), and later want to perform a calculation with the numeric part of the data.

Movie Title	November Breeze
Stars	Jason Blade, Jennifer Harmony
Length	146 minutes
Minutes	146

In this layout, for example, movie lengths were entered with "minutes" after them, so the data is text. To find the average length of the movies in the database, however, we must first convert the Length field's data to numeric information. This is done in the Minutes field with the formula =TEXTTONUM('Length').

 If the text field in the argument contains two numbers, the TEXTTONUM function combines them. For example, if the Length field above read "3 hours, 20 minutes," the Minutes field would contain the value 320.

TRIM(text)

The TRIM function eliminates extra spaces from a text string. This function is especially handy when you import a file from another application and it includes extra spaces at the beginning or end of each entry.

Orig. Name	Verde Valley Ceramics
New Name	Verde Valley Ceramics

Here, for example, the Orig. Name field's data has extra spaces in front of it, but the New Name field eliminates them with the formula =TRIM('Orig. Name').

TRIM eliminates extra spaces from anywhere in a text string, so you can also use this function to clean up extra spaces between words or sentences in a text field or spreadsheet cell.

Trigonometric functions

This section explains ClarisWorks' trigonometric functions. If you know enough about trigonometry to understand these functions, the examples below will give you all you need to use them in ClarisWorks spreadsheets or databases. Otherwise, you'll need a trigonometry textbook, because this book is about ClarisWorks, not about trigonometry.

The *number* argument required for most trigonometric functions can be a single number, an expression that evaluates to a number, or a cell reference. Most of these functions produce results expressed in radians, but you can use the DEGREES function to convert radians to degrees. You can also convert a value expressed in degrees into radians with the RADIANS function.

Note: Many of the calculated results from trigonometric functions are lengthy decimal fractions. These numbers have been rounded off in the examples in this section.

ACOS(number)

The ACOS (Arc Cosine) returns the inverse of a cosine, which is an angle expressed in radians. The argument must be a number in the range -1.0 to 1.0. For example:

Formula	Result
=ACOS(5/9)	1.0989
=DEGREES(ACOS(5/9)	62.96

ASIN(number)

The ASIN (Arc Sine) function returns the inverse of a sine, which is an angle expressed in radians. The argument must be a number in the range -1.0 to 1.0. At the top of the next page for example:

Formula	Result
=ASIN(4/7)	0.60824
=DEGREES(ASIN(4/7)	34.849

ATAN(number)

The ATAN (Arc Tangent) function returns the inverse of a tangent value, which is the number supplied in the argument. For example, =ATAN(1.5) returns 0.0982.

ATAN2(x-number,y-number)

The ATAN2 (Arc Tangent 2) function returns the angle (in radians) between the positive X-axis and a line starting at coordinates 0,0 and passing through the *x-number* and *y-number* coordinates in the argument. For example:

Formula	Result
=ATAN2(2,5)	1.19
=DEGREES(ATAN2(2,5)	68.19

COS(number)

The COS (Cosine) function returns the cosine of a number expressed in radians. For example, =COS(1.0989) returns 0.454576.

DEGREES(radians-number)

The DEGREES function converts a value from radians to degrees. This function is demonstrated in other function examples in this section.

EXP(number)

The EXP (Exponent) function calculates the value of *e* to the power of its argument. *e* is a transcendental mathematical constant used as the base of natural logarithms. Its value is approximately 2.7182818. For example, =EXP(1) returns 2.7182818....

LN(number)

The LN (Natural Logarithm) function returns the natural logarithm of a number. The number in the argument must be positive. For example:

Formula	Result
=LN(1)	0
=LN(10)	2.30

LOG(number{,base})

The LOG (Logarithm) function returns the logarithm of the number supplied. ClarisWorks assumes the base to be 10 unless you supply a value in the optional *base* argument. The *base* argument value can be any number except 1. For example:

Formula	Result
=LOG(1000)	3
=LOG(1000,5)	4.292

LOG10(number)

The LOG10 (Logarithm to base 10) function calculates the logarithm to base 10 of the number supplied. This function produces the same result as the LOG function when you don't use the optional *base* argument with it. For example, =LOG10(1000) returns 3.

PI()

The PI function has no argument. It calculates the value of *pi* (π), which is the ratio of a circle's circumference to its diameter. Pi equals approximately 3.14159.

RADIANS(degrees-number)

The RADIANS function converts a number from degrees to radians. For example, =RADIANS(45) returns 0.785398.

SIN(number)

The SIN (Sine) function calculates the sine of a number, which is an angle expressed in radians. For example, =SIN(45) returns 0.8509.

TAN(number)

The TAN (Tangent) function returns the tangent of the argument, which is an angle expressed in radians. For example, =TAN(4500) returns 2.905.

Troubleshooting

Most calculation errors occur because you've entered the formula wrong in the first place, or because conditions in the spreadsheet or database have changed since you entered the formula so that it now produces an incorrect result. We'll look at these scenarios separately.

The Bad Formula message

The message *Bad Formula!* appears when you try to enter an incorrect formula into the spreadsheet or database. This message nearly always occurs when you've made a syntax error as you type the formula. Here are some things to look for:

The wrong function name. Spelling counts with function names (although capitalization doesn't). Don't put function names inside single or double quotation marks.

The wrong number of parentheses or commas. Don't use commas to separate thousands in numbers (enter 1000, not 1,000), and don't use a comma before any optional arguments if you don't enter the optional arguments themselves. Check the function's format earlier in this chapter and check that each end of the function has the same number of parentheses, and that they're in the right place. When you've nested one or more functions in the same formula, work your way from the inside out: check the format of the innermost function and its parentheses, then move outward to the next function.

The wrong number of arguments. Check the formula examples earlier in this chapter and make sure you've included all the arguments you need, and that they're each separated by commas. If you paste a function into a formula, remember to delete all the text abbreviations that get pasted with it— these are just guides to help you remember which arguments are required.

The wrong format for an argument. Check that text arguments have double quotation marks around them, and that commas separating multiple text arguments are outside (not inside) the double quote marks that mark the ends of the text itself. Don't use dollar signs for numbers, and don't use commas to separate thousands within large numbers.

Incorrect references. Check the field or cell references themselves, and make sure the cells or fields you're referring to contain the data you want.

Calculation error messages

If ClarisWorks doesn't display the *Bad Formula!* message as you try to enter a formula in the spreadsheet, it means the formula's format is acceptable. Sometimes, however, the formula produces a calculation error when you put inappropriate values or text in certain cells. When this happens, ClarisWorks displays various error messages to describe what's wrong. Here's what those messages mean, and what to do about them.

#NA! The result isn't available, probably because the formula refers to a cell or field (or specific data in a cell or field) that doesn't exist. Check the formula's references.

#DIV/0! The formula is trying to divide by zero. Check the contents of the cells or fields being referred to and change the values in them.

#VALUE! A value in the formula is invalid. There may be text, dates, or times in a cell or field referred to in a numeric formula, for example. Check the result type in a database formula, and make sure the data type being referenced in the formula is what the formula requires.

#NUM! A number in the formula is invalid. The formula may call for a certain kind of number, and that's not what it's getting. Check the cell or field referred to in the formula. For example, the formula needs a negative number, and you've entered a positive one.

#REF! A cell reference in the formula is invalid. This error often occurs when you've deleted a row or column that contained a cell referenced in a formula.

#ARG! The argument is incorrect. Check, the number of parameters or syntax in the argument to make sure they're the same as the sample shown earlier in this chapter.

#USER! A user-defined error. This message is produced with the ISERROR function. Check the formula in the cell or field to see what sort of error condition has been specified to cause this.

#DATE! The date in the formula is invalid. Check the format of the date in the referenced cell or field.

#TIME! A time in the formula is invalid. Check the format of the time in the referenced cell or field.

#PRECISION! There aren't enough digits to display the formula's result. Use the ROUND function to reduce the number of digits produced by the formula.

A spreadsheet cell isn't wide enough to display the value. Either widen the cell or use the ROUND function to round the value off so it can be displayed with fewer digits.

#ERROR! Something's wrong, but ClarisWorks doesn't know exactly what it is. Carefully check the formula and the contents of cell referred to in the formula.

Using frames

Frames are special objects that you create in a ClarisWorks document to work with data in a different way than the document normally allows. You can create text, spreadsheet, or paint frames using their respective tools in the tool panel, and you can create these frames in every type of ClarisWorks document except communications documents. ➤➤

Frame basics

A frame starts out as a rectangular object you draw using one of the frame tools in the tool panel, just as you might draw a rectangle with the rectangle tool.

Adding a frame

To add a frame to a document:

1. Display the tool panel in the document (if it isn't already showing) by choosing *Show Tools* from the View menu.

2. Select the text, spreadsheet, or paint tool in the tool panel. (See p. 22 in Chapter 2 if you can't remember which tool is which.)

3. Draw a rectangle in the document where you want the frame to go. The frame appears, like this:

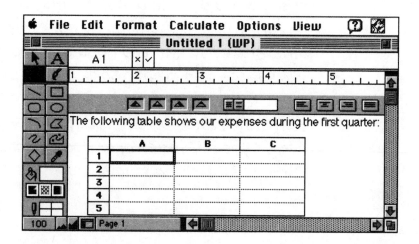

When you first add a frame, ClarisWorks automatically switches to the frame's data environment so you can work with data inside it. Here, for example, we're working in a word processor document, but cell A1 is selected inside the new spreadsheet frame and the spreadsheet's menus are showing in the menu bar.

 If you want to add text to a spreadsheet, database, draw, or paint document, you don't have to actually draw a frame; you can just select the text tool, click in the document, and start typing.

 You can only add a frame to a database document when you're in Layout mode.

Switching among data environments

Once you have a frame in a document, there are three different data environments you can choose: the document's data environment; the frame's data environment; and the draw environment, where frames are graphic objects.

You can switch among these environments by clicking.

- Click anywhere in the document (outside a frame or other object) to select the document environment.

- Double-click inside a frame to switch to its environment.

- Click once on a frame or on another graphic object, or click on the pointer tool, to switch to the draw environment.

 Because a frame is just another graphic object in the draw environment, you can select it and choose options with the fill or pen tool to change the frame's fill color or pattern or its border. You can also use the commands on the Arrange menu to move one frame or other object in front of or behind others. The draw environment's flexibility allows you to do things like draw lines, boxes, or circles on top of frames, add a text frame on top of a spreadsheet frame, or add a paint frame on top of a text frame. See *Managing objects in layers* on p. 248 in Chapter 8 for more information.

Moving, resizing, copying, and deleting frames

Because frames are treated like other objects in a document's draw environment, you can select, move, and resize them just as you would other objects.

1. Click on the frame once to select it. The draw environment is activated (if it isn't active already), and selection handles appear at the frame's corners, like this:

2. Drag the whole frame to move it, or drag one of its selection handles to resize it.

When a frame is selected like this, you can also use the *Cut, Copy, Paste, Clear,* and *Duplicate* commands on the Edit menu to copy, paste, delete, or duplicate it. Pressing Delete while a frame is selected also deletes it. (See *Selecting, cutting, copying, and pasting data* on p. 57 in Chapter 3 for more information about these commands.)

Opening a frame

Frames are limited to the size you make them, and they don't have scroll bars. Although you can always resize a frame to reveal a little more of it, you can also open a frame to display it as a full-screen window, complete with scroll bars, zoom controls, and pane controls as described in *The document window* on p. 17 in Chapter 2.

To open a frame, select it and choose the *Open Frame* command from the View menu, or hold down the Option key and double-click on the frame. The frame opens as a full-screen window.

To close a frame and reduce it back to its original size in the document, just click the window's close box.

 You can't open a spreadsheet or text frame's window when you're working in a paint document, because frames become part of the paint document's environment once you create them.

Special situations

The basic procedures discussed above should cover most situations where you'll use or work with frames. However, some types of frames behave a little differently in specific document environments.

Adding text frames to word processing documents

You can add a text frame to spreadsheet, paint, draw, and database documents using the basic procedures outlined earlier, but since you're already in a text environment in a word processing document, adding a text frame there takes an extra step: hold down the (Option) key as you draw the frame or click in the document.

Using frames in paint documents

Everything you create in a paint document becomes part of the paint environment. When you create a spreadsheet or text frame in a paint document, you can add text or numbers inside it only when you first create the frame. Once you click away from the frame to select the paint environment, the frame and its data become paint images and can only be edited with the paint tools (see Chapter 9). You can't create a paint frame in a paint document.

Making a chart in a spreadsheet frame

When you work in a spreadsheet frame, you can make a chart just as you can in a spreadsheet document. However, you can choose whether you want the chart to appear inside the spreadsheet frame or outside it as a separate object. Either way, the chart is linked to the spreadsheet data inside the frame.

To make a chart inside a spreadsheet frame:

1. Select the frame and choose *Open Frame* from the View menu.

2. Select the data you want to chart and then choose the *Make Chart...* command from the Options menu.

3. Choose the chart options you want and then press [Return]. The chart appears inside the window.

To make a chart outside of a spreadsheet frame, either:

- Select the data you want to chart without opening the frame; or

- Open the frame, select the data, then close the frame before choosing the *Make Chart...* command.

When you make a chart without the frame window open, the chart appears as a separate object in the document.

Changing the display in spreadsheet frames

Spreadsheet frames normally display row and column headings, grid lines, and other information, and they normally show the upper left corner of a spreadsheet (beginning at cell A1). However, you may want the frame to show a different spreadsheet area, and you may want to hide the headings and grid lines.

To change how data is displayed inside a spreadsheet frame, select the frame and choose the *Modify Frame...* command from the Options menu. You see the Display dialog box, like the one at the top of the next page:

```
Display
☒ Cell grid          ☒ Column headings
☐ Solid lines        ☒ Row headings
☐ Formulas           ☒ Mark circular refs

Origin  [A1    ]      (Cancel)    [ OK ]
```

Type a different cell address in the Origin box to change which cell shows in the frame's upper left corner, and click the other checkboxes to hide or show column headings and change other display attributes. See *Setting display options* on p. 149 in Chapter 5 for more information on these options.

Setting a paint frame's resolution and depth

When a paint frame is selected, you can use the *Modify Frame…* command to change its resolution and color depth. When you select the frame and choose the *Modify Frame…* command, you see the Resolution and Depth dialog box, and you can change these options there. See *Changing the document size, resolution, and depth* on p. 281 in Chapter 9 for more information.

Linking frames

You can create as many frames as you like in any document. You can have several frames of the same type or frames of different types. Each frame's data is separate from the others' data, so individual text frames are like individual text documents. But when you create more than one frame of the same type, you can link these frames to show different parts of the same frame's data environment.

When you link text frames, text flows automatically from one frame to the next, like this:

| Rainy Days | rainy day aggravates a |
| Many people suffer from rain-induced depression. Somehow the gloom of a | natural tendency in such people toward pessimism. |

When you link spreadsheet or paint frames, on the other hand, you simply display a different part of the frame's environment, like this:

	A	B		A	B
1	123	234	5	400	500
2	345	345	6	432	543
3	300	400	7	321	432
4			8		

Frame links give you extra flexibility for displaying data. You can move or resize linked frames just as you would individual frames, and you can create links between frames on different pages of a document. However, there are some key limitations on frame linking:

- You can't link frames in a paint document;

- You can't link text frames in a word processing document;

- You must create and link frames in the same operation—you can't link frames that already exist in a document; and

- The only way to break a frame link is to delete the linked frame.

Let's see how all this works.

Linking text frames

To create linked text frames, you must be working in a spreadsheet or draw document, or in the Layout mode of a database document, and you must be in the draw data environment.

1. Open the document where you want the linked frames.

2. Click on the pointer tool in the tool panel to switch to the draw environment (unless you're working in a draw document anyway).

3. Choose *Frame Links* from the Options menu.

4. Choose the text tool, draw the first frame, and then click once outside the frame. The frame looks like this:

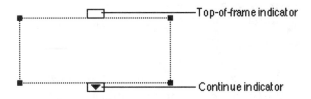

5. Click on the continue indicator at the bottom of the frame.

6. Draw the next frame. It looks like this:

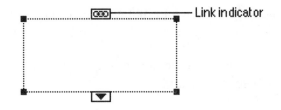

The link indicator shows that this frame is linked to another.

7. Repeat steps 5 and 6 until you've created all the frames you want.

The first linked frame's outline becomes invisible when you draw the second one, so you'll just have to guess about where you want the second one. To see all linked text frames at once, (Shift)-click on them.

When you've created all the linked frames, double-click inside the first one to switch to the text environment, and then type or paste in your text. Any text that won't fit inside the first frame automatically flows into the next one, and so on. If the last of your linked frames is filled with text but there's still more text below it, you'll see an overflow indicator, like this:

Many people suffer from rain-induced depression. Somehow the gloom of a rainy day aggravates a natural tendency in such ⊠——Overflow indicator

To remedy this problem, you can always add another linked frame (click on the continue indicator and draw another one), enlarge the existing frames, delete some text, or make the text a smaller size.

Linking spreadsheet or paint frames

The basic procedure for linking spreadsheet or paint frames is the same as in the steps above. The only differences are:

- The frame outlines don't disappear when you draw new linked frames; and

- Data doesn't flow from one linked spreadsheet or paint frame to the next; instead, you see an adjacent part of the same frame.

Using linked and unlinked frames in the same document

When creating a flyer or newsletter layout, you may want different groups of linked frames (three frames containing one article and two containing another, for example), or you may want to combine linked and unlinked frames in the same document.

The only way you can link one frame to another is to click the continue indicator at the bottom of the previous frame before drawing the next one. To create a second set of linked frames that isn't linked to the first set, therefore, just don't click the previous frame's continue indicator. Instead, choose the frame tool and draw a new frame. Once you click away from the new frame, you' see a continue indicator on it, and you can click the indicator to create a second frame linked to this one. Both of these frames won't be linked to the original group of linked frames, however.

To create an unlinked frame after making several linked frames, you need to turn frame linking off. Click in the document itself to switch to the draw environment, choose *Frame Links* from the Options menu to remove the check mark next to its name, then select a tool and create the new frame.

Troubleshooting

You can't work inside a frame. You need to double-click inside a frame to switch to its data environment. If the frame's selection handles are showing, you're in the draw environment instead. Once you click away from a frame in a paint document, the frame becomes an image and you can't work in its data environment anymore.

You can't find the *Frame Links* or *Modify Frame...* command on the Options menu. You must be in the draw environment to see these commands, not in the frame's data environment. Click once outside the frame to switch to the draw environment.

Text frame edges disappear when you click outside the frame. That's just the way it is. It's best to enter or paste text into a text frame as soon as you create it, so you can tell roughly how big the frame is from looking at the text. When you select the frame again, you'll see handles at its corners.

You can't add a frame to a database document. You must be in Layout mode to add a frame in the database. Choose *Layout* from the Layout menu.

You paste text into a linked frame and you can't see the end of the text. The text has overflowed the frame and is displayed in one of the subsequently linked frames. Check the other frames.

You make a chart in a spreadsheet frame's open window, but then you close the window and you can't see it anymore. Resize the frame to display the chart, or reopen the frame window, select the chart, and paste it into the document's data environment.

13

Using macros and shortcuts

Macros and shortcuts can save you a lot of time and keystrokes as you use ClarisWorks. Macros speed up your work by automatically executing a series of keystrokes or mouse movements. Shortcuts are macros that appear as buttons on a palette—you can play one back by just clicking a button icon. ➦

All macro and shortcut features are available from the Shortcuts submenu, which appears when you choose Shortcuts from the File menu.

About macros

A macro is a stored series of keystrokes or mouse movements, or a combination of them. You can record keyboard commands, text you type, or mouse events such as selecting objects; choosing menu commands; moving, scrolling, or resizing windows; or clicking dialog box options.

To create a macro, you name the macro and assign keys to execute it, turn on the macro recorder, perform the events you want to record, and then stop recording. The series of events is recorded, and can be played back by pressing the keys you assigned to that macro.

You can create macros that work in all ClarisWorks applications, in just one application, or even in just one document. Once you've created a macro, you can play it, change the way it plays, add it to the shortcuts palette, or delete it.

Recording a macro

To record a macro:

1. Choose *Record Macro…* from the Shortcuts submenu. You see the Record Macro dialog box, like the one at the top of the next page.

2. Type a descriptive name in the Name box.

```
┌─────────────────────────────────────────────────────────────┐
│  Record Macro                                                 │
│  ───────────────────────────────────────────────────────     │
│                                           ┌─Play In ──────    │
│   Name  [Untitled 1            ]          │ ☐ All Environments │
│                                           │ ☒ Word Processing  │
│   ○ Function Key            ┌──────┐      │ ☐ Drawing          │
│   ◉ Option + ⌘ + Key        │      │      │ ☐ Painting         │
│                             └──────┘      │ ☐ Database         │
│   ┌─Options ───────────────────┐          │ ☐ Spreadsheet      │
│   │ ☐ Play Pauses              │          │ ☐ Communications   │
│   │ ☐ Document Specific        │          └─────────────────── │
│   │ ☐ Has Shortcut      ┌────┐ │                               │
│   │ ☐ In Shortcuts Palette│    │ │        ( Cancel ) (( Record ))│
│   └───────────────────────────┘          └──────────────────   │
└─────────────────────────────────────────────────────────────┘
```

3. Click in the Key box and type a key that will execute the macro when you press it while holding down (Option) and (⌘). You can define separate macros with uppercase and lowercase keys, such as S and s. If you're using a Macintosh Extended Keyboard, you can also click the Function Key button and then press a function key to assign it as the macro key.

4. Click checkboxes to select other options from the Options area, or to specify a ClarisWorks application in which the macro will work.

By assigning macros to specific applications, you can reuse the same macro key. For example, (Option)(⌘)(S) might split a window in spreadsheet documents but apply a superscript character style in word processing documents.

5. Click the Record button or press (Return). You' see a blinking microphone icon where the menu icon normally appears, indicating that your mouse and keyboard actions are now being recorded.

6. Perform the operation you want to record.

7. Choose *Stop Recording* from the Shortcuts submenu. The macro is recorded.

Recording a log-on macro

To record a macro that automatically connects your Mac to an online computer service and enters your user name and password, follow these steps.

1. Open a communications document and set it up to dial the number of the online service, then turn on your modem, if necessary.

2. Choose *Record Macro...*, type a macro name and macro key in the Record Macro dialog box, then click Record. ClarisWorks begins recording the macro.

3. Choose *Open Connection* from the Session menu. ClarisWorks dials the online service's number.

4. Wait for the Modem Status box to show that you're connected, then click the OK button in it.

5. Wait for the online service's user name prompt to appear on your screen, then select it and choose the *Copy* command.

6. Choose *Macro Wait...* from the Shortcuts submenu. You see a dialog box like this:

```
┌─────────────────────────────────────────────┐
│ Macro Wait                                    │
│ ──────────────────────────────────────────── │
│                                               │
│  ● Wait for "┌──────────────────┐"           │
│              └──────────────────┘             │
│     to appear on the data stream.             │
│                                               │
│  ○ Wait for │2.0│ seconds of line inactivity. │
│                                               │
│                   ┌────────┐  ┌────────────┐  │
│                   │ Cancel │  │     OK     │  │
│                   └────────┘  └────────────┘  │
└─────────────────────────────────────────────┘
```

7. Choose *Paste* to put the user name prompt in the Wait For box.

8. Click the OK button to put this dialog box away.

9. Type your user name at the prompt in the communications document. If there's a password prompt after it, copy the prompt and paste it into the Macro Wait dialog box, as in steps 5 through 7.

10. Type your password at the password prompt and finish logging onto the online service.

11. Choose *Stop Recording* from the Shortcuts submenu to complete the macro.

 Before you record a macro to handle a common task, check the Available Shortcuts list to make sure there isn't a shortcut for this operation already. See *Editing the Shortcuts palette* on p. 392.

Playing a macro

To play a macro, just press the combination of keys assigned to that macro.

If you can't remember a macro key or which macros you've recorded, choose *Play Macro...* from the Shortcuts submenu. You see the Play Macro dialog box, like this:

Play Macro

Double space	⇧
Single space	
	⇩

(Cancel)   (**Play**)

The list shows all the macros you've recorded for this particular document or application. To play a macro in this dialog box, either double-click on its name or select it and then press (Return) or click the Play button.

Editing a macro

Once you've recorded a macro, you can change its name or its macro key, or you can change its other options.

1. Choose *Edit Macros…*from the Shortcuts submenu. The Edit Macros dialog box appears, like this:

```
┌─────────────────────────────────────────────────────────────┐
│                                                               │
│  Edit Macros                                                  │
│  ─────────────────────────────────────────────────────────   │
│                                       ┌─Play In ──────────┐   │
│  Macro  [Double space ▼]              │ ☐ All Environments │   │
│                                       │ ☒ Word Processing  │   │
│  Name   [Double space      ]          │ ☐ Drawing          │   │
│                                       │ ☐ Painting         │   │
│   ○                        ┌───┐      │ ☐ Database         │   │
│   ◉ Option + ⌘ + Key       │ 2 │      │ ☐ Spreadsheet      │   │
│                            └───┘      │ ☐ Communications   │   │
│  ┌─Options──────────────────────┐     └────────────────────┘   │
│  │ ☐ Play Pauses                │                             │
│  │ ☐ Document Specific          │                             │
│  │ ☐ Has Shortcut      ┌───┐    │     ┌────────┐ ╔════════╗   │
│  │ ☐                   │   │    │     │ Cancel │ ║  Done  ║   │
│  └──────────────────────────────┘     └────────┘ ╚════════╝   │
│                                                               │
└───────────────────────────────────────────────────────────────┘
```

2. Choose the macro you want to edit from the Macro pop-up menu.

3. Type a different name or macro key, or choose different options by clicking the checkboxes.

4. Click the Done button to confirm the changes and put the dialog box away.

As this process indicates, however, you can't edit the actual events recorded in a macro. To change the events you've recorded, delete the macro you want to change and then record a new one with the events you want. (See *Deleting a macro* on p. 390.)

About macro options

Let's take a quick look at the macro options available in the Record Macro and Edit Macros dialog boxes. The *Play In* checkbox options are pretty obvious, but let's go through the checkboxes in the Options area.

Play Pauses tells ClarisWorks to play all the pauses between keystrokes or mouse movements. ClarisWorks usually doesn't play pauses because it assumes you're just pausing between events to decide what you want to do next.

Document Specific makes a macro specific to the current document. You'll want to limit a macro's action to a specific document when it resizes a particular object or selects a particular block of text, a group of records, or a range of spreadsheet cells.

Has Shortcut creates a button for the macro. This button is automatically added to the Available Shortcuts list in the Edit Shortcuts dialog box (see p. 393). The button is initially blank, but you can create a custom button design by editing it:

1. Click the button sample to the right of the Has Shortcut option. You see a dialog box like the one at the top of the next page:

```
┌─────────────────────────────────────┐
│≡≡≡≡≡≡≡≡≡ Edit Button Icon ≡≡≡≡≡≡≡≡≡│
│                                     │
│  ┌─────────────────┐      □         │
│  │                 │                │
│  │                 │                │
│  │                 │   ┌──┬──┬──┬──┐ │
│  │                 │   │  │  │  │██│ │
│  │                 │   ├──┼──┼──┼──┤ │
│  │                 │   │██│██│██│██│ │
│  │                 │   ├──┼──┼──┼──┤ │
│  │                 │   │██│  │██│██│ │
│  │                 │   ├──┼──┼──┼──┤ │
│  │                 │   │  │  │██│██│ │
│  └─────────────────┘   └──┴──┴──┴──┘ │
│                                     │
│               ( Cancel )  (  OK  )  │
│                                     │
└─────────────────────────────────────┘
```

2. Click on a color or shade in the palette at the right and then click or drag the pointer on the grid at the left to create a button design.

3. Click OK or press (Return) to save the new design and return to the Edit Macros dialog box. The new design appears as the button sample.

In Shortcuts Palette adds the shortcut button to the current Shortcuts palette. (See *Editing the Shortcuts palette* on p. 392.)

Deleting a macro

To delete a macro:

1. Choose *Delete Macros...* from the Shortcuts submenu. You see a dialog box like the one at the top of the next page:

```
┌─────────────────────────────────────────┐
│ Delete Macros                             │
│  ┌─────────────────────────────────┬──┐  │
│  │ Double space                    │ ⬆ │  │
│  │ Single space                    │  │  │
│  │                                 │  │  │
│  │                                 │  │  │
│  │                                 │ ⬇ │  │
│  └─────────────────────────────────┴──┘  │
│  ( Delete )      ( Cancel )   (( Done ))  │
└─────────────────────────────────────────┘
```

2. Select the name of the macro you want to delete, then click the Delete button.

3. Click the Done button or press (Return) when you're finished.

About shortcuts

Shortcuts are macros that have been turned into graphic buttons and placed on the Shortcuts palette, so you can execute a sequence of events by simply clicking a button. ClarisWorks comes with dozens of predefined shortcuts for common operations like opening a file, selecting a cell format, making a connection in the communications document, or sorting a database file. These shortcuts can't be edited with the *Edit Macros...* command. However, you can change the collection of shortcut buttons on the palette, and as you record other macros of your own you can add them to the Shortcuts palette and create graphic buttons for them. (See *Editing a macro* on p. 388.)

Using shortcuts

To use a shortcut, choose *Show Shortcuts* from the Shortcuts sub-menu off the File menu. The Shortcuts palette appears, like this:

The shortcuts you see on this palette depend on the type of ClarisWorks document you have open at the time. Some general shortcuts are available when you have no documents open, and each document type has its own specific shortcuts.

Once the Shortcuts palette is showing, just click a button for the shortcut you want to execute.

Tip

The shortcut buttons are cute, but it's hard to remember which one does what. If you have trouble determining which shortcut button is which, display shortcut names instead of buttons by choosing the Show Names option in the Palettes Preferences dialog box. See p. 394.

Editing the Shortcuts palette

Each ClarisWorks application has its own preset selection of shortcut buttons, but you can customize the Shortcuts palette at any time. You can add or remove shortcuts, or create a custom palette just for the document you're currently working in. To edit the palette:

1. Choose *Edit Shortcuts...* from the Shortcuts submenu. You see the Edit Shortcuts dialog box, like the one at the top of the next page:

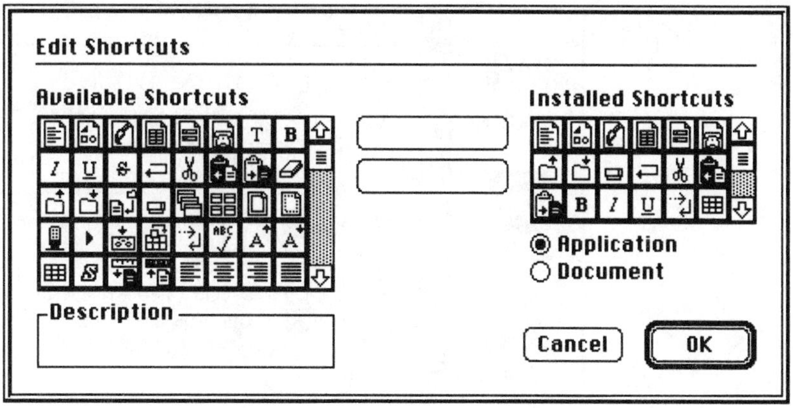

Edit Shortcuts

Available Shortcuts　　　　　　　　　**Installed Shortcuts**

⊙ Application
○ Document

[Cancel]　[OK]

─Description─

2.　Click a button in either the Installed Shortcuts or the Available Shortcuts list. You may have to scroll one of these lists to display the button you want. As you click a button, a description of its function appears in the Description box.

To add a button, double-click on it in the Available Shortcuts list, or select it and click the Add button.

To remove a button, select it in the Installed Shortcuts list and click the Remove button.

To create a document-specific shortcuts palette, click the Document button below the Installed Shortcuts list. The Installed Shortcuts list becomes empty, and you can add shortcuts to it.

Setting other Shortcuts preferences

Along with showing shortcut names instead of buttons, you can set other options to control how shortcuts operate. When you choose the *Preferences...* command from the Edit menu and click the Palettes icon, the Shortcuts preferences appear at the right below the color palette options, as shown at the top of the next page:

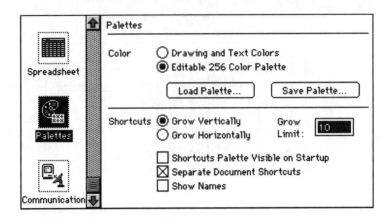

Here's what the options do.

Grow Vertically expands the Shortcuts palette vertically as you add buttons or names to it, while *Grow Horizontally* expands the palette to the right. The *Grow Limit* box lets you set a limit on the number of shortcuts you can add to the palette.

Shortcuts Palette Visible On Startup displays the palette automatically when you create a new document or open a document. Normally the palette is hidden.

Separate Document Shortcuts is usually checked. This tells ClarisWorks to create a separate palette for document-specific shortcuts, rather than adding them to the same palette as general shortcuts for that document type.

Show Names displays shortcut names rather than buttons. The preset option is to display buttons, but it's not always easy to remember which button does what.

Troubleshooting

You press a macro key but the macro won't play. Choose *Play Macro...* from the Shortcuts submenu to make sure the macro name is listed. If the macro isn't listed, you're probably in the wrong document type (trying to play a spreadsheet macro in a database document, for example). If the macro name is listed, you may have defined the macro key as an uppercase letter and you're trying to execute it by typing a lowercase letter. Choose *Edit Macros...* and choose the macro name to see which key you defined for it.

You can't choose the *Macro Wait...* command. This command is available only when you're connected to another computer with a communications document. You must be completely connected (not dialing the phone or waiting to connect) before the command becomes active.

You can't find a shortcut button on the Shortcuts palette. Some buttons only appear in certain types of ClarisWorks documents. Choose *Edit Shortcuts...* from the Shortcuts submenu and check the Installed Shortcuts list for the document type you're in to see if the button is there. If it's not, you can add it to the palette.

You can't remember what a shortcut button does. Choose *Edit Shortcuts...* from the Shortcuts submenu and click the button you want to know about in one of the two lists. A description appears in the Description box. Remember, to display shortcut names in your document instead of buttons, choose *Preferences...* from the Edit menu, click the Palettes icon, and then click the Show Names checkbox.

14

Using mail merge

Mail merge allows you to automatically pull data from records in a ClarisWorks database file and insert it in a word processor or spreadsheet, or in a text frame in a spreadsheet or draw document. Most of the time, you'll use mail merge with the word processor to produce groups of form letters, invoices, or other individualized documents. ➤➤

This chapter covers the details of using mail merge. This process involves using both word processing and database documents, however, so if you need more information about those documents, consult chapters 4 and 7.

· ·

About mail merge

Performing a mail merge involves these steps:

1. Create a ClarisWorks database document and store the data you want to merge, if the document doesn't already exist.

2. Open the database file.

3. Create a new word processor, spreadsheet, or graphics document, or open an existing one in which you want to merge data. This will be the *merge document.*

4. Select the location in the merge document where you want the merged data to appear. (You'll have to create a text frame in a spreadsheet or graphics document first.)

5. Use the *Mail Merge...* command to select the database file from which you want to merge data.

6. Select the database fields whose data you want to merge. ClarisWorks places *merge markers* in the document to show where data will be merged.

7. Select the merge markers and choose the appropriate character and paragraph formats. (The merged data will have these formats.)

8. Print the merge document.

You can merge data from any field (except summary fields) in any ClarisWorks database document, as long as the document is open at the time. You can also merge data from the same database field into more than one location in a merge document.

When you merge data from a database document, ClarisWorks merges the data from the indicated fields from every record that's currently visible in that document. Database documents can contain hundreds or thousands of records, but you can use the database's find and match features to select only the records you want to be showing at any given time, so you can be very specific about which data you merge.

To see how this works, let's go through the procedure for merging data into a new word processing document.

Creating a merge document

Let's assume that we want to merge name and address data from a database named Employees into a form letter document called Attaboys. For this example, we'll assume that the database and the form letter already exist, and that we need only merge the data and print the letters.

1. Open the Employees database. In this case, we'll assume that we want to merge data for all the employee records in this file, so we don't need to select specific records.

2. Open the Attaboys word processor document. It appears on the screen, on top of the database document.

3. We want to merge data to create the address block of the letter, so we'll move the insertion point to the top of the document, two lines below the date, as shown at the top of the next page:

```
┌══════════════ Attaboys (WP) ══════════════┐
│ 1       2       3       4       5       6  │
│                                            │
│  [△] [△] [△] [△]   [≡≡] 1 li   [■] [≡] [≡] [≡]   [□□] │
│ January 12, 1995                           │
│                                            │
│ |                                          │
│                                            │
│ Dear :                                     │
│                                            │
│ Acme Novelty has just experienced the biggest sales quarter in its histor│
│ to thank you, , for helping to make it possible. As a token of my appreciat│
│ enrolled you in the Vegetable of the Month Club, through which you'll re│
│ exotic vegetable each month for the next year. Thanks again for helping │
│                                            │
│ 100  [△▲][□] Page 1        [←][▥]         [→][▣] │
└════════════════════════════════════════════┘
```

4. Choose *Mail Merge...* from the File menu. The Select Data dialog box appears, like this:

```
┌────────────────────────────────────────┐
│                                          │
│  Select Data                             │
│ ─────────────────────────────────────── │
│ ┌──────────────────────────────────┬──┐ │
│ │ Employees                        │⇧ │ │
│ │                                  ├──┤ │
│ │                                  │  │ │
│ │                                  │  │ │
│ │                                  │  │ │
│ │                                  ├──┤ │
│ │                                  │⇩ │ │
│ └──────────────────────────────────┴──┘ │
│                                          │
│              ( Cancel )   ┌─ OK ─┐      │
│                           └──────┘      │
└────────────────────────────────────────┘
```

5. Every open database document is listed in this dialog box. Double-click on the Employees document name to select it. ClarisWorks displays the Mail Merge window, like the one at the top of the next page:

```
╔═══════════════════════ Mail Merge ═══════════════╗
║ □                                               □ ║
║  Field Name              Merge Database:          ║
║  ┌──────────────────┐┌─┐                          ║
║  │ FirstName        ││⬆│  Employees               ║
║  │ LastName         ││☰│                          ║
║  │ Street           ││ │                          ║
║  │ City             ││⬇│  ┌──────────────────┐    ║
║  └──────────────────┘└─┘  │   Select Data... │    ║
║  ┌──────────────────┐     └──────────────────┘    ║
║  │   Insert Field   │     ┌──────────────────┐    ║
║  └──────────────────┘     │   Print Merge... │    ║
║                           └──────────────────┘    ║
╚═══════════════════════════════════════════════════╝
```

You can move the window around the screen to reveal portions of the document underneath. Also, notice that this window has a gravity zoom box in its upper right corner. When you click this box, the window shrinks so that only its title bar shows, and ClarisWorks automatically moves it to the upper right corner of the document.

6. We want to merge the FirstName, LastName, Street, City, State, and Zip fields from this database file. The FirstName field is already selected in the list, so double-click on it, or click the Insert Field button below the list. A merge marker for the field appears in the document at the insertion point, like this:

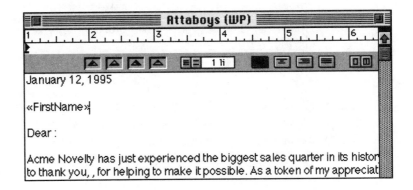

7. Press the ⌸Spacebar⌸ once to put a space after the marker, then double-click on the LastName field name in the Mail Merge

window. ClarisWorks inserts the LastName field's merge marker in the document.

8. Press ⌐Return¬ to move the insertion point to the next line, then double-click on the Street field name in the list to insert a merge marker for it in the second line of the address block.

Get the idea? You move the insertion point to the place where you want the data to appear and then select the field to merge from the Merge Fields window.

After merging the address block, you'll need to merge the FirstName data in the greeting line, and also in the second line of the letter text. The finished letter looks like this:

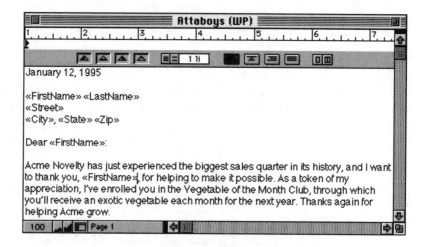

```
≣▓█▓≣════════════ Attaboys (WP) ═══════════▓⊠
1 . . . . .|2. . . . .|3. . . . .|4. . . . .|5. . . . .|6. . . . .|7. . . ▲
▲ ▲ ▲ ▲  ▣▤ 1 li  ▮▮ ▤ ▤ ▤  ▯▯
January 12, 1995

«FirstName» «LastName»
«Street»
«City», «State» «Zip»

Dear «FirstName»:

Acme Novelty has just experienced the biggest sales quarter in its history, and I want
to thank you, «FirstName», for helping to make it possible. As a token of my
appreciation, I've enrolled you in the Vegetable of the Month Club, through which
you'll receive an exotic vegetable each month for the next year. Thanks again for
helping Acme grow.

100  ▮▮▯ Page 1       ⟨▮▮▮▮
```

If you know the names of the database fields you want to merge, you can also insert merge markers by typing them. To enter the « and » symbols that enclose a merge field name, press ⌐Option⌐\¬ and ⌐Shift⌐Option⌐\¬, respectively.

Formatting merge markers

Once you have merge markers in a document, you can select them and change their font, size, or style just as you would other text. When the merge document is printed, the merged text will have the same format characteristics as the merge marker did.

 Unlike inserted date or time markers, merge field markers can be edited one character at a time. Be careful not to delete either of the merge symbols (« or ») or any portion of a merge field's name, or the data won't merge properly.

Since merge markers will be replaced by data, make sure to add the appropriate spaces and punctuation before and after each one so the data will look right when the document is printed. To format the third line of the address block of our sample letter on the previous page, for example, you would:

- Merge the City field, then type a ⌐,⌐ and press the ⌐Spacebar⌐ once;

- Merge the State field, then press the ⌐Spacebar⌐ once; and then

- Merge the Zip field.

Printing a merge document

To print a merge document, you again use the *Mail Merge...* command, and you must also open the database file from which data will be merged.

1. Open the database document.

2. Open the merge document.

3. Choose *Mail Merge...* from the File menu.

4. Select the database file as the source of data, if necessary. (If you didn't close the database file after merging the fields into the document, you don't have to select it again.)

5. Click the Print Merge... button in the Mail Merge window. You see the standard Print dialog box, and you can then print the document. ClarisWorks prints one copy of the document for each record that's currently showing in the source database file.

Troubleshooting

You can't find the database document you want in the Merge Data window. The document isn't open. It has to be open before you'll see its name in the Merge Data window.

The wrong field names are showing in the Mail Merge window. Try scrolling the list to see if they're simply out of view. If the names aren't on the list, you have the wrong database document selected. Check the document name in the upper right corner of the Mail Merge window to see which document is open.

Your merge document prints, but it contains data from the wrong records. Use the database's Find mode, Match Records, or selection features to display only the records you want printed, then try the print merge again.

The data doesn't merge, even though the database document is open. Make sure you're using the *Print Merge...* command to print, not the regular *Print...* command. Next, check the Merge Database name in the Mail Merge window; you may have the wrong database selected. You can have several database documents open at once, but only one can be selected when you print the merge document. If the correct database is selected, look at the merge markers in your merge document and make sure you haven't edited their names. Marker names must be exactly the same as the field names in the database, or the data won't merge.

C H A P T E R

15

Publishing
and subscribing

If you're using Macintosh System 7, you can
take advantage of its publish and subscribe
capability in ClarisWorks documents. Basically,
publish and subscribe is an automatic
cut-and-paste link. You select data in one
document, publish it, and then subscribe to
it in other documents. Whenever the original
data changes, the subscriber documents
change as well. ➤➤

Publishing and subscribing require three elements:

- A *publisher*, which is a selection of data from a document;

- An *edition*, which is a file on your disk that contains a current version of the publisher's data; and

- A *subscriber*, which is the area in a document that displays data from the edition file.

Each publisher has its own edition file. As you change data inside the published selection, the edition file is automatically updated. You can set options to decide how often changes in the publisher are sent to the edition file—see *Setting publisher options* on p. 408.

An edition file can have as many subscribers as you like. You might publish part of a budget spreadsheet and subscribe to it in an annual report, for example, and then subscribe to the same data in a profit-loss statement. You can set options to determine how often the subscriber reads information from the edition file—see *Setting subscriber options* on p. 410.

Note: If you're using Macintosh System 6, you can still work with documents containing publishers and subscribers, but the data won't be updated automatically.

To see how all this works, let's go through the process a step at a time.

Selecting and publishing data

To publish something, you select the data you want to publish and then create an edition file. Publish and subscribe works in every ClarisWorks document type except communications documents. You can select data (text, spreadsheet cells, data in database fields) or objects (charts, draw objects, frames, or paint images).

1. Select the data you want to publish, then choose *Create Publisher...* from the Publish submenu at the bottom of the Edit menu. You see a dialog box like this:

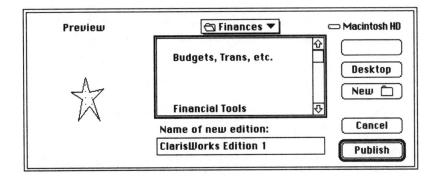

The Preview area shows the data you've selected—in this case, a draw object.

2. Type a name for the new edition file in the Name Of New Edition box and choose a location for it.

3. Click the Publish button or press Return. ClarisWorks creates an edition file and the data is published. To indicate this in the original document, the published data is surrounded by a gray border, like this:

 Choose *Hide Borders* from the Publishing submenu to hide a publisher's or subscriber's gray border.

Setting publisher options

Once you've published an edition file, any changes you make to the publisher are sent to the edition file whenever you save the document. However, you can send updates manually at any time, set ClarisWorks so the edition is not updated when you save the file, or cancel the publisher to break the link between it and its edition file. To do any of these, use the *Publisher Options...* command.

1. Click inside the border of the published area to select the publisher.

2. Choose *Publisher Options...* from the Publish submenu. You see the Publisher dialog box, like this:

```
┌─────────────────────────────────────────────────────────────┐
│                                                               │
│  Publisher to:   ☐ Star Logo Edition  ▼                       │
│ ─────────────────────────────────────────────────────────── │
│  ┌─Send Editions:────────────────────┐                       │
│  │  ◉ On Saue                         │   ┌─────────────────┐ │
│  │  ○ Manually    ┌──────────────────┐│   │ Cancel Publisher │ │
│  │                │ Send Edition Now  ││   └─────────────────┘ │
│  │  Latest Edition: Thursday, January 12, 1995 12:24:47 PM  │ │
│  │                                    │   ┌────────┐ ┌──────┐ │
│  └────────────────────────────────────┘   │ Cancel │ │  OK  │ │
│                                            └────────┘ └──────┘ │
└─────────────────────────────────────────────────────────────┘
```

The Publisher To pop-up menu at the top shows the name of the edition file. By clicking on this menu, you can see the directory path that shows exactly where the edition is located on your disk.

3. Click the Send Edition Now button to update the edition file immediately; click the Manually button to set the edition for manual updates only, or click the Cancel Publisher button to break the link between the publisher and the edition. You can also see the date and time when the latest edition update was sent.

4. Click OK or press (Return) to close the dialog box and save the changes you've made.

Edition files have gray icons when you view them in the Finder (like the one shown on the Publisher To menu in the example above), so you can always distinguish an edition file from a normal document file.

Once you've published an edition, you can close the publisher's document if you like. The publisher's document doesn't have to be open in order for you to subscribe to the edition you created.

Subscribing

To subscribe to an edition:

1. Open a document and select the area where you want the subscriber to appear, then choose the *Subscribe To...* command. You see the Subscriber dialog box, which looks amazingly like the Publisher dialog box shown on the previous page.

2. Select the edition to which you want to subscribe.

3. Click the Subscribe button or press (Return). ClarisWorks inserts the subscriber in your document. It's outlined in gray, like this:

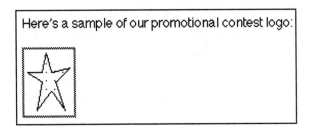

When you subscribe to cells in a spreadsheet, make sure you select enough cells in the subscriber area to contain the cells in the edition. If you don't, ClarisWorks subscribes to the whole edition anyway and overwrites as many cells as necessary to contain the edition's data.

Setting subscriber options

Normally, subscribers are set to automatic updates, so they change whenever the edition file changes. Also, subscribers normally exist as complete entities and they can't be modified in the subscribing document. However, you can change these options with the *Subscriber Options...* command.

1. Click inside the gray border of the subscriber's area. If you don't see the gray border, choose *Show Borders* from the Publishing submenu.

2. Choose *Subscriber Options...* from the Publishing submenu. You see the Subscriber dialog box, like this:

Subscriber to: ▢ **Star Logo Edition**   ▼

┌─ **Get Editions:** ──────────────────────────
   ● **Automatically**   [**Cancel Subscriber**]
   ○ **Manually**   [**Get Edition Now**]   [**Open Publisher**]
   Latest Edition : Thursday , January 12, 1995 12:33:45 PM

                                    [Cancel]   [**OK**]

As with the Publisher dialog box, the Subscriber To pop-up menu at the top shows the name of the edition file. Click on it to see the edition file's location on your disk.

3. Click the Get Edition Now button to update the subscriber immediately; click the Manually button to set the subscriber for manual updates only; or click the Cancel Subscriber button to break the link between the subscriber and the edition.

You can also open the publishing document by clicking the Open Publisher button in this dialog box.

If the data you subscribed to is text or numbers, there's an Allow Modification checkbox at the bottom of the Subscriber dialog box. By checking it, you permit changes to the subscriber data from within the subscribing document. Otherwise, the data can only be changed when it's changed in the publishing document.

Even if you allow modifications and make them, the subscriber will still be updated with new data as long as the link remains between it and the edition file.

4.   Click OK or press ⟨Return⟩ to close the dialog box and save the changes you've made.

Deleting a subscriber

If a subscriber contains a graphic, you can delete it by simply backspacing over it or selecting it and pressing the Delete key. This includes text frames or text objects from documents. If a subscriber contains text, however (spreadsheet or database data, or text from a word processing document, for example), you can't delete it unless you first allow modification of the subscriber or cancel the subscriber in the Subscriber dialog box.

Once you allow modification to a text subscriber, you delete the text as you normally would in that document's data environment.

Viewing an edition in the Finder

Edition files can't be opened by ClarisWorks, and they're invisible in the directory dialog box you see when you use the *Open...* or *Insert...* command. However, when you're working in the Finder you can view information about an edition and even open its publisher quickly:

1.   Double-click on the edition file in the Finder. You see a window like the one at the top of the next page:

Star edition

PICT   [**Open Publisher**]

2. The window shows the data the edition contains. Click the
   Open Publisher button or press [Return] to open the
   publisher's document.

Troubleshooting

**You try to reformat a subscriber or change its position in a document, but
a message says that you can't modify it.** Select the subscriber and choose
Subscriber Options... from the Publishing submenu, then click the Allow
Modification checkbox at the bottom of the Subscriber dialog box.

**You publish some spreadsheet cells and subscribe to them in a word
processing document, but the columns of data don't line up properly.**
You have to set custom tabs in a word processing document to properly align
columnar data in a subscriber. Before you can select the subscriber data and
set tabs for it, though, you have to allow modifications to it. Open the
Subscriber dialog box and check the Allow Modifications box (see the
previous solution).

As an alternative to subscribing to spreadsheet data directly in a word processing document, create a spreadsheet frame in the word processing document and then subscribe to the spreadsheet data inside the frame. Because you're subscribing to spreadsheet cells inside another spreadsheet, the data will be formatted properly and you won't have to worry about tabs.

You published text or numbers with custom character formats, but the formats don't appear in the subscriber. Publish and subscribe doesn't maintain custom data or text formats. You have to reformat the data in the subscriber. If you see a message saying that you can't modify the subscriber, select the subscriber, choose *Subscriber Options...*, and check the Allow Modifications box in the Subscriber dialog box, then reformat the data.

A message says the edition is missing. The edition file has been moved to another disk, renamed, or deleted. Doing any of these prevents ClarisWorks from locating the edition. However, ClarisWorks can find the edition if you've simply moved it to another folder on the same disk.

The Open Publisher button is dimmed in the subscriber dialog box. Either the edition has been renamed, deleted, or moved to another disk, or the publishing document (or the application that created it) has been moved, renamed or deleted. Use the *Find...* command on the File menu in the Finder to search for the missing file or program.

16

QuickTime
and slide shows

QuickTime and slide shows are two options you
can use to jazz up ClarisWorks documents on
your screen. With QuickTime you can view
movies inside documents, and slide shows let
you display pages of documents as individual
slides. You need Apple's QuickTime extension
and Macintosh System 7 software to display
movies, but you can display any document
as a slide show. ➤➤

Using QuickTime

QuickTime is Apple's software technology for displaying movies and sounds on a Mac. In order to display QuickTime movies, you must have the QuickTime extension installed in your System Folder.

In ClarisWorks, a QuickTime movie is an object, just like a frame or a draw object. A movie looks like this:

└─Control badge

When a movie is selected, you see selection handles at its corners, just as you would with other objects. Clicking the control badge displays a set of controls you use to play the movie, as described later in this chapter.

Putting a movie in a document

You add a QuickTime movie to a document just as you do a picture. There are three ways to do this:

- Paste the movie from the Clipboard;

- Insert the movie with the *Insert...* command; or

- Import the movie.

When you import a movie, ClarisWorks creates a new Draw document and puts the movie in it.

You can insert QuickTime movies into word processing, spreadsheet, database, draw, or paint documents, but you can't always play them. Here are the exceptions:

- If you don't have QuickTime installed, you can see a Quick-Time movie object but you can't play the movie.

- In a paint document the first frame of the movie is converted into a painted image, so you can't play the movie.

- In a database document you can see the movie object in either Layout or Browse mode, but you can only play a movie in Layout mode.

Playing a movie

To play a movie:

1. Click the control badge. The movie controls appear below the movie frame, like this:

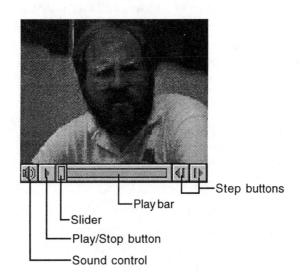

2. Click the Play/Stop button. The movie begins playing. As it plays, the slider moves to the right across the play bar. When the slider reaches the right edge of the play bar, the movie either stops or begins playing all over again, depending on the movie options you've set. (See *Setting movie options* on the next page.)

The other controls let you stop the movie, advance or reverse it, or adjust the sound volume.

• Click the sound control to reveal a pop-up slider you can drag to adjust the movie's sound volume.

• Click the Play/Stop button to stop the movie when it's playing, or to start a movie when it's not playing.

• Drag the slider to advance or reverse proportionally through the movie.

• Click one of the step buttons to advance or reverse one frame at a time.

Selecting or playing part of a movie

You can select part of a movie and play only that part by Shift-clicking in the play bar. The play bar darkens to show which part of it is selected. Once you've made your selection, click the Play/Stop button to play only that part.

Editing a movie

When it comes to editing, think of a movie as a flip book of individual pictures that you can select, cut, paste, or rearrange as you like. Use the step controls or the slider to select the frame or frames you want and then cut or copy them.

You can cut a group of frames from a movie and paste them into another movie, rearrange the frames within one movie, or cut some frames from a movie and paste them elsewhere in a document as a separate movie.

Setting movie options

To change the size, playback speed, or other movie options, select the movie (so the handles appear—don't click on the control badge) and then choose the *Movie Info...* command from the Options menu. You see the Movie Info dialog box, like this:

```
┌──────────────────────────────────────────────────────┐
│  Movie Info                                            │
│ ─────────────────────────────────────────────────     │
│ ┌Playback Options─────────────────────────┐           │
│ │ ☒ Normal size      ☐ Loop                │           │
│ │ ☐ Selection only     ◉ Forward only      │           │
│ │                      ○ Forward & backward │           │
│ │ Speed  [1      ]                          │           │
│ └──────────────────────────────────────────┘           │
│                                                        │
│  Durations –                                           │
│  Movie       0:00:12.3       ( Cancel )  ┌──────┐      │
│  Selection   0:00:00.0                   │  OK  │      │
│                                          └──────┘      │
└──────────────────────────────────────────────────────┘
```

If you've resized the movie, you can check the *Normal Size* box to return the movie to the size it had when you first added it to the document.

The *Selection Only* box tells ClarisWorks to play only the selected part of the movie.

The *Loop* box tells ClarisWorks to play the movie in an endless loop (repeating over and over) instead of stopping at the end. The *Forward Only* button repeats the movie from beginning to end only; the *Forward & Backward* button tells ClarisWorks to play the movie forward, then backward, then forward again, over and over.

The *Speed* box lets you set the playback rate. The normal speed is 1, but you can play the movie faster by entering other positive values. By entering a negative value, you play the movie faster only when it is playing backward.

Finally, the *Durations* information at the bottom tells you the total length of the movie and the length of the current selection.

. . . .

Displaying a slide show

ClarisWorks slide show option lets you display each page of a document as a slide. Slides appear by themselves on the screen, so this option is great for presentations. The *Slide Show...* command on the View menu lets you control how the slides in a multipage document are displayed.

 The *Slide Show...* command isn't available in Communications documents.

When you choose the *Slide Show...* command, you see the Slide Show dialog box, like this:

Slide Show

Order

  ⊞ Page 1   ⇧
  ⊞ Page 2
  ⊞ Page 3
  ⊞ Page 4
          ⇩

┌ **Slide Options** ─────────────
│ ⊠ **Fit to window**   ☐ **Fade**
│ ⊠ **Center**   ☐ **Loop**
│ ⊠ **Show cursor**   ☐ **Advance every**
│
│ ☐ **Background**   **5** seconds
│ ■ **Border**

⊞ = **Opaque**
⊟ = **Transparent**
☐ = **Hidden**

┌ **QuickTime Options** ─────────────
│ ☐
│ ☐   ☐

**To end show,
press q.**

(**Done**)   (**Cancel**)   (**Start**)

To display the pages in your document as slides, press Return or click the Start button. Each page of your document will appear on the screen as a slide, with a solid background and no menus showing. If you've simply clicked the Start button to accept the defaults in this dialog box, your slides will be changed once every 5 seconds, and they'll play in a continuous loop.

If you don't want to change any of the options in the Slide Show dialog box, you can skip over it by holding down the Option key when you choose the *Slide Show...* command. The slide show will start immediately, using the current options in the Slide Show dialog box.

To stop a slide show and return to the Slide Show dialog box, press Q, ⌘., or Esc.

Setting slide show options

Now let's look at the options in the Slide Show dialog box.

At the left, the *Order* list shows each of the pages in your document. You can rearrange the order in which pages are displayed by selecting the page name and dragging it up or down in the list. The icon at the left of each page name is normally opaque, which means that the slide will appear by itself. However, you can also make pages transparent (so they appear on top of the previous slide), or you can make them invisible so they don't appear at all.

- Click once on the icon to make the page transparent, so it overlays the previous slide.

- Double-click on the icon to make the page invisible, so it's skipped in the slide show.

- Click again to return the icon to its opaque mode, so the slide appears by itself.

In the *Slide Options* area, the *Fit to Window, Center,* and *Show Cursor* options are normally checked, and they do what they say: they resize the slide to fit the document window, center the slide on the screen, and show the cursor on the screen during the slide show.

The *Background* and *Border* options are pop-up palettes in which you choose the background and border colors for your slides. You set one color for each of these options for every slide in the show. (You can't set a red background for one slide and a green background for another, for example.)

The *Fade* option produces a fade effect between slides.

The *Loop* option displays the slides in an endless loop. When you uncheck this option, the slides are shown only once, and the last slide in your document remains on the screen at the end of the show until you press Q.

The *Advance Every* option is normally unchecked. It tells ClarisWorks to automatically change the slides at specific intervals. The default interval is 5 seconds, but you can enter any number of seconds you want. When the Advance Every box is unchecked, slides advance only when you click on the screen.

You can always advance slides manually, even if you have the Advance Every option set. Along with clicking the mouse button, you can advance a slide by pressing ⌃⌘↓ or ⌃⌘→. To back up a slide, press ⌃⌘↑ or ⌃⌘←.

In the *QuickTime Options* area, you have three choices that affect how QuickTime movies are played in slide shows. These options are available only if you have the QuickTime extension installed in your System Folder and if the document you're working with contains one or more QuickTime movies.

The *Auto Play* option tells ClarisWorks to automatically play any QuickTime movies that are in the slide being shown. As soon as the slide is displayed, the movie begins playing. If this option isn't checked, you have to play the QuickTime movie manually as discussed earlier in this chapter. If a slide contains more than one QuickTime movie and Auto Play is checked, the movies are played one after the other, in the objects' order on the slide from top to bottom or left to right.

The *Simultaneous* option is available only if the Auto Play option is checked. This tells ClarisWorks to play all the Quick-Time movies in one slide at the same time, rather than playing them one after the other.

Finally, the *Complete Play Before Advancing* option tells Claris-Works to automatically advance to the next slide as soon as all the QuickTime movies in the current slide are played. This setting overrides the Advance Every option, and it's available only if the Advance Every option is checked. For example, suppose you have the Advance Every option set to advance slides every 5 seconds, but it takes 10 seconds to play a QuickTime movie. If Complete Play Before Advancing isn't checked, ClarisWorks advances the slides every 5 seconds even if the QuickTime movie on the slide isn't finished playing. With the Complete Play Before Advancing box checked, however, ClarisWorks waits until the movie is finished playing before advancing the slide.

Troubleshooting

A QuickTime movie's control badge isn't showing. This means you're either viewing the movie frame in a Paint document, or you don't have the QuickTime extension installed in the Extensions folder inside your System Folder. If you've just dragged the QuickTime extension into your Extensions folder, you have to restart the Mac before QuickTime becomes active.

You try to play a movie, but a message says the movie isn't available. The object in a ClarisWorks document isn't the actual QuickTime movie—it's a pointer that tells ClarisWorks where to find the movie and that displays the movie's first frame. If the movie file itself has been moved to another disk, renamed, or deleted, ClarisWorks can't find it.

A movie plays, but it's jerky and the sound is choppy. QuickTime is very sensitive to the speed at which it can access the data in the movie file. It tries to play movies back at the same speed at which they were recorded, but sometimes it can't access the data quickly enough to do this. If the movie file is located on a CD-ROM disk, the CD-ROM player may be too slow to access the data at the speed QuickTime needs it. The same problem occurs when you play a movie file that's located on another disk across a network or on a magneto-optical disk.

The movie plays over and over. Click the Start/Stop button to pause the movie, then click on the movie frame to select it (so handles appear). Choose *Movie Info...* from the Options menu, uncheck the Loop option, and press Return. Now the movie will play only once.

The *Movie Info...* command doesn't appear on the Options menu. This command won't appear if you select a movie in a paint document, and it doesn't appear on the menu when you're working in a document that doesn't contain a QuickTime movie. Also, the command won't appear if you don't have QuickTime installed (see above).

A document page isn't displayed as a slide, or it's displayed as a transparent image on top of the previous slide. Press Q to display the Slide Show dialog box, then click the icon next to the hidden or transparent page until it shows opaque, as in the example on p. 420.

17

Mailing documents

If you have Apple's PowerTalk software installed on your Mac, you can use ClarisWorks to exchange electronic mail with other PowerTalk users. ➤➤

About PowerTalk

PowerTalk is desktop communications technology built into advanced versions of Macintosh system software like System 7 Pro. If you have PowerTalk installed, you can create and send mail, locate other users or servers on your network quickly, and affix or verify digital signatures on documents you send or receive. PowerTalk is made possible through system software extensions, and any program that supports PowerTalk can also be used to send and receive mail. ClarisWorks version 2.1 supports PowerTalk.

Using PowerTalk involves several new features and concepts. This chapter is no substitute for the *PowerTalk User's Guide* supplied by Apple, but we'll begin by going over some basic PowerTalk concepts, as it's necessary to understand these before you can use mail in ClarisWorks.

Sending electronic mail and faxes from the desktop has become a popular activity for many Mac users. The problem is that there are several different ways to do this, depending on which electronic mail or fax software you're using. In some cases, you might have to use two or three different programs to send the same letter to two or three different people, and you'd have to maintain separate address books for each mail system.

PowerTalk lets you send and receive mail in just one way with one set of addresses, no matter where your mail correspondent is located. By implementing PowerTalk at the system software level and providing the proper connections (or gateways) to other electronic mail systems, Apple makes sending and receiving mail as simple as creating and printing documents. Along with the basic PowerTalk services it provides with certain versions of system software, Apple includes a simple electronic mail program called AppleMail, so you can create and send messages from the desktop.

With PowerTalk, you can send messages from your Mac to other Macs, but the messages can't be delivered unless the other Mac is running. If the other Mac isn't running, the message is saved on your Mac until it can be sent. However, another Apple product called PowerServe lets you set up mail servers on a network. If you set up PowerServe mail servers, messages you send to others can be sent to the server (which is running all the time), and then forwarded to the addressee the next time that person starts up his or her Mac.

Basic PowerTalk components

In order for PowerTalk (or any mail system) to work, each mail user must have a unique address. In PowerTalk, each user is iden-tified with an *information card* that can contain not only the person's name and electronic address, but a physical address, phone number, and other information as well. Part of setting up PowerTalk on your Mac is creating an information card for your-self. Once you've done that, you can make your information card available to others and collect other cards from your electronic correspondents, much like you'd exchange business cards.

Along with information cards, PowerTalk adds some new fea-tures to your Mac's desktop and menu.

A *Mailbox* icon lets you access an In Tray and an Out Tray. If you've received mail, the In Tray lists the *letters* (messages) you've received and allows you to open them. The Out Tray lists letters you've sent and shows their status—whether each letter has been transmitted yet or not.

A Catalogs icon shows *catalogs*, or lists of mail servers and network users on every network or network zone you can access from your Mac. Catalogs are maintained on these mail servers, and you can browse through them to find user addresses you don't have. (See Chapter 4 in the *PowerTalk User's Guide* for more information.)

You can also create *personal catalogs* on your Mac to store fre-quently used information cards. The *Personal Catalog* item on the menu lets you open your personal catalog or add new information cards to it. The *Find In Catalog* item on the menu lets you search network catalogs for specific user addresses or file servers by name. If you have more than one personal catalog, you specify the *preferred personal catalog*, the one that opens each time you open your personal catalog.

The *PowerTalk Key Chain* icon on your desktop lets you prevent unauthorized access to your mail, and also lets you specify an *access code* (password) by which you can connect to many different network services. Before you can use PowerTalk, you must "unlock" this key chain each time you start up your Mac by entering your access code. If you leave your Mac temporarily, you can lock your keychain to prevent others from accessing your mail.

Finally, another Apple-supplied utility called *DigiSign* lets you create your own digital signature so you can "sign" the letters you send to verify their authenticity. See Chapter 8 in the *PowerTalk User's Guide* for more information.

Setting up PowerTalk

You set up PowerTalk by giving your Macintosh a unique network name, defining your PowerTalk Key Chain access code (or password), creating an information card for yourself (so others can send you letters), and choosing any PowerShare mail servers to which you want access (if you're on a network that has PowerShare servers).

Additionally, you can add other users' information cards to your personal catalog, either by creating them from scratch or by copying them from a network catalog.

For more information about these procedures, see Chapter 2 in the *PowerTalk User's Guide*.

Once you've set up PowerTalk, ClarisWorks version 2.1 automatically recognizes it and you can send mail right from inside your ClarisWorks documents.

Using mail in ClarisWorks

Any ClarisWorks document except a communications document can be used to create a letter. You turn a document into a letter by attaching a *mailer* to it. A mailer is a special header that specifies the message's sender (you), its recipient(s), and its subject. You can send a letter to as many different people as you like by adding their addresses to the mailer. You can also use the mailer to add enclosures to your letter, such as other documents or folders.

When you send a letter, you can send it in its native Claris-Works format, or you can use various foreign file formats, much as you would when exporting a document. For example, if you're mailing a letter to someone who has Microsoft Word but not ClarisWorks, you can send the letter in Microsoft Word format. When you're sending a letter to several different people, you can send it in multiple formats simultaneously. Finally, you can send the document as a *snapshot* (a bitmapped picture of the document that can be viewed but not edited), and as *AppleMail* (a format compatible with the AppleMail program).

You also set a priority designation for each letter you send. This doesn't affect the speed at which the letter is delivered, but the designation appears with the letter in the recipient's In Tray, so the person can have some idea of its urgency (see *Sending Letters* and *Viewing Mail* later in this chapter for more information).

When you receive mail, you open the mailbox icon on your desktop, open the In Tray, and then open each letter there. Once you've opened a letter, you can easily reply to it, save it, or forward it to someone else.

There are four new shortcut buttons you can use to add or delete mailers, send letters, forward letters, or reply to letters. Use the *Edit Shortcuts...* command on the Shortcuts submenu and scroll to the bottom of the Available Shortcuts list to find these new shortcuts and add them to your Shortcuts palette.

ClarisWorks' mail functions are handled from the Mail sub-menu off the File menu, and from within the mailer you attach to a document. You can also streamline some ClarisWorks mail activities with the Mail options in the Preferences dialog box. Let's look at these procedures now.

Creating and sending letters

To create a letter with ClarisWorks, you add a mailer to it.

1. Open the document you want to send, or create a new document. (You can't mail communications documents.)

2. Type the text of your message in the document. (If you're mailing an existing document, you'll probably want to type the text of your message at the top of the document and then separate it from the rest of the document's contents with a row of dashed lines or some extra spaces.)

3. Choose *Add Mailer* from the Mail submenu off the File menu. ClarisWorks adds a mailer to your document, like the one at the top of the next page:

```
┌─────────────────────────── Weekly Reminder (WP) ───────────────────────────┐
│ ▽  ⬚ From                              Subject                               │
│   ┌──────────────────────┐           ┌──────────────────────┐              │
│   │ Charles Rubin        │           │                      │              │
│   └──────────────────────┘           │                      │              │
│   ⬚ Recipients                        │                      │              │
│   ┌──────────────────┐ ┌─┐           └──────────────────────┘              │
│   │                  │ │⇧│                                                   │
│   │                  │ └─┘           ⬚ Enclosures                           │
│   │                  │               ┌──────────────────┐ ┌─┐              │
│   │                  │               │                  │ │⇧│              │
│   │                  │ ┌─┐           │                  │ └─┘              │
│   │                  │ │⇩│           │                  │                  │
│   └──────────────────┘ └─┘           │                  │ ┌─┐              │
│                                      └──────────────────┘ │⇩│              │
│ 0    1    2    3    4    5    6                                             │
│                                                                             │
│   [▲][▲][▲][▲]  [≡│≡]  [     ]  [≡][≡][≡][≡]  [□|□]                          │
│                                                                             │
│                                                                             │
│       *Nag, Nag, Nag....*                                                   │
│                                                                             │
│       Just your weekly reminder to turn in expense reports by noon          │
│       on Friday if you want the reimbursement included in next week's       │
│ [100] [▄▄] [□] Page 1              [⇦][     ]                               │
└─────────────────────────────────────────────────────────────────────────────┘
```

4. If you've set up your Mac properly to use PowerTalk, the *From* box automatically contains your name.

If you have more than one PowerTalk address, you can change the From address by clicking the *From* button and entering the PowerTalk Key Chain access code for the PowerTalk address you want.

5. Click in the *Subject* box and type the message's subject. Keep the description to a few words or less (you'll see why in *Reading and responding to mail* later in this chapter). Every message must have a subject, or PowerTalk can't send it.

6. Press (Tab) to move the insertion point to the Recipients list.

Addressing letters

To address your letter, add one or more addresses to the Recipients list in the mailer. There are two basic ways to do this.

- If you have information cards stored in a folder on your desktop or in an open catalog on your desktop, you can drag one or more of them from the desktop into the *Recipients* box.

- To addresses from inside the mailer, click the *Recipients* button and select user names from the address panel that appears. (If you haven't entered your PowerTalk Key Chain access code since you started up your Mac, you'll be asked to enter it before the address panel is displayed.)

Adding names from the address panel

The address panel lets you add names to the Recipients list from your personal catalog or from a network catalog. You can also enter a recipient name and address by typing it, or search a network catalog to find the address you want.

The address panel appears when you click the Recipients button. It looks like this:

The panel lists addresses in either your personal catalog or in a network catalog (depending on which of these you last used). When you select a recipient name and add it to the Recipients box, you also choose whether to send the letter *To* that person, to send it as a carbon copy (*CC*), or to send it as a blind carbon copy (*BCC*). BCC recipient names don't show up in the Recipients box when you add them.

To add a name to the Recipients list from the address panel, either:

- Double-click the name to add it as a To address, or

- Select the name and then click the To or CC button, or hold down the (Option) key and click the BCC button.

 When you drag addresses into the Recipients list from the desktop, they are also added as To addresses.

Deleting recipients from a mailer

If you add a name to the Recipients box and then change your mind, just drag the information card to the Trash.

Using address panel options

The four buttons in the address panel give you different options for locating and adding addresses to the Recipients list in the mailer.

- Click the book button to view your personal catalog. The names appear as shown on p. 432.

- To view and browse through network catalogs, click the globe button and then navigate to the catalog you want and select a user name from it.

- To locate an address by searching for the user's name, click the magnifying glass button to display the Find Address panel, like the one at the top of the next page:

```
                        Find Address
  ┌───┐
  │ 📖 │      Find  ┌──────────────────────────┐
  └───┘            └──────────────────────────┘
  ┌───┐
  │ 🌐 │    Search ┌─────────────────────┬───┐
  └───┘           │ everywhere          │ ▼ │
                  └─────────────────────┴───┘
  ┌───┐    ┌──────────────────────────────┬──┐
  │ 🔑 │    │                              │⇧ │
  └───┘    │                              ├──┤
  ┌───┐    │                              │  │
  │ ✏ │    │                              │⇩ │
  └───┘    └──────────────────────────────┴──┘

         ┌──────────┐      ┌────────┐ ┌────────┐
         │  Done    │      │        │ │        │
         └──────────┘      └────────┘ └────────┘
```

Enter the user's name in the *Find* box, and use the Search menu to specify a particular network catalog or disk where you want to search, if you like. (If you know that the address is in a particular catalog or on a particular disk, specifying one makes the search go faster.) Click the *Find* button to conduct the search. Any addresses that match the name you typed appear in the list, and then you can select the specific address you want to use.

• To enter an address manually, click the pencil button to display the Type-In Addressing panel, like this:

```
                     Type-In Addressing
  ┌───┐
  │ 📖 │      Address
  └───┘
  ┌───┐    ┌──────────────────────────────────┐
  │ 🌐 │    │                                  │
  └───┘    │                                  │
  ┌───┐    │                                  │
  │ 🔍 │    │                                  │
  └───┘    └──────────────────────────────────┘
  ┌───┐
  │ ✏ │    Catalog ┌─────────────────────┬───┐
  └───┘            │ AppleTalk           │ ▼ │
                   └─────────────────────┴───┘

         ┌──────────┐      ┌────────┐ ┌────────┐
         │  Done    │      │        │ │        │
         └──────────┘      └────────┘ └────────┘
```

Type the address in the *Address* box, choose the network catalog where the address is located, then click the To, CC, or BCC button to add this name to the Recipients list.

When you're through adding names to the Recipients list, click the *Done* button in the address panel to put it away.

 If you select a name in the Catalog Browser panel and hold down the (Option) key, the To button changes to Save…. Clicking the Save button saves an alias of the selected address into your preferred personal catalog.

Adding enclosures

To add enclosures to your letter, drag a document or folder from your desktop into the *Enclosures* box, or click the *Enclosures* button in the mailer. When you click the Enclosures button, you see a directory dialog box where you can navigate among your disks and folders and select files or folders to enclose. To enclose an item, double-click it in the list or select it and then click the *Enclose* button.

You can enclose up to 50 different items with each letter you send. Once you've added an enclosure, a paper clip icon appears in the mailer's upper right corner to remind you of this.

To delete an enclosure, just drag it from the Enclosures list to the Trash. This doesn't delete the item from your disk—it just deletes it from the Enclosures list.

Sending letters

When you've finished entering a subject, addresses, and enclosures in the mailer, you're ready to send the letter.

1. Choose *Send…* from the Mail submenu. You'll see the Send Document dialog box, like the one at the top of the next page:

```
┌─────────────────────────────────────────────────────────────┐
│ ┌───────────────────────────────────────────────────────┐   │
│ │ Send document "Weekly Reminder"          ┌──────────┐  │   │
│ │                                          │   Send   │  │   │
│ │ Send as: [ ClarisWorks        ▼]  ☐ Sign Letter       │   │
│ │                                          ┌──────────┐  │   │
│ │                                   Priority: ○ High    │   │
│ │                                          │  Cancel  │  │   │
│ │                                             ● Normal  │   │
│ │                                             ○ Low     │   │
│ │          ☐ Multiple Formats                           │   │
│ └───────────────────────────────────────────────────────┘   │
└─────────────────────────────────────────────────────────────┘
```

2. Choose a letter format from the pop-up menu. If you want to send the letter in multiple formats or in AppleMail or Snapshot format, click the *Multiple Formats* checkbox. You'll see additional buttons for AppleMail and Snapshot formats, and you can then choose one or both of these and select one or more of the formats from the pop-up menu.

3. If you've created a digital signature, you can sign your letter by clicking the *Sign Letter* checkbox. (See Chapter 8 in your *PowerTalk User's Guide* for more information.)

4. Click a button to set the priority level for the letter. (Remember, this doesn't affect the speed of the letter's delivery, it only identifies the letter's priority in the recipient's In Tray.)

5. Press [Return] or click the *Send* button to send the letter. A copy of it appears in your Out Tray.

Saving letters

Any letter you open is stored in your In Tray until you delete it from there. However, you may not want to clutter your In Tray with a bunch of old mail, so you can also save letters elsewhere.

You can save letters you create or open just as you would any other ClarisWorks document, using the *Save* or *Save As...* command on the File menu (see *Saving documents* on p. 27 for more information). Along with saving letters as ClarisWorks documents or in foreign file formats, however, you can also save them in

Letter or Letter Stationery formats. In fact, the default file format for any letter you save is Letter format.

Here's how the Letter and Letter Stationery formats differ from standard ClarisWorks formats:

ClarisWorks format saves the document but not its mailer.

Letter format saves the document along with its mailer.

Letter Stationery format saves the document and its mailer as stationery, so you can create standard mail documents that you can reuse easily.

Collapsing or deleting a mailer

You won't always want to retain mailers with documents, and even if you do, you won't always want the whole mailer displayed, since they take up so much room on the screen. Fortunately, you can collapse a mailer or delete it when you no longer need it.

To collapse a mailer, click the triangle next to the From button. The mailer shrinks to a ribbon at the top of your document, like this:

Clicking the triangle again expands the mailer.

One of the mail preferences options lets you decide whether messages open with expanded or collapsed mailers. See *Setting mail preferences* on p. 442.

To delete a mailer, open the document that contains the mailer and then choose *Delete Mailer* from the Mail submenu.

Reading and responding to mail

PowerTalk notifies you when you receive mail, either by flashing an icon in the menu bar, playing a sound, or displaying a message, depending on how you've set the preferences for your mailbox (see Chapter 5 in the *PowerTalk User's Guide* for more information).

Viewing mail

To view mail you've received, you use the mailbox icon on your desktop. Double-click the mailbox icon on your desktop. The In Tray opens automatically, like this:

✓	Subject	Sender	Date Sent	Location	Priority
	🖂 Status Report	Dick Searle	1/12/95, 1 :55 PM	local	normal

In Tray for Charles Rubin — 1 item

Here you can see each letter's subject, sender, and other information. (You can see why it's a good idea to keep subject information relatively short—there's not much room in which to display it here.)

To help organize your In Tray when it contains many letters, you can sort items in the In Tray by subject, sender, date sent, location, priority level, or whether the item has been read or not. As in other desktop windows, you can switch views by choosing them from the View menu, or by clicking the name of the category by which you want to view.

You can also control which letters are displayed in the In Tray by adding descriptive *tags* to them. Tags are invisible markers, identified by keywords, that you can attach to letters. For example, you could tag letters associated with different projects with different keywords, and then display only letters with a particular tag. To add tags to mail in the In Tray, you use the Mailbox menu (see Chapter 5 in the *PowerTalk User's Guide*). You can add tags to your letters from within ClarisWorks by setting a mail preferences option (see p. 442).

Opening mail

To open a letter in the In Tray, double-click it. The letter opens with its mailer. (The mailer may be expanded or collapsed, depending on how you've set your mail preferences. See p. 442.)

When the letter is open, you can save it elsewhere on your disk if you like, using the *Save* or *Save As...* command on the File menu. If the message has enclosures, you can double-click their names in the Enclosures list to open them.

You must actually open a new mail message to cancel the mail notification features. If you open your In Tray without opening a new message inside it, your Mac will continue to notify you that you have new mail. If mail notification really begins to bug you, you can turn off all notification with the *Preferences* command on the Mailbox menu that appears in the Finder when your In Tray is open. See Chapter 5 in the *PowerTalk User's Guide* for more information.

After you've opened a letter, a check mark appears next to its name in the In Tray so you can distinguish it from unopened letters.

Deleting mail

To delete a letter from your In Tray, drag it to the Trash. You can also Shift-click or drag a selection rectangle around groups of letters to delete them.

By setting your mailbox preferences, you can also tell your Mac to automatically delete mail once it has been in the In Tray for a certain number of days. Open the mailbox icon on the desktop and then choose *Preferences* from the Mailbox menu; or see Chapter 5 in the *PowerTalk User's Guide* for more information.

Replying to a letter

You can always create a new letter from scratch and send it in reply, but you can also have ClarisWorks do some of the work for you by using the *Reply* or *Reply to All* command on the Mail submenu. To automate the reply process:

1. Open the original letter and choose *Reply* or *Reply to All* from the Mail submenu. (*Reply* sends your answer only to the person who sent you the letter; *Reply to All* sends your answer to everyone on the original letter's Recipients list.) ClarisWorks opens a new, untitled word processor document with a mail header already attached, and already filled out to respond to the original message, like the one at the top of the next page:

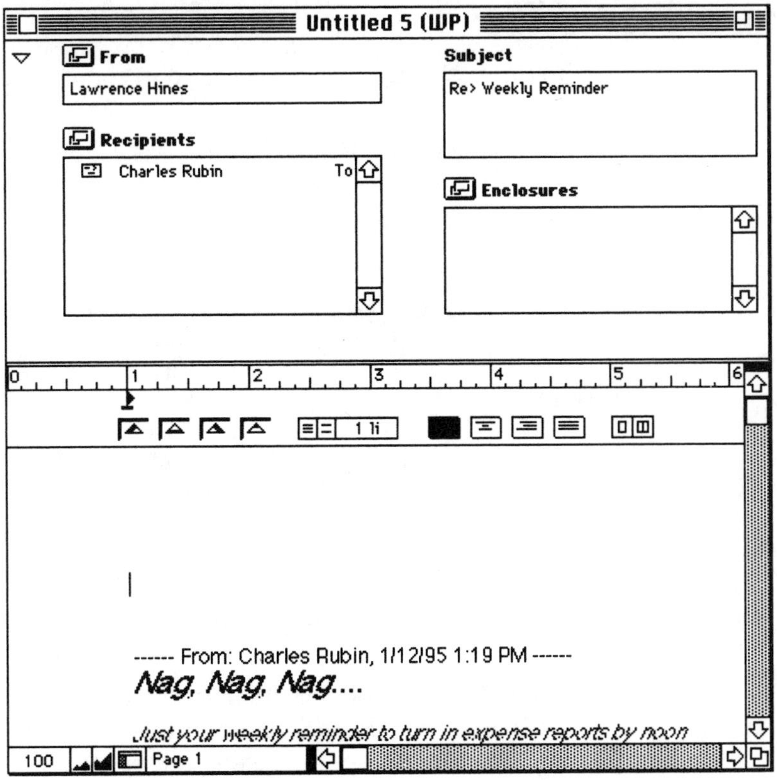

2. If the letter you're replying to was a word processor document, the text of that message is included in your reply, and is separated from your reply by a dashed line, as shown above. (If the original message was another type of document, its contents aren't included in your reply.) Also, notice that ClarisWorks has added *Re>* in front of the message's subject.

3. Type the text of your reply.

4. Expand the mailer and add any new recipients or enclosures, if necessary.

5. Send the message.

Forwarding a letter

To forward a letter you've received to someone else:

1. Open the letter and choose *Forward* from the Mail sub-menu. A new mailer is added on top of the letter's original mailer, like this:

```
┌──────────────────────────────────────────────────────────────┐
│▤□══════════════ Weekly Reminder (WP) ══════════════▤▤│
├──────────────────────────────────────────────────────────────┤
│ ▽   🖃 Forwarded by              Subject                       │
│     ┌─────────────────────┐▽    ┌───────────────────────────┐ │
│     │ Charles Rubin       │     │ Fwd> Weekly Reminder      │ │
│     └─────────────────────┘     │                           │ │
│     🖃 Recipients                │                           │ │
│     ┌─────────────────────┐⇧    └───────────────────────────┘ │
│     │                     │                                    │
│     │                     │     🖃 Enclosures                  │
│     │                     │     ┌───────────────────────┐⇧   │
│     │                     │     │                       │     │
│     │                     │⇩    │                       │     │
│     └─────────────────────┘     │                       │     │
│ ◹                               └───────────────────────┘⇩   │
└──────────────────────────────────────────────────────────────┘
```

   Notice that the From label has changed to *Forwarded by*, and the message's subject now has *Fwd>* in front of it. This mailer is added on top of the original mailer—it doesn't replace it. To see the original mailer, click the dog-ear icon in the lower left corner of the mailer.

2. Add one or more addresses to the Recipients box in the mailer, add any new enclosures if you like, and then send the letter as you would any other message.

• •

Setting mail preferences

There are a number of options you can set for how mail is handled in ClarisWorks. To view and change these options, choose the *Preferences…* command from the Edit menu, scroll the palettes list at the left until you see the Mail icon, and then click the Mail icon. The Mail preferences appear, like this:

```
┌─────────────────────────────────────────────────────────┐
│ Preferences                                               │
│  ┌──────────┬──┬──────────────────────────────────────┐  │
│  │       ⬆  │ Mail                                     │  │
│  │ [Palettes]│     ☐ Include contents of original letter in reply │
│  │ Palettes │       ◉                                  │  │
│  │          │       ○                                  │  │
│  │          │     Style [Plain Text ▼]                 │  │
│  │[Communic.]│    ☐ Close a letter after it has been sent │
│  │Communication│   ☒                                    │  │
│  │          │     ☐ Show options when closing a letter │  │
│  │          │     ☐ Expand mailer when creating a letter │  │
│  │  [Mail]  │     ☐ Expand mailer when opening a letter │  │
│  │   Mail   │     ☒ Delete movie files when letter is closed │
│  │       ⬇  │    ( Movies Folder... ) Cirrus 85-Q :    │  │
│  └──────────┴──┴──────────────────────────────────────┘  │
│            (Make Default)  ( Cancel )  (   OK   )         │
└─────────────────────────────────────────────────────────┘
```

If you have a letter open when you set these preferences, they'll apply to that letter only. If you want the options you set here to apply to every letter you work with, either:

- Click the *Make Default* button before clicking OK to save the preferences; or

- Set the options when no letters are open.

Here's what the options do.

Include contents of original letter in reply tells ClarisWorks to copy the contents of the original letter to your reply letter when you use the *Reply* or *Reply to All* command. When the box is checked, you can choose to have the entire contents of the original letter included in your reply, or to have only the contents you've selected in the original letter included in your reply. Also, the Style menu below the two buttons lets you select a character style for the original letter's contents. Choosing a different style like Italic or Underline helps distinguish the original letter's text from the reply you type.

Close a letter after it has been sent tells ClarisWorks to automatically close a letter after you send it. You're usually finished with the letter at that point anyway, so this saves your having to close it yourself. If you check the box below this option, ClarisWorks will remind you to save the letter before it automatically closes it.

Show options when closing a letter tells ClarisWorks to display two options when you close a letter you've just opened from your In Tray. When you check this option and then close a letter you've opened from the In Tray, ClarisWorks displays a dialog box like this:

```
┌─────────────────────────────────────────────┐
│  ┌──┐    Close letter and:                    │
│  │▫▫│                                          │
│  └──┘    □ Add tag  ┌──────────────────────┐   │
│                     └──────────────────────┘   │
│          □ Move to Trash                       │
│                                                 │
│                    ( Cancel )  [ Close ]        │
└─────────────────────────────────────────────┘
```

The *Add Tag* box lets you add a tag to the letter. If you've already created one or more tags, they appear on the pop-up menu next to the text box, and you can add them by using the menu after you check the Add Tag box. If you specify a new tag, it is automatically added to the pop-up menu and will appear there next time you use the Add Tag option. (For more about using tags, see Chapter 5 in the *PowerTalk User's Guide*.)

The *Move to Trash* box tells ClarisWorks to automatically move the letter to the Trash when you close it. If you know you don't want to keep the letter in your In Tray, check this option to delete it automatically.

Expand mailer when creating a letter tells ClarisWorks to add a mailer in its expanded form when you use the *Add Mailer* command. If the box isn't checked, the mailer is added in its collapsed form.

Expand mailer when opening a letter tells ClarisWorks to display an opened letter with the mailer expanded. If the box isn't checked, letters open with their mailers collapsed.

Delete movie files when letter is closed tells ClarisWorks to delete any QuickTime movie files that were enclosed with a letter once the letter is closed. When you enclose a QuickTime movie with a letter you send, the movie isn't in its playable format. When the letter is opened by its recipient, however, the movie is converted into its playable format and is saved on your disk. By checking this option, you avoid saving every movie file contained in letters you open. Since QuickTime movie files are quite large, this is a good option to check (which is why a checked box here is the default option). The *Movies Folder...* button below the movie file option lets you select a different disk or folder on which to store movie files if you opt to store them. The default location is your startup hard disk.

Troubleshooting

There's no Mail menu on your File menu. You're not using version 2.1 or later of ClarisWorks. Contact Claris at 408-987-7000 for an upgrade.

The Mail item on your File menu is dimmed. You're running ClarisWorks on a Mac that hasn't been set up to use PowerTalk. Install the PowerTalk system software and then the Mail menu will become active. If you don't have PowerTalk, consult your Apple dealer or software vendor.

You can't find a user's name or address in the address panel. Either you're looking in the wrong catalog, the user has moved his or her information card to another catalog, or you've got the user's name wrong.

If you can't find a user's name in your personal catalog, it means you either haven't added that person's address to your personal catalog, or you've stored it in a different personal catalog. You can create more than one personal catalog with PowerTalk, so you may need to look in others. Check your disk for other personal catalogs. If you find one and find the user's name in it, drag the information card from that catalog into the Recipients list in your mailer.

To change which personal catalog ClarisWorks displays when you use the address panel, select the icon for the catalog you want on the desktop, choose *Get Info...* from the File menu, and click the *Set Preferred* button. See Chapter 4 in the *PowerTalk User's Guide* for more information.

Rather than hunting around your disk, you can also have your Mac search for the user's address. Click the magnifying glass icon to display the Find Address panel. Type in the user's name there and click the Find button. If the user's name exists on your network, the address appears in the Find Address panel's address list. If you click the Find button to search for an address and no addresses are found, you probably have the user's name wrong, or the user hasn't yet set up his or her Mac for PowerTalk.

A letter is not delivered. Either the letter can't be delivered because it has been sent directly to a Mac that isn't turned on, or the address can't be found.

If you're not using PowerShare servers on your network, you send letters from one Mac to another, but the delivery can't take place if the recipient's Mac is off. When this is the case, the letter has the status *waiting* when you view it in your Out Tray. The only thing you can do in this case is to wait for the user to start up his or her Mac.

If the letter couldn't be delivered because the address can't be found, you'll see a trouble message in your Out Tray indicating this. If you used an address that has worked before, the user may have moved his or her information card to a different catalog or network zone or changed his or her

Macintosh name, so the address on the information card you used is no longer valid. Check with the user.

If you used the Type-In Addressing panel to enter an address from the keyboard, make sure you've spelled the address properly, and that you've included the network zone name if the user is in a different zone. For example, if the user *JoJones* is in a zone called *Siberia*, the address should be *JoJones@Siberia*. You must always include the zone name preceded by the @ sign to send mail to a different zone when you type an address by hand.

You can't find the Mailbox icon on your desktop. PowerTalk isn't turned on. Use the PowerTalk Setup control panel to turn it on. See Chapter 2 in the *PowerTalk User's Guide* for more information.

Your Mailbox icon is showing, but you're unable to send or receive any mail. Either you have AppleTalk set to Inactive in the Chooser or you've become physically disconnected from the network. If you can send mail but you can't receive it, it's possible that your Macintosh name has been changed in the Sharing Setup control panel.

To check the network connection, make sure your network adapter cable is securely plugged into the back of your Mac. If it looks loose, shut the Mac down and reconnect it. If the connection looks okay, open the Chooser and click the *Active* button in the AppleTalk area in the lower right corner of the Chooser window.

To check your Macintosh name, open your local network catalog and look at the name on your own information card. This name should match the Macintosh Name information listed in the Sharing Setup control panel. If it doesn't, change the Macintosh Name information in the Sharing Setup control to match the name on your PowerTalk information card.

The AppleTalk or other network catalog names are missing from the address panel when you click the Catalog button—you see disk and folder names instead. This means you aren't connected to the network or you don't have AppleTalk turned on. See the previous problem.

You get a "Disk Full" message when you try to send a letter. PowerTalk requires at least 1.5 megabytes of free space on your startup disk. If you get a full disk message when you try to send a letter, you'll have to delete some files from your disk to make more room. Check the Out Tray and In Tray in your PowerTalk mailbox. If you have some old, large messages there, you should be able to delete them, particularly if you've saved the information someplace else. One of the problems with mail is that you can have two or three different versions of the same document: one saved in ClarisWorks, one saved in a different format, and one saved in your In Tray or Out Tray. Watch for these duplications and eliminate them to conserve disk space.

You get low memory messages when using mail features. PowerTalk hogs over 500K of memory by itself, so if you're running close to the limit of your Mac's memory when you try to open your mailbox or send mail, you may run low on memory. The temporary solution is to close other windows, documents, or applications you're not currently using, or disable other large system extensions like QuickTime or file sharing if you're not using them. The long-term solution is to buy more memory for your Mac.

A

Installing
and running
ClarisWorks

*This appendix covers options and
strategies for installing ClarisWorks
and for adjusting the amount of
disk space and memory it uses.* ➡

Installing ClarisWorks

ClarisWorks comes with an Installer program that automates the process of installing all of the program's files on your disk. The full installation includes dozens of files:

- The ClarisWorks program.

- An onscreen introduction to the program.

- A folder of Assistants files.

- A folder of stationery documents.

- A folder of translators that let you work with files from other programs.

- Main and user spelling dictionaries (the user dictionary is empty).

- A Thesaurus file.

- Help system files.

- The Macintosh Communications Toolbox and associated files.

- A Labels file containing various label layouts for the database.

- Macro, shortcuts, and preferences files.

To install all these files:

1. Insert Disk 1 in your floppy disk drive and then double-click the Install ClarisWorks icon in the disk window that appears. You see the Installer program's title screen.

2. Press (Return). You see the Easy Install dialog box, like the one at the top of the next page:

```
╔══════════════════ Install ClarisWorks ══════════════════╗
║  ┌─────────────────┐                    ┌─────────────┐  ║
║  │ Easy Install  ▼ │                    │  Read Me... │  ║
║  └─────────────────┘                    └─────────────┘  ║
║  ┌────────────────────────────────────────────────────┐ ║
║  │ Installs the ClarisWorks 3.0 application program,   │ ║
║  │ Assistants, Introduction to ClarisWorks, onscreen   │ ║
║  │ Help, stationery files, clip art, spell-checking,   │ ║
║  │ thesaurus, hyphenation, XTND import and export      │ ║
║  │ translators, and communications tools.              │ ║
║  │                                                     │ ║
║  └────────────────────────────────────────────────────┘ ║
║   Disk space available: 136,152K   Approximate disk space needed: 12,038K ║
║   Install Location                                        ║
║                      ┌──────────────────┐  ┌───────────┐ ║
║                      │ Macintosh HD   ▼ │  │   Quit    │ ║
║      ┌──────┐        └──────────────────┘  └───────────┘ ║
║      │ ⌐    │    ┌──────────────────┐      ┌───────────┐ ║
║      └──────┘    │   Switch Disk    │      │  Install  │ ║
║  on the disk "Macintosh HD"  └──────────────────┘  └───────────┘ ║
╚══════════════════════════════════════════════════════════╝
```

3. The Installer proposes to install ClarisWorks on the hard disk you used to start up your Mac. If you want to install the program on a different disk or inside a folder on your hard disk, click the Switch Disk button and navigate to the disk where you want ClarisWorks installed.

4. Click the Install button or press (Return). The Installer goes to work and prompts you to insert other disks as it needs them. When the installation is complete, you see a message saying so. You will need to restart your Macintosh to properly install all the ClarisWorks files before running the program for the first time.

• •

Saving Disk Space

The full ClarisWorks installation occupies about 12 megabytes of disk space. If you'd like to save some space on your hard disk, you can eliminate many of the ClarisWorks files that aren't essential to running the program.

There are two ways to save space on your disk:

1. Perform the full installation and then delete unwanted files or folders from your disk.

2. Perform a custom installation and install only some of the ClarisWorks files.

Let's look at each process in detail.

Deleting unwanted files

If you've already performed a full installation, you can free up some disk space by deleting files you know you won't use. In the ClarisWorks 3.0 folder, you can eliminate the Read Me file, the Introduction to ClarisWorks file, and some or all of the files in the Clip Art folder. By eliminating all the clip art and the other files, you'll save nearly 2 megabytes of disk space.

To save even more space, open the Claris folder inside your System Folder. There you'll find the Claris Translators, Claris-Works Assistants, and ClarisWorks Stationery folders, along with help, dictionary, macro, preferences, and other files.

The Claris Translators folder contains several dozen translators for different programs. If you know you won't need to share files with certain programs, you can delete those specific translator files from inside this folder, keeping only the ones you might really need.

In the ClarisWorks Stationery folder, check out each of the stationery documents and then delete the ones you don't think you'll use. Do the same with the ClarisWorks Assistants folder.

Finally, you can delete individual files. The ClarisWorks Help file is 3.5 megabytes by itself, so as you master the program you might want to eliminate this file. You might also delete the US Thesaurus file to save another 150K if you don't plan to use this feature.

With some judicious pruning, you can easily save several megabytes of space by deleting unwanted files from the Claris-Works folder and the Claris folder. If space on your disk is really, really tight, you can save even more space by deleting communications tools you won't use from inside the Extensions folder in your System Folder. For example, if you never use the Kermit error-checking protocol, you could delete the ClarisWorks Kermit Tool file and save 63K.

None of these suggested deletions will interfere with your abilities to run ClarisWorks and work with documents. And if you find you've deleted a file that you want to use later, you can always perform a custom installation or copy individual files from the ClarisWorks installation floppy disks.

Performing a custom installation

If you know in advance which files you want and don't want to install, you can avoid having to delete unwanted files by installing only those you do want with a custom installation. You can also use a custom installation to add a few more documents or features to an existing installation of ClarisWorks on your disk. To customize an installation:

1. Open the Install ClarisWorks program, as described on p. 426. When you see the Installer title screen, press (Return) to display the Easy Install dialog box.

2. Choose Custom Install from the pop-up menu in the upper left corner of the dialog box. You see the Custom Install dialog box, like the one at the top of the next page:

```
┌──────────────────── Install ClarisWorks ────────────────────┐
│  ┌─────────────────────┐                      ┌────────────┐ │
│  │ Custom Install    ▼ │                      │ Read Me... │ │
│  └─────────────────────┘                      └────────────┘ │
│  ☐ ClarisWorks for any Macintosh              [i] ⬆         │
│  ☐ ClarisWorks for Macintosh                  [i]           │
│  ☐ ClarisWorks for Power Macintosh            [i]           │
│  ·············································                 │
│  ☐ ClarisWorks Assistants                     [i]           │
│  ☐ ClarisWorks Stationery                     [i]           │
│  ☐ ClarisWorks Clip Art                       [i]           │
│  ☐ Introduction to ClarisWorks                [i] ⬇         │
│        Disk space available: 136,125K     Approximate disk space needed: OK │
│  ┌─ Install Location ──────────────────────┐                 │
│  │         ┌─────────────────────┐         │   ┌──────────┐  │
│  │         │ Macintosh HD      ▼ │         │   │   Quit   │  │
│  │         └─────────────────────┘         │   └──────────┘  │
│  │    ┌────┐       ┌─────────────┐         │   ┌──────────┐  │
│  │    │    │       │ Switch Disk │         │   │ Install  │  │
│  │  on the disk "Macintosh HD"   └─────────┘   └──────────┘  │
│  └──────────────────────────────────────────┘               │
└──────────────────────────────────────────────────────────────┘
```

The scrolling list contains the names of individual files or groups of files. Beneath the list you can see the amount of available disk space you have and a running tally of the disk space you'll need to install the items you select.

3. Scroll the list and select the first item you want to install. [Shift]-click to select additional items.

4. When you've selected all the items you want, click the Install button. ClarisWorks performs the installation, prompting you to insert other disks as necessary.

As with a full installation, you are prompted to restart your Mac when the custom installation is finished.

Running ClarisWorks

ClarisWorks will run on any Macintosh Plus or later model with 1 megabyte or more of RAM (random access memory) running Macintosh System 6.0.5 or later software. The program will run from a floppy disk, but for best performance you should run it from a hard disk. If you're running System 7.0 or later software, you'll need at least 2 megabytes of RAM. If you want to use PowerTalk mail features in ClarisWorks, you'll need a Macintosh II or Classic or later model with System 7 Pro or System 7.5 or later and at least 5 megabytes of RAM.

Beyond these basic hardware requirements, however, you can set up ClarisWorks to run most efficiently on your Mac, depending on the amount of RAM you have installed and the types of documents you work with. In this section, we'll look at configuring ClarisWorks to make the best use of your Mac's available memory.

Starting the program

Once you've installed ClarisWorks, you start the program by opening it or by opening one of its documents.

- Double-click the ClarisWorks icon in the Finder (or select the ClarisWorks icon in the Finder and choose the *Open...* command from the File menu). ClarisWorks starts and you see the Welcome dialog box. (See Chapter 2 for more information.)

- Double-click a ClarisWorks document icon in the Finder (or select the document icon and choose the *Open...* command from the File menu). ClarisWorks starts and then the document opens.

If you're using Macintosh System 7 (or MultiFinder under System 6), each program you open asks the Mac's system software for a certain amount of RAM in which to operate. ClarisWorks requests varying amounts of RAM for its use, depending on which Mac you install it on. If there isn't enough RAM available when you open ClarisWorks, you see a message saying so, and you have to close other documents or quit other programs to free up enough RAM for ClarisWorks to run.

Changing the program's memory size

If you can run ClarisWorks but you need to conserve your Mac's available RAM for other uses, you can reduce ClarisWorks' RAM requirement to as little as 800K, depending on which Mac you have. On the other hand, if you're working with lots of large documents at once in ClarisWorks, or if you find that paint documents won't open at full size, you should increase ClarisWorks' RAM requirement.

To adjust ClarisWorks' RAM requirement:

1. Quit ClarisWorks, if it's currently running, and locate the ClarisWorks folder on your disk in the Finder.

2. Open the ClarisWorks folder and click once on the ClarisWorks icon to select it.

3. Choose *Get Info* from the File menu or press ⌘I. You see the ClarisWorks 3.0 Info window, like the this:

ClarisWorks 3.0 Info

ClarisWorks 3.0
ClarisWorks 3.0

Kind : application program
Size : 1.5 MB on disk (1,655,944 bytes used)
Where : Macintosh HD : Applications : ClarisWorks 3.0 Folder :

Created : Tue, Oct 11, 1994, 3:00 PM
Modified : Fri, Nov 11, 1994, 12:14 PM
Version : ClarisWorks 3.0 October, 1994
Comments :

Memory Requirements

Suggested size :	2289	K
Minimum size :	2114	K
Preferred size :	2289	K

☐ **Locked**

Note : Memory requirements will decrease by 1,314K if virtual memory is turned on in the Memory control panel.

The *Memory Requirements* area at the bottom of this window shows the *Suggested Size* (as specified by Claris); the *Minimum Size* suggested by the program; and the *Preferred Size*.

Note: If you're running System 6 or System 7.0, the Preferred Size box is called *Current Size* or *Application Memory Size*.

4. Double-click in the Preferred Size box and type a different RAM amount. If your computer has less than 4 megabytes of RAM, try increasing the memory size to 1450K. If you have 4 megabytes of RAM, try increasing it to 1900K. If you have more than 4 megabytes of RAM or you're using a Power Macintosh, try adding 2000K to the current setting. To find out the minimum memory size ClarisWorks will allow on your Mac, type in 800K or less in the Minimum Size box and click the Info window's close box. You'll see a message that tells you what the minimum size really is.

5. Click the close box to put the window away. The next time you run ClarisWorks, it will use the amount of memory you specified in the Preferred Size box, unless there isn't that much memory available on your Mac at the time. In that case, ClarisWorks will open using the minimum memory size, assuming there's that much available on your Mac at the time.

Adjusting memory in other ways

Along with changing ClarisWorks' memory size with the *Get Info* command, you can also change the amount of memory it uses by adjusting other system software features or by changing preferences inside ClarisWorks itself. Here's a quick rundown.

• If you're using a Mac that has built-in color video, open the Monitors control panel (or click on the Monitors option in the Control Panel DA if you're using System 6) and set your Mac to display fewer colors or gray shades. It takes far less memory to display black and white or 16 colors than it does to display 256 colors.

- Open the Memory control panel (or use the Control Panel DA under System 6) and set the RAM cache size to its minimum. You can even try turning the cache off if you're using System 6. If you're using System 7 or later, turn on the Virtual Memory feature. This will reduce the amount of actual RAM you need to run the program.

- If you're using System 7 but you don't plan to share files from your disk with others on a network, open the Sharing Setup control panel and make sure file sharing is turned off to save 300K or so of memory.

- If you're not viewing QuickTime movies in ClarisWorks or using QuickTime in other programs, drag the QuickTime extension out of your System Folder (it's inside the Extensions folder in the System Folder if you're using System 7). When you store this extension outside the System Folder, it won't load when you start your Mac and you'll save from 400 to 700K of memory, depending on which version of QuickTime you're using.

- Change the Communications preference option in Claris-Works from an Unlimited scrollback area to one of a fixed size. This will reduce the amount of memory used by communications documents. See p. 302 in Chapter 10.

- Use the *Resolution & Depth...*command in paint documents to set the pixel depth to Black & White, 4 colors, or 16 colors, rather than thousands or millions of colors. As you click different options in the Resolution and Depth dialog box, you can see how much memory each option requires. See p. 282 in Chapter 9.

B

Keyboard Guide

ClarisWorks has dozens of keyboard alternates you can use to choose menu commands. Here's a complete list of them. ➸

. . . .

General commands

These commands work in all ClarisWorks documents, although they're not always available. For example, the Spelling submenu's commands aren't available when you're working in the draw or paint environment.

	Command	**Keys**
File Menu	New...	⌘N
	Open...	⌘O
	Close	⌘W
	Save	⌘S
	Save As...	⌘ Shift S
	Show Shortcuts	⌘ Shift X
	Record Macro...	⌘ Shift J
	Mail Merge...	⌘ Shift M
	Print...	⌘P
	Quit...	⌘Q
Edit Menu	Undo	⌘Z
	Cut	⌘X
	Copy	⌘C
	Paste	⌘V
	Select All	⌘A
Edit Menu (**Find/Change submenu**)	Find/Change...	⌘F
	Find Again	⌘E
	Find Selection	⌘ Shift E
Edit Menu (**Writing Tools submenu**)	Check Document...	⌘ =
	Check Selection...	⌘ Shift Y
	Thesaurus...	⌘ Shift Z
View Menu	Page View	⌘ Shift P
	Show/Hide Tools	⌘ Shift T
	Show/Hide Rulers	⌘ Shift U
? **Menu**	ClarisWorks Help	⌘ ?

You can use ⌘-key shortcuts instead of clicking buttons in ClarisWorks dialog boxes. If a button has a heavy black outline, of course, you can press Return to select it. If a button doesn't have a heavy black outline, you can select it by pressing ⌘ and the first letter of the button's name.

Word processing commands

The following commands work in word processing documents, in text frames, and whenever you edit text objects in drawing documents or database layouts. (Outline menu commands are available only in word processing documents.)

	Command	Keys
Size Menu	Other…	⌘ Shift O
Style Menu	Plain Text	⌘ T
	Bold	⌘ B
	Italic	⌘ I
	Underline	⌘ U
	Superscript	⌘ Shift +
	Subscript	⌘ Shift −
Outline Menu	Outline View	⌘ Shift I
	New Topic Left	⌘ L
	New Topic Right	⌘ R
	Move Left	⌘ Shift L
	Move Right	⌘ Shift R
	Move Above	⌘ Shift A
	Move Below	⌘ Shift B

Spreadsheet commands

These commands work in spreadsheet documents and spreadsheet frames.

	Command	Keys
Edit Menu	Copy Format	⌘ Shift C
	Paste Format	⌘ Shift V
Format Menu	Left	⌘ [
(Alignment submenu)	Center	⌘ \
	Right	⌘]
	Number...	⌘ Shift N
Calculate Menu	Insert Cells...	⌘ Shift I
	Delete Cells...	⌘ Shift K
	Calculate Now	⌘ Shift =
Options Menu	Make Chart...	⌘ M
	Protect Cells	⌘ H
	Unprotect Cells	⌘ Shift H
	Go To Cell...	⌘ G

Database commands

These commands work in the database Browse and Find modes. When you're in Layout mode, ClarisWorks switches to the draw environment—see *Draw commands*, next.

	Command	Keys
Edit Menu	New Record	⌘R
	Duplicate Record	⌘D
Layout Menu	Browse	⌘ Shift B
	Find	⌘ Shift F
	Layout	⌘ Shift L
	Define Fields...	⌘ Shift D
Organize Menu	Show All Records	⌘ Shift A
	Hide Selected	⌘ Shift 9
	Hide Unselected	⌘ Shift 0
	Go To Record...	⌘G
	Sort Records...	⌘J
	Match Records...	⌘M

Communications commands

These commands work only in Communications documents.

	Command	Keys
Settings Menu	Info...	⌘I
	Show Scrollback	⌘L
	Phone Book...	⌘B
Session Menu	Open/Close Connection	⌘ Shift O
	Wait For Connection	⌘ Shift W
	Save Lines Off Top	⌘T

Draw commands

These commands work in draw documents, in database Layout mode, and whenever the draw environment is active in other documents.

	Command	Keys
Edit Menu	Reshape	⌘R
	Smooth	⌘ Shift 9
	Unsmooth	⌘ Shift 0
Arrange Menu	Move Forward	⌘ Shift +
	Move Backward	⌘ Shift –
	Align To Grid	⌘K
	Align Objects...	⌘ Shift K
	Rotate	⌘ Shift R
	Group	⌘G
	Ungroup	⌘ Shift G
	Lock	⌘H
	Unlock	⌘ Shift H
Options Menu	Turn Autogrid Off/On	⌘Y
	Object Info...	⌘ Shift I
	Frame Links	⌘L

Paint commands

The only keyboard command in paint documents and paint frames is *Turn Autogrid On* (⌘Y) on the Options menu.

Index

More from Peachpit Press

Icons for the Masses
David Lai

This entertaining and informative book shows you how to use icons to quickly enliven and personalize your Macintosh computer. Includes a disk of 1,000 icons and ICON Wizard, a shareware icon editor. $17.95 *(154 pages, includes disk))*

Illustrator 5.0/5.5 for Macintosh: Visual QuickStart Guide
Elaine Weinmann and Peter Lourekas

Written in the same style as Elaine Weinmann's award-winning, best-selling QuarkXPress Visual QuickStart Guide, this indispensable step-by-step guide covers the basics of Illustrator and the latest features of Illustrator 5.5. $17.95 *(240 pages)*

The Little Online Book
Alfred Glossbrenner

A beginner's guide to everything you need to begin exploring the electronic universe from your desktop. Covers modems, the Internet, and online services. Also includes a step-by-step cookbook explaining common online tasks. $17.95 *(380 pages)*

The Mac is not a typewriter
Robin Williams

Covers the top twenty things you need to know to make your documents look clean and professional, including em dashes, curly quotes, spaces, indents, white space, and more. $9.95 *(72 pages)*

The Macintosh Bible, 5th Edition
Edited by Darcy DiNucci

Now completely updated, this classic is crammed with tips, tricks, and shortcuts that cover the most current software and hardware. New chapters highlight multimedia, children's software, PowerPCs, and more. $30.00 *(1,170 pages)*

The Macintosh Bible CD-ROM
Jeremy Judson, Editor

A dazzling array of special goodies, featuring more than 600 MB of utilities, games, sounds, video clips, digitized photos, clip art, fonts, and demos. Also includes selections from Peachpit books in Acrobat format. $25.00 *(CD-ROM)*

The Non-Designer's Design Book
Robin Williams

This book is for anyone who needs to design, but who has no background or formal training in the field. Follow these basic principles and your work will look more professional. Full of design exercises and quizzes. $14.95 *(144 pages)*

The Photoshop Wow! Book (Mac Edition)
Linnea Dayton and Jack Davis

This book is really two books in one: an easy-to-follow, step-by-step tutorial of Photoshop fundamentals and over 150 pages of tips and techniques for getting the most out of Photoshop version 2.5. Full color throughout, *The Photoshop Wow! Book* includes a disk containing Photoshop filters and utilities. $35.00 *(208 pages, includes disk)*

Protect Your Macintosh
Bruce Schneier

A hands-on guide that discusses all aspects of Macintosh security: backups, viruses, data protection, encryption, network security, and physical security. Includes reviews of useful products that can help you avert or recover from disaster. $23.95 *(350 pages)*

Real World Scanning and Halftones
David Blatner and Steve Roth

Here's a book that will save you time and money as you master the digital halftone process, from scanning images to tweaking them on your Mac to imagesetting them. $24.95 *(275 pages)*

Zap! How Your Computer Can Hurt You and What You Can Do About It
Don Sellers

Learn about the variety of potential hazards of using your computer and how to reduce your risk. Includes chapters on backache, headache, radiation, and much more. $12.95 *(150 pages)*

For a complete list of Peachpit Press titles call 1-800-283-9444 and request our latest catalog.

⊘ Order Form

to order, call:
(800) 283-9444 or (510) 548-4393 or (510) 548-5991 (fax)

Qty	Title	Price	Total

Shipping .... **UPS Ground**	Subtotal
First Item .... **$ 4**	Add applicable state sales tax
Each Additional .... **$ 1**	Shipping
	TOTAL

Name

Company

Address

City   State   Zip

Phone   Fax

❑ Check enclosed   ❑ Visa   ❑ MasterCard   ❑ AMEX

Company purchase order #

Credit card #   Exp. Date

What other books would you like us to publish?

Please tell us what you thought of this book:

Peachpit Press • 2414 Sixth Street • Berkeley, CA • 94710

MAC